DRY  NG

Analy ation

Umberto Pelizzari • Federico Mana • Roberto Chiozzotto

DRY TRAINING FOR FREEDIVING

Analysis and management of physical preparation

IDELSON-GNOCCHI

Photographers:
Alice Cattaneo
Giovanni Contessa
Igor Liberti
Stefano Tovaglieri
Riccardo Trianni
Paolo Zanoni
Michele D'Incà

Translator:
Ilaria Molinari

Reviser:
Tiffany Porter

IDELSON-GNOCCHI Srl – Editori dal 1908 - **www.idelsongnocchi.it**
Sorbona • Grasso Morelli • Liviana Medicina • Grafite • Idelson Gnocchi Ltd.
Via M. Pietravalle, 85 - 80131 Naples, Italy - Tel +39-081-5453443 - Fax +39-081-5464991

Idelson Gnocchi Publisher, Ltd.
1316 King's Bay Drive, Crystal River FL 34429, USA - Tel. +1 352 361 9585 - Fax +1 561 207-7132

To freediving,
our source of energy and passion,
which allowed us to write this book with unity,
cooperation and even
a bit of healthy confrontation.

TABLE OF CONTENTS

PREFACE

Freediving is a wonderful world!

I discovered it while following the black line on the bottom of the pool during the 40,000 km I have covered in 25 years of swimming.

Freediving is so natural that many people do not consider it a sport, but rather a technique that helps swimmers hold their breath while exploring the seabed or spearfishing.

But it is a real, technical and well-structured sport, rewarding those who practice it by putting them in touch with themselves and with nature.

Freediving means freedom. I'm sure everyone has, at least once, dreamt of being a dolphin, playing with the school, riding a wave and taking a dip in the deep blue. Almost everyone has put his or her head underwater for a few seconds and said afterward, "I made it!"

Freediving is essential in many sports and a great way to further develop and improve technique and performance. I devote a large part of my swimming training to dynamic apnea exercises to improve turns and starts.

But while freediving can be of significant help in many sports, this book shows the other side of the coin, and that is, how other sports can help freediving and those who practice it.

I believe there is still a lot to learn about how to train your body for apnea, simply because it completely overturns the physiological laws that are the basis of all other sports: When you practice freediving, you hold your breath! *Dry Training for Freediving* helps us understand how to incorporate other sports into our freediving training.

The absolute truth may still be far from being known, but I think this book will help us move in the right direction.

And I hope it can help you, even unintentionally, become like Pelizzari more easily.

Now it's time to hold your breath ...without fear!

Massimiliano Rosolino

Winner of the 2000 Sydney Olympics and of the 2001 World Championships gold medal in the 200 mt. individual medley

World champion in the 200 mt. individual medley at the 2001 World Championships in Fukuoka

Winner of 60 medals in international and continental championships, four Olympic medals, five World Championship medals and 10 World Short-Course Championships medals

INTRODUCTION

Freediving and spearfishing have millions of followers in Europe. Italy is often considered the cradle of these sports, boasting hundreds of instructors and thousands of trainees. Italian schools churn out more than 4000 licenses each year.

Nevertheless, freediving is still regarded as a recreational, amateur sport. It is uncommon to see groups of professional freedivers doing exercises and training with a coach.

Training usually consists of a couple of evening gatherings a week, at most, where participants follow improvised training schedules that do not include the cornerstones of a real workout for any sport: planning, workload, rest, etc.

Even the few professional freedivers find it difficult to determine the best training program to follow. They often try their hands at several methods, while attempting to identify the strengths and weaknesses, advantages and disadvantages of each.

The leading professionals follow training programs very different from one another, confirming how much work still needs to be done to determine the best training method for freediving.

Most top athletes in other competitive sports, such as swimming, skiing, basketball and volleyball, follow well-structured and well-tested training programs that are very similar to those used by their peers from a technical and physical point of view.

Maybe for freediving all this is not feasible yet, but the aim of this book and the book that will follow it, *Specific Training for Freediving: Deep Freediving, Dynamic and Static Apnea*, is to present a method for freedivers and spearfishers to identify and customize a training path specifically designed for freediving.

FOREWORD

Many of you may wonder why, although there are already hundreds of books about training, we wrote another book on the topic. This book is different from all the others. It is not so different in its contents, but rather in its approach. It is not directed toward doctors or experts, but toward people who play sports for competitive satisfaction and well-being. This book is also unique in that, until now, no book has been written specifically about freediving training.

During more than a decade of training young athletes, we noticed that most people wanted to do "something else" in addition to freediving – maybe something linked to it and for the benefit of it. Besides being beneficial to freedivers, these alternative sports have proved to be irreplaceable panaceas, giving peacefulness and pleasure outdoors, in the water or at the gym.

The goal of this book is to give some guidelines to ensure that participation in other sports is beneficial to freediving training, while giving the satisfaction and well-being that only sports can give.

We will deal with traditional and well-known sports, such as running, cycling, swimming and workouts at the gym, intentionally omitting activities, such as cross-country skiing, for example, which have seasonal and/or logistical limitations.

This book does not replace a trainer or coach; it simply presents the experience and advice of high-level freedivers who have directly experienced and tested dry-land training models and have analyzed their effectiveness.

A word to the wise: If you are hoping that the following pages will reveal the secret to quickly achieve record performances, you will be disappointed. Much of what you need is already in your possession. We are talking about the perseverance, willingness, enthusiasm, diligence and competitiveness that are inside each of us and are absolutely necessary for achieving our goals.

Athletic success brings with it feelings of great satisfaction that make all the sacrifices, hard work and time you devote to training worthwhile. To achieve that success, it is important that you give your best when your best is required. It is up to you to decide whether to do that every day.

The examples, tables, time schedules, figures and so forth presented in this book are merely guidelines to help you easily understand what we are talking about. Obviously, the program will have to be adjusted to suit your individual level and needs.

We wish you good reading… and enjoy your training!

Chapter 1
TRAINING STAGES

The word "training" has several meanings. It is sometimes used to mean simply a recreational activity performed only occasionally and not properly regulated.

By stating the above, we do not want to belittle those who approach freediving as a recreational activity. However, the workout proposed below is meant to aid followers of this wonderful discipline so that they can better understand how to train to become good freedivers and develop the most suitable workouts for their specific conditions, goals, interests, etc.

We hope that after reading this book, both recreational and would-be professional freedivers can design their own athletic profiles and set their own individual training or maintenance paths.

1.1 Why train: general remarks

The first thing to understand about training is why we do it, or at least why we think it is worth doing it.

It is true that having a natural talent for a specific sport depends on genetics, but it is also true that most anyone can see improvement with proper training. This is sacrosanct in every sport, and freediving is no exception. We reach our maximum level of performance only after a set of training sessions – in or out of the water. Be suspicious of those who say they can achieve best performances without training. Either they train and hide it, or their best performances are actually far below their potential.

Training allows us to shape and change our bodies through adjustments and adaptations. We are able to respond to external stress and adapt so that the stress does not unbalance our life in a functional way. This is why we train. We can modify our body through adaptation. Take, for example, the principle of survival: We adapt our body to withstand certain conditions in order to stay alive.

The human body is a perfect machine that can bear massive workloads. It can also quickly adapt to unfavorable environmental conditions. These adaptations are made possible through proper training.

The human body has its own autonomous intelligence that is separate from the conscious intelligence. This autonomous intelligence helps preserve the human being's life and, regardless of its willingness, it governs the physiological and metabolic activities of our body. In freediving, the physiological stimulation for the maintenance of life is very strong, since the athlete is doing something extremely unnatural – holding his breath.

When we go to the gym and lift weights, our muscles start to swell. This is adaptation. When we swim using very high-performance fins, our leg muscles gradually change to accommodate the stressors created by the fin. This is also adaptation.

Training is necessary to recruit as many motor units (muscles) as possible, and training provides our body with a series of both external and internal stimuli (loads), leading the body to give immediate and suitable responses to such stresses.

These responses, if properly steered and stressed, cause adaptation (the so-called "supercompensation," which we will see in detail below), enabling our bodies to achieve increasingly better performance for each action they are required to perform.

One definition of training might be: the educational process that takes place through regularly scheduled workouts designed to increase in quantity and intensity, often with increasingly heavier loads, which stimulate the physiological process of supercompensation and improve physical, mental, technical and tactical abilities, thereby enhancing the athlete's performance.

In a training session, there are two players: the person who trains (**the athlete**) and the person who teaches how to train (**the trainer**).

The trainer is generally in charge of athletes' training and preparation for competition. But in freediving, the number of professional athletes is very low. Even lower is the number of trainers. It is difficult to find people with experience as high-level freedivers who can train new generations of athletes. This illustrates that freediving is still far from being considered a popular organized sport.

Therefore, freediving's potential for growth from a technical point of view is enormous, and that is one of the reasons we wrote this book. That being said, let's get back to the main subject.

Training is nothing more than the repetition of a series of exercises that leads to structural, metabolic and functional changes.

In physiological terms, training could be described as a set of procedures carried out to cause temporary adjustments in the functioning of our bodies. These functional adaptations allow you to more effectively perform specific activities that are analyzed in terms of figures and referred to as sports performance. Training is a stimulus that causes temporary adaptations. If training is discontinued and there is no stimulus, our bodies tends to return to their regular level of functioning, also called the baseline.

One characteristic of a healthy body is a balance of bodily functions known as homeostasis. The typical stress of everyday life does not bring about significant change in this balance.

However, when stress becomes more significant and greater than what we are used to, homeostasis is thrown out of balance and the systems that govern our body are no longer able to ensure its stability.

The body responds to significant external stress by making biochemical, physiological-functional and morphological changes and adaptations. These adjustments allow the body to handle new situations and possibly reach new potentials. This is supercompensation: the basis of all adaptation processes.

1.2 Energy systems

Although we do not want to get into a lot of scientific details, we cannot refrain from considering some key concepts about training. We will explain these concepts in the simplest possible way to help you better understand the content of the following chapters.

Training involves both aerobic and anaerobic energy systems. When we train, we cause muscular actions. The muscles use adenosine triphosphate (ATP) as cellular fuel for their contraction.

There is a limited supply of ATP in muscle cells (2.5 g/kg of muscle, for a total amount of 50 g). This supply is used up after about one second of exercise. Our body, however, uses other energy systems to continually resynthesize ATP.

When ATP is used, it loses a phosphate and breaks down to form (adenosine diphosphate (ADP). At this stage, it cannot be used as fuel by the body, unless ATP is rebuilt through the addition of another phosphate.

This rebuilding process can be triggered through three fundamental metabolic pathways.

1. **Alactic anaerobic pathway:** In the muscle, as in other cells, there is an important supply of active phosphate groups called phosphocreatine or creatine phosphate (CP). When this energy pathway is used, ATP is produced using the stored CP.
   In the alactic anaerobic system, oxygen is not involved, hence we use the word "anaerobic". No lactic acid is produced, hence we use the word "alactic" to describe such a system.
   The alactic anaerobic system is an immediate source of energy, but a limited one in terms of time and a very limited one in terms of capacity. CP supplies in the muscles are quickly depleted (in approximately 4-5 seconds). However, the supply varies from person to person, and the more you work out, the more CP you have. During a short, intense workout, the decrease in strength is directly linked to the depletion of the CP stores in the muscles. Sprinters know this very well, as they see their speed decline during the final meters.
   ATP and CP stored in the muscles are used simultaneously during both short and intense efforts. In total, they give energy lasting 4-8 seconds at the most.
2. **Lactate anaerobic pathway:** ATP is produced by the breakdown of stored sugar, called glycogen, which is located primarily in the muscles and in the liver. This process is referred to as anaerobic glycolysis. It is a system capable of providing a

great amount of ATP, but only for short to intermediate periods of time (ranging from 15 seconds to 2 or 3 minutes).
This system produces a waste product called lactic acid, which is the main cause of muscular fatigue (acidosis). The production of lactic acid has a "toxic" effect on the muscles, making them heavy and sore and preventing their normal and prolonged motion. Our muscles, however, can be trained within certain limits to tolerate lactic acid, and in other sections of this book you will learn how the muscles do it. This system does not need a great quantity of oxygen, so it is considered to be anaerobic.
Very short exercises (lasting a minute or less) require almost exclusively anaerobic effort. In track, for example, these are the sprints, the 100 meters, 200 meters and 400 meters. The 400 meter discipline is particularly challenging because the body is required to support the anaerobic effort for the maximum duration possible. Lovers of this discipline call it the "death lap" (since 400 meters equals one lap) and it is not uncommon to see athletes who have consumed too much energy in the first half of the race fall behind in the final straight.

3. **Aerobic system:** During resting conditions or during moderate exercise, ATP is resynthesized through aerobic metabolism. This is the most beneficial way to produce ATP, which comes from the breakdown of fatty acids and sugars. All this happens in the presence of oxygen, which is the decisive factor in the process of ATP re-synthesis. The oxygen taken in through breathing is used for the production of energy through a series of complex chemical reactions called "aerobic processes."
   The aerobic system is used extensively in physical efforts that range from a few minutes to several hours; the intensity level can vary from low (aerobic capacity) to medium-high (aerobic power).

1.3 Aerobic and anaerobic thresholds

Aerobic and anaerobic energy systems run in parallel, that is to say at the same time. What varies, primarily, is the percentage of contribution by each of the energy pathways during the exercise.

When we start running, we begin at a very slow pace. The aerobic system is still "cold" and cannot provide all the energy needed. The anaerobic systems make up for this lack and consequently, the amount of lactate in the blood increases.

Once the aerobic system starts to work, it is able to provide all the energy we need, while the alactic anaerobic system virtually "turns off" and the lactate level in the blood decreases. In this case, we are running at a pace lower than the aerobic threshold. But what happens when we reach it? The lactate anaerobic system turns on again, and the concentration of lactate in the blood increases, reaching a value of approximately 2 mmol/L (millimoles per litre of blood).

The aerobic threshold (AT) is the minimum speed at which the lactate levels remain steady.

If we increase the speed above that threshold, the heart rate increases, as does the lactate, rising from 2 mmol/L to 3 mmol/L, for example. But the lactate, once it reaches a new balance value, remains steady over time. If we continue to speed up, at a certain point the lactate will be produced faster than it can be metabolised. Its concentration continues to increase, even if the speed is steady, until the body is no longer able to tolerate the high concentration and is forced to slow down.

The highest speed at which the lactate remains steady is called the anaerobic threshold. The level of lactate at this stage is about 4 mmol/L.

The anaerobic threshold (ANT) is the maximum speed at which the lactate levels remain steady.

When we get above the anaerobic threshold, the heart rate does not increase linearly with speed anymore. It increases more slowly. (Otherwise, the heart would blow up!) This happens because the aerobic system can no longer keep up with our body's energy demand, and the lactate anaerobic system kicks in to help out. This speed/heart rate curve is used in a popular test – the Conconi Test – to measure the anaerobic threshold.

Graph 1.1 shows the heart rate as it relates to speed during aerobic exercise, in this case, running. Similar graphs for other sports might show somewhat different figures.

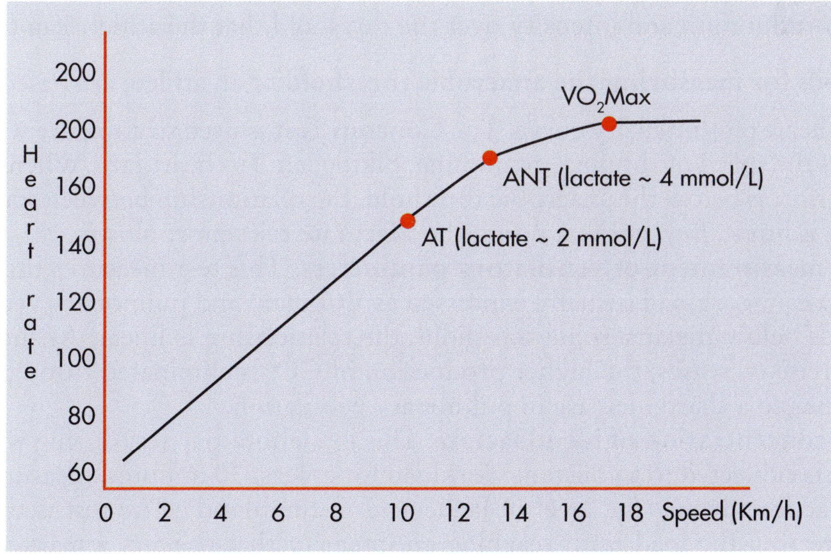

Graph 1.1 *cibo360.it*

If you increase the running speed, the heart rate increases in an almost linear way. This is quite natural: In performances longer than 3 or 4 minutes, energy is mainly produced by the aerobic system, which requires oxygen supplied by oxygenated blood being pumped by the heart. The more oxygen required by the muscles, the more blood the heart must pump. Therefore, the heart rate increases.

In sports medicine, the anaerobic threshold is the maximum level of physical exertion that our body can bear without accumulating lactic acid in the blood. Below this threshold, the athlete's metabolism is supported exclusively, or almost exclusively, by the aerobic system, and physical exertion can be tolerated for long periods. Above the threshold, the anaerobic systems kick in, using their limited energy supplies. An athlete can therefore sustain exertion above the threshold only for very short periods. After a few minutes at most, the athlete will need to stop, or at least reduce the intensity of the exercise.

The anaerobic threshold can be measured in terms of heart rate (using a heart rate monitor) or power output. The anaerobic threshold for a trained athlete lies at approximately 80% to 85% of the maximal heart rate. (For example, if the maximal heart rate is 210 beats per minute, the threshold will be between 165 and180 beats per minute.) Throughout this book, we will often refer to the heart rate with acronyms such as HR or HR max, which mean heart rate and maximal heart rate, respectively.

On the other hand, the power output values may vary according to the sport and to the athlete's level of fitness. Roughly speaking, the anaerobic threshold for a professional cyclist is around 400 or 500 watts (while the maximal power can reach up to 1700 watts).

The anaerobic threshold can be trained with specific exercises. The most suitable ones for this purpose are "repeats," short series of exercises performed at maximum intensity, several times in succession, alternating short recovery periods with cool-down intervals. These exercises increase the anaerobic threshold as well as increasing the effort duration and intensity over the threshold that the athlete can tolerate.

Methods for measuring the anaerobic threshold of an athlete are based on:

- the heart rate/intensity curve. The **Conconi Test** is used to compare workload (and thus the speed of running, swimming, biking, etc.) to heart rate. When the intensity of effort is below the anaerobic threshold, the relationship between speed and heart rate is linear. Beyond that point, the heart rate rises more slowly.
- the **measurement of ventilatory parameters**. This test measures the relationship between workload (usually expressed as VO_2max) and pulmonary ventilation. For loads below the anaerobic threshold, the relationship is linear. As the intensity of exercise increases, the higher production of CO_2 is eliminated through exhalation, thanks to a sharp increase in pulmonary ventilation.
- the **concentration of blood lactate**. This is a laboratory test during which the athlete is subjected to a constant workload for at least 30 minutes, measuring the value of lacticacidemia (the level of lactic acid in the blood). The test is then repeated, increasing the load until reaching an intensity that triggers a marked increase in lactic acid accumulation.

1.4 Vo_2max. Maximal oxygen consumption

VO_2max is the maximum rate of oxygen consumed in one minute.

The aerobic process needs oxygen in order to produce energy. Therefore, oxygen consumption can be considered proportional to the energy produced by the aerobic process.

It can be easily measured by studying the air inhaled and the air exhaled by the athlete and analyzing the variation in the concentration of oxygen. **The maximal oxygen consumption occurs when the speed exceeds the anaerobic threshold**, as showed in the table above. This speed corresponds to the maximum heart rate.

An athlete is able to prolong his effort in a condition of maximal oxygen consumption for almost 7 minutes. In such a situation, the amount of blood lactate can range from 5 to 8 mmol/L, depending on the individual. Maximal oxygen consumption occurs when the aerobic energy production system is "squeezed" to its maximum level and is not able to give more.

This state cannot last more than a few minutes, because the body has already simultaneously started up the anaerobic process that increases lactate concentration to unbearable levels.

1.5 Supercompensation

Supercompensation is a theory explaining how a body adapts to a specific training stimulus.

As explained previously, the body lives in a state of balance called homoeostasis. Any condition disturbing that balance is immediately offset, if possible, by an equal and opposite reaction.

Fatigue and deterioration caused by physical exertion are offset by an automatic set of reactions as the body's defense system tries to reconstruct the lost balance.

Supercompensation is therefore the physiological response of the training stimulus to homeostasis breakdown. Our body starts up the supercompensation process to improve and to avoid such a level of training load. The metabolic reserves, the metabolism and the different anatomical structures, for a short period of time, reach a slightly higher value than the original level. That's the basis of the concept of supercompensation (the process through which our body adapts to increasingly heavier workloads). We will try to explain it using a simple example.

When an athlete first takes up running, friction between the shoes and the feet causes blisters. Eventually, the skin in those areas will harden and thicken, allowing the athlete to run without pain. This example clearly illustrates the concept of supercompensation, or how the body excessively compensates for damage caused by stressful activity.

The body does not only repair the damaged skin but also confronts the friction with a stronger defense by creating a callus. In order to allow the callus to form, the athlete needs a period of rest. Otherwise, the blister will turn into a sore.

Supercompensation is based on three principles:

- effort gradualness
- adequate recovery time
- a high level of frequency

In order for supercompensation to occur, the training must meet three fundamental conditions.

First of all, the physical effort must reach or cross a specific threshold, so that enough physical stress is induced. If the workload is too low, the process of supercompensation does not occur.

In this framework, the recovery period is extremely important. The body needs a period of rest during the training program in order to generate physiological adaptations so that the athlete will be able to start again and perform better. The training process is based on a stimulus-adaptation ratio and stimulus features. Its effectiveness depends on the type of adaptation and how well the training is maintained.

It is by no means easy to design a training program. When the training outcome depends on alternating between physical workloads and recovery breaks (necessary to

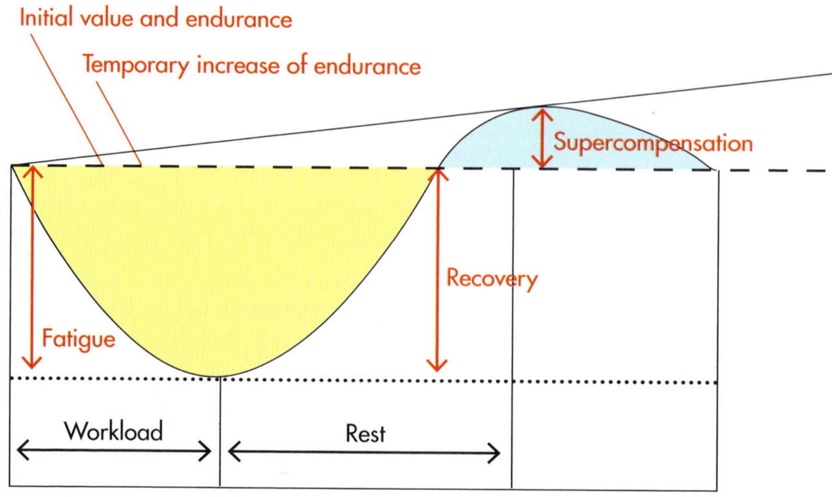

Graph 1.2 *muscolab.net*

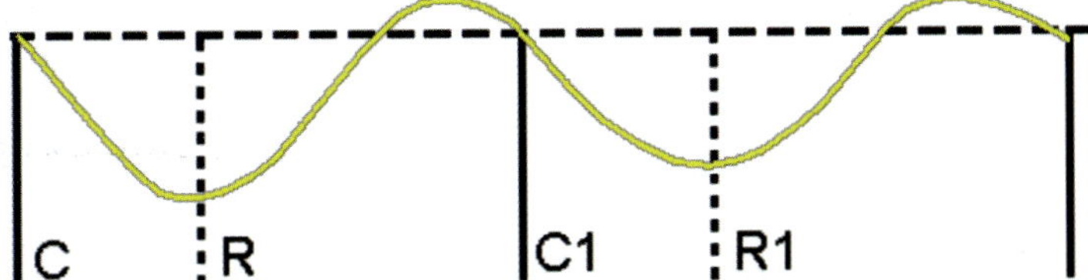

When the period of rest (R-R1) is too long, the new workload (C1) starts late. This will not lead to the positive effects of supercompensation.

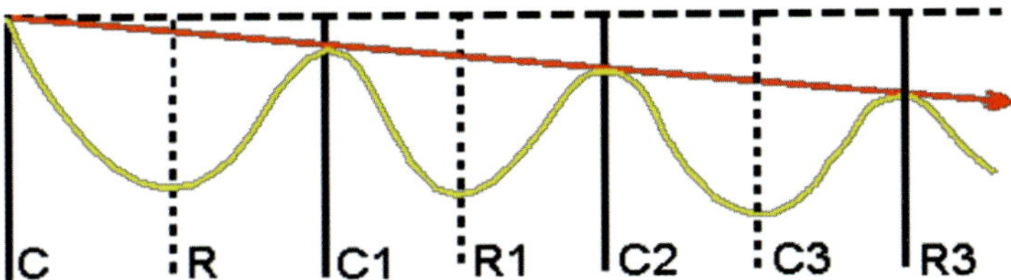

When the workout is repeated before the body completely recovers, the athlete will progressively underperform.

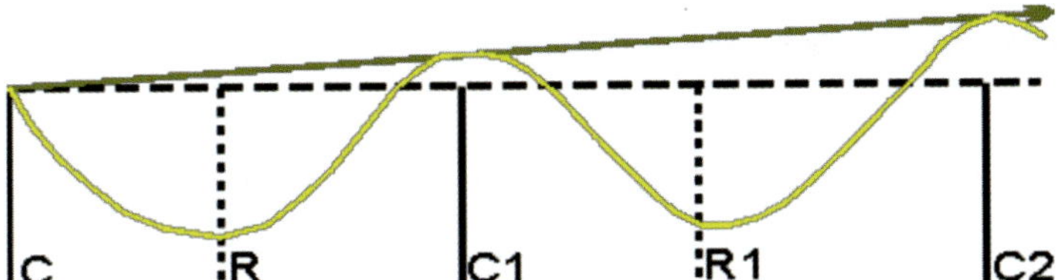

Supercompensation pathway with an optimal period of rest. When the new workload (C1, C2) starts at the peak of supercompensation, the athlete will outperform.

Graph 1.3 *ski-nordik.it*

bring about the positive effects of supercompensation), it can be difficult to synchronize the sequence of the various training steps. This is where the skill and professionalism of the trainer come into play.

1.6 Training stimulus

Training stimulus is the means by which a training workload (physical workload) is presented. The following important elements should be taken into account:

- **intensity**: The amount of force with which the stimulus acts on the athlete's body, leading to different fatigue levels. It is calculated by maximal percentage.
- **duration**: The length of time of each exercise or set of exercises.
- **density**: The stimulus frequency; the ratio between workout duration and recovery duration.

- **volume**: The workout quantity; the duration of every single stimulus multiplied by the number of stimuli.

Physical workload is the set of stimuli that the body receives during the training session.

As we saw earlier with regard to supercompensation, if the stimuli are too weak, they are useless; if they are too strong, they can do damage. In order to achieve maximum training potential, the workload must be constantly and gradually increased. All four workload factors (volume, density, intensity and duration) can be intensified. However, it is best to increase them one by one.

Workload is divided into two types:

- **external:** the measurable, objective value (lifted kilograms, covered distance, speed, repeats, etc.). In a training session, external workload refers to the quantity of work performed by the athlete.
- **internal:** the effect the workout has on the individual's body.

If the training workload is too high and is not balanced with adequate recovery periods, it can result in overtraining, which can lead to performance stasis or decline.

1.7 Biomotor abilities: strength, speed and endurance

Biomotor abilities are traditionally divided in strength, endurance and speed.

They are usually treated separately, even though their specific attributes can be interchanged, creating additional intermediate categories, such as fast strength, strength endurance, etc.

1.7.1 *Strength*

The human body is a complex structure made of bones, muscle tissue, tendons, ligaments, etc. Thanks to a complex system of levers, we are able to perform a wide range of movements. These levers, however, require strength in order to be moved. In physiology, **strength** is "the motor capability to overcome or oppose resistance using muscular tension" (Manno).

It is linked to muscle contraction features, and it depends on structural and nervous system factors.

In every sport, it is important to have physical strength, motor coordination and elasticity. It is completely useless to have mighty musculature if you have rigid joints and tightly contracted muscles.

Many freediving disciplines require sinuous movements and hydrodynamic positions. Therefore, good joint mobility and muscle flexibility is essential.

Strength is divided into:

- **maximal strength:** the highest level of strength that the neuromuscular system can produce through voluntary contraction (Harre). Workload component prevails over speed component;
- **speed strength:** the ability to overcome resistance with maximum contraction (Harre). Or, how quickly the neuromuscular system can produce the greatest possible force.
- **endurance strength**: the ability to oppose fatigue (Harre). Workload and speed maintain average values, and in addition to muscle involvement, cardiovascular and respiratory support is needed.

1.7.2 *Speed*

Speed is the ability to make fast movements. It is linked to the efficiency of the nervous system, and it is the least trainable biomotor ability because it has a strong genetic basis. Speed depends on the amount of white muscle fiber, on the transmission speed of impulses through nerve fibers, on the ability to quickly relax the muscles and, most important of all, on cyclic actions. Of the three abilities, speed is surely the least important one for freedivers. A fast athlete usually has a strong, hypertrophic musculature, and this is not an essential feature for being a top freediver.

1.7.3 *Endurance*

Endurance is the physical ability that enables us to exert ourselves and remain active for a long period of time. It is directly linked to the efficiency of the energy systems used in movement. Any movement requires that a specific quantity of ATP (our body fuel) be released in a specific interval of time. Having more energy means being able to maintain the physical effort for a longer period of time. Energy involves both power and endurance. A marathoner, for example, needs a high and steady ATP output over a long period of time (3 to 4 hours). A sprinter needs a large quantity of ATP, but only for a very short period of time (about 10 seconds). A 100-meter runner reaches maximum speed within about 40 meters, and he has to keep it up to the finish line, therefore he has to maintain the effort. These examples show that there are many types of endurance. Therefore, there are many methods for training and developing it.

Endurance can involve a limited muscle group and its related energy substrates (muscular endurance) or huge muscle masses and the whole cardiovascular and respiratory system (general endurance).

GENERAL ENDURANCE is the ability to sustain an effort that is not linked to the athletic gesture for which the athlete is training. The most common example of a builder of general endurance is running.

SPECIAL ENDURANCE is the ability to sustain a specific effort similar to the one performed during a competition.

General endurance is important for everybody, even for those who do not play sports at a competitive level. For those who do play sports at a competitive level, general endurance is the basis upon which all types of specific endurance are developed.

The human body, by nature, needs to move, and for this reason regular physical exercise is essential to good health.

Strength endurance and speed endurance are two additional types of endurance. For freedivers, speed endurance is an extremely important quality.

STRENGTH ENDURANCE is the ability to oppose the dynamic and static endurance as long as possible.

SPEED ENDURANCE is the ability to keep a specific maximal or submaximal speed for relatively long periods (8 to 45 seconds).

1.8 Scheduling a training program

When designing a training program, it is extremely important to include the following steps:

1. **Tests** to record and measure starting level
   Starting-level tests are extremely important in training programs. In order to completely understand their importance, it is necessary to clarify the concept of training. We all agree with famous trainers who say sports training is a complex process designed to enhance physical performance. In order to make this process efficient, it is essential to know one's physical capability and starting level. This will prevent wasting energy and time by starting with a workout that is too easy – or too hard. Tests can be used to determine an athlete's personal fitness level so you can design a training profile that fits the person and the disciplines that he or she will be performing. In each chapter related to the various training disciplines, we will describe the most common and useful starting tests.
2. Setting training **targets**
   Training targets must be set to meet the athlete's specific needs. A freediver should carefully establish his training targets using the following steps.
   When an athlete performs a discipline other than his own, it is quite normal to get in touch with other professionals and share training sessions with them. This enables professional athletes to challenge each other. Not only can it be stimulating, but also it can lead to a mutual shift of respective targets.
   It is up to the freediver to keep within his scope of work. This will make it easier to set specific, in-the-water training goals.

3. Setting the **training method** to reach any goal
   Once a goal has been set, it is important to know how to achieve that goal. The scheduling of weekly training sessions, workouts and recovery times plays a fundamental role in building a sound and achievable program. In training for freediving, there may be several types of goals, starting with goals for general overall physical preparation and continuing on to goals specific to freediving that will be focused on during in-the-water training.
4. **Time** schedule (long and short term)
   While a training program needs to be future-oriented, establishing the actual training schedule requires starting from the date of a future goal and working backward. Since it is almost impossible to maintain maximum fitness for a long period and to achieve this status many times during the year, each athlete will choose a specific period during which to be most fit. This will affect the schedule of the athlete's individual training program. Given a final deadline for maximum fitness, the athlete, in this case the freediver, can work backward, determining intermediate deadlines for various physical preparation goals. For example, if a freediver needs to be fit for deep freediving in September, he will have to start from that month and work backward, fitting the various training steps into his schedule. He will have to choose when to start and conclude his pressure adaptation training, specific training in the water, freediving training and general physical training. Within each section of training, he will have to schedule sub-deadlines, which will enable him to train at his best during each training unit. Training scheduling is a priority.
5. Evaluation tests
   Training tests are nothing but intermediate evaluations of physical condition.
   Training tests help evaluate whether the training is on track to meet the set goals and deadlines. This is easy to assess with the average athlete, who competes often. For the freediver, who trains for a long period in different fields before doing underwater training, the results of such tests are more difficult to evaluate. In each training session, the freediver should be able to gradually evaluate improvement in his physical condition in order to properly manage the training process.
   In addition to the elements described above, two additional factors are essential for making the freediver's training schedule sound, feasible and focused.
6. Time available
   The first step to organizing a training session is to decide how much time we want to devote to it. Fewer than 3 sessions per week is not enough to achieve the necessary workout/adaptation/growth stages. In addition, training should be stepped up during the different stages of conditioning/stabilization/fatigue. Therefore, one can't start with a specific number of training sessions per week and keep that number all year round. If we are not professional athletes, we should carefully evaluate our leisure time so that we can use the time devoted to training most efficiently.
7. Age
   Many freedivers, including the professional ones, are often older than 25 years old. When it comes to training, we often forget an important factor: our age. This should be carefully considered when we undertake a training program that includes work-

out, recovery and growth. The training program should help guard us against traumas and problems caused by overtraining with too short a recovery period. Recovery periods must be set according to our age. We are continuously aging and changing from an organic, muscular and skeletal point of view. We cannot do anything about it, so we must carefully exercise our passion for sports by accepting physical changes and trying to mitigate the effects of aging with age-appropriate workouts.

1.8.1 *Training program framework*

Dividing time into periods and sub-periods is the best way to organize a year-round training program that will take place both at the gym and in the water. Periods and sub-periods are the following:

- macro-cycle
- meso-cycle
- micro-cycle

The longest sub-period is the macro-cycle. It is often a year-long period of time consisting of several meso-cycles. During the year, one or more meso-cycles can be introduced. Macro-cycle planning is usually used in sports where the most important goal is reached at the end of the training season. Nowadays, the trend of extending the competition season, even in freediving, has caused a yearly schedule to be divided into three to five macro-cycles, or even more. A yearly training program divided into one or more macro-cycles aiming at off-season maximum athletic training can be structured in four periods:

- overall preparatory training period
- special preparatory training period
- competitive training period
- transition or recovery period

We need to analyze which exercises are included in these four periods.

- **Transition period**: This is when we gradually start swimming, doing strengthening workouts at the gym, running or cycling. The transition period lasts 4 to 6 weeks. It is important not to overdo with exercises in the pool in order to avoid the frustration and lack of motivation that can come with overtraining. Having a strong desire to train is essential.
- **Overall preparatory training period**: After we have worked on our body (muscular system) and our engine (cardiovascular system), a second training period begins. During that period we will enhance some basic qualities and lay the foundation to improve our performance. We will work on overall endurance and aim for an adequate amount of stress generated by robust running, swimming, cycling or workout sessions. This period lasts from 8 to 16 weeks. Those who cannot forgo evening swimming with friends should reduce their workouts.
- **Specific preparatory period**: In this period the training is focused on improving specific qualities such as threshold frequency, aerobic power and specific strength.

- **Competitive period:** At this stage, the athlete trains himself in his discipline and performs some isolated cross-training sessions at the gym. The athlete will perform specific workouts that train specifically for the athlete's particular discipline.

The competitive period has been included in order to provide a complete framework, even though, according to freedivers, it is not so important. The competitive period of the sport we are using for training purposes (swimming, for example) should not overlap with freediving competitions. Often, there is no need to participate in the competitive period of the sport we are using for training. We will explain why in the next chapter. We intentionally did not go into detail about the meso-cycle and the micro-cycle. This book is not designed for such an in-depth analysis.

1.9 Setting a training session

Each standard training unit is divided in three parts:

- Warm-up
- Main part
- Cool-down

1.9.1 *Warm-up*

In sports, we often to hear the word "warm-up." Athletes warm up before the match in sports such as basketball, volleyball, rugby, football, swimming or cycling,

just as cars and motorbikes warm up their engines before a race. The word "warm-up" refers to the various forms of activation taking place before each session with the aim of performing at one's best. By increasing its internal temperature, our body, like any other machine, is able to perform better, thanks to the following:

- More blood flow because of vasodilation of the circulatory system and HR increase;
- Faster and more complete O_2 release from haemoglobin (Bohr effect);
- Muscle viscosity and connective tissue elasticity increase;
- Increase in flow of synovial fluid to joints;
- Faster conduction of nerve impulses and increase in sensitivity of neuromuscular receptors with improved coordination processing;
- Increased and improved metabolic exchanges and energy substrates;
- Adrenaline increase.

It is important to know that the metabolic "ignition" time, that is, the time needed to launch oxygen consumption, is at least 5 minutes. After this period of time, the training can begin in an optimal condition from a neuromuscular and organic point of view, thereby reducing physical suffering caused by a cold start, as well as possibly avoiding joint and muscle traumas.

1.9.2 *Main part*

During this stage, the body is stressed to stimulate adaptations and consequently to perform at its highest level. This stage can last anywhere from 30 minutes to 3 hours,

depending on the session. This part includes the appropriate exercises to provide the stimuli described in the previous chapters.

1.9.3 *Cool-down*

This is a very important and delicate stage. After a prolonged period of maximal exercise, we produce a high quantity of lactic acid. Performing at a submaximal level during a cool-down period allows lactic acid to drain from the muscles more easily. Meanwhile, lactic acid is being used as a fuel and therefore continues to be metabolized. In addition, performing the cool-down can help avoid a sharp decrease in blood pressure after a training session.

While HR remains high after a training session because of the presence of adrenaline and noradrenaline, a quick drop in blood pressure can often lead to dizziness, nausea or even ischemic heart diseases.

Furthermore, a cool-down period provides time to enjoy a few minutes of active relaxation and reflect on the good training session we have just performed. This helps us feel good about the goals we have achieved and allows us to start the next training session with more enthusiasm.

Now that these general concepts have been described, we will discuss the practical and specific applications of training for freedivers.

Chapter 2

PHYSICAL TRAINING FOR FREEDIVERS

For freedivers, as for all athletes, it is important to train at one's best, using methods that help the body respond to the specific challenges of his or her sport.

To that aim, athletes often perform parallel training activities in addition to following training regimens designed for their particular sport. Those activities enable the athletes to improve strength, endurance, muscle elasticity and the cardiovascular system. In more advanced sports, athletes work not only with trainers who strive to obtain athletes' best from a technical and strategic point of view, but also with other trainers whose aim is to achieve a high level of general athletic fitness through weight-lifting and/or circuit training and/or calisthenics.

In most major sports, a lot of research has gone into creating the best possible physical training routine for each particular discipline. Since freediving training is still under study, this book aims to analyze and determine which out-of-the-water training activities will most benefit the freediver.

A fit and elastic body can better perform the specific technical tasks required in freediving. General athletic training aims to create the optimal physical condition so that, during more individualized training sessions, the athlete is supported by a strong, reactive body that can handle the workload and is less affected by fatigue. Compared to other disciplines, freediving is unique because it is performed while holding one's breath. This peculiarity cannot be ignored because of its effects on the body from a chemical, physiological and functional point of view. We cannot live without oxygen. Therefore, in a discipline like freediving, where a basic survival element is missing, a unique physiological defense system comes into play. This defense system consists of energy and metabolic conditions generated by the athletic techniques specific to the performance (dynamic, constant, variable, etc.).

According to famous physiologists, researchers and trainers such as Enrico Arcelli, Vladimir N. Platanov and Yurij Verchoshanskij, the science of training is not based on any mathematical formula. It is based instead on the biomechanical, bioenergetic and psychophysiological aspects of one of the world's most complex machines: the human body. This is why training design is not an exact and well-defined science. It becomes even more complex when this human machine trains in the unnatural condition brought about by holding one's breath. In addition to attaining a maximal level of general fitness, we also have to bring this unnatural feat to its highest limit.

In more common sports, it is easy to identify the main traits that the athlete should develop in order to improve and stand out. Trainers know that marathoners need to train their aerobic system, sprinters need to focus on their anaerobic system, and volleyball players need to build up their explosive strength, which enables them to jump up.

In freediving, it is not as easy to identify which characteristic must be focused on. There is not yet a so-called "performance model," which **carefully** defines the metabolic pathways that are essential to our discipline. We don't have as much statistical information about the specific involvement of the aerobic and anaerobic systems, the type of muscle fibers used, the amount of "fuel" consumed, etc.

Since we do not know this, what do we rely on in order to formulate theories and plan effective physical training programs? The following tips are based on the experience of high-level freediving athletes who have singled out a specific approach after testing many different types of training regimens.

2.1 The model freediver

It is still very difficult to identify the perfect body for the "ideal" freediver, even though an increasingly precise profile is being drawn up.

Since freediving followers are relative few in number, a natural selection of people physically inclined to excel in freediving is difficult to determine. Freedivers stand out mainly because they are strong-willed and highly motivated to spend countless hours in water training.

Athletes from other sports have their own specific physical structure, and they are the living expression of a physical specialty because of the diligent training they fol-

low for their discipline. Marathoners are all long-limbed, very slim and have lengthened muscle bundles. Even their cardiovascular and pulmonary systems have adapted to the specific needs of marathon running. By contrast, sumo wrestlers and weight lifters have physically developed to make the most of their massive muscle strength. The outstanding freediver is usually a long-limbed athlete with not excessively hypertrophic muscles, but with well-developed joint mobility and great muscle elasticity, as well as an above-average pulmonary volume. These physical traits enhance his ability to perfect the necessary technical skill, movement plasticity and reactivity. There are a few high-level freedivers who have a completely different structure and are characterized by physical prowess and capability to perform hard workouts at the gym.

These freedivers do not necessarily stand out for their grace, elegance and familiarity with water. Instead, they most often compete in disciplines that require almost no muscle intervention (no limits variable weight).

2.2 Freediving and athletic training: what to train

Water is denser than air. That is why we move with more difficulty in the water. When we deep-dive, in the first 20 meters we are buoyant and our bodies are pushed upward (Archimedes' principle), so we must make a significant effort to swim away from the surface. In dynamic apnea, our body must move horizontally and, at the same time, break resistance against the upward push. When the freediver is about to dive, or while he is performing dynamic apnea, he has to face two forces. One force – resistance, caused by the water he must move – tends to restrain him. The other force – propulsion, generated by the muscles involved in the whole movement of the fin-stroke – moves him forward. This simple but important concept is at the foundation of the functional analysis of muscles involved in freediving.

In freediving, both the anaerobic and aerobic systems are involved, but we do not know in which percentages.

Both of them must be developed during training. The current trend prefers focusing on aerobic training, with a lower percentage (about 30%) of anaerobic training in the last part of the session.

According to almost all popular freedivers, who include extensive general athletic training in their training programs, anaerobic exercises must be done for a period of time as close as possible to the freediving performance time.

For instance, if a competition in constant weight or in dynamic apnea lasts almost two minutes, it will be more useful to perform 200 meters in freestyle instead of a 50-meter sprint. In weight-lifting, we would perform multiple sets of squats with a not-too-heavy workload, rather than doing one squat and lifting massive workload. After an initial training period, the trend is to aim for maximal aerobic power. According to freedivers like us, the most useful dry training is one that moves us to the limits of the aerobic and anaerobic systems while trying not to surpass the anaerobic threshold. Regardless of various athletes' opinions or scientific data that may one day allow us to know what and how to train, there is an indisputable fact: It is essential to be a fit, well-trained, skilled athlete before becoming a skilled freediver. A freediver needs good threshold values, a good recovery system, flexibility and muscular agility. Those features help the aspiring freediver to cultivate his passion with more enthusiasm. Blood shift and the connected elasticity of blood vessels require a well-functioning cardiovascular system, helped by a well-trained heart that pumps and drains blood to and from the lungs efficiently. While from the organic point of view we focus on improving aerobic power (VO_2max), from the muscle point of view we will focus on the muscle areas that are most involved in water test.

Here is how a well-structured training program can be beneficial to freediving:

- **High-level freediver, close to his potential:** Neophyte or amateur freedivers can improve their water performances very quickly during the initial stages. As freedivers reach higher levels of training, improvement in performance will slow down until it levels off. Therefore, freedivers need to change their training stimuli to further improve their performances. This can be done through harder and more focused training. To this aim, it is very important to have a well-designed physical training program.
- **Adding basic physical preparation sessions during the earliest stages of the process:** For a freediver undertaking one year of specific training in the pool, it is helpful to add some basic workload training.
- **Improving pulmonary and cardiovascular systems' efficiency and muscle-building:** These are the main attributes needed by high-level freedivers. Physical training can help improve them.

- **Adapting muscle structure to the athletic gesture**: When the freediver is training to undergo a specific kind of effort, he can work on the muscle areas involved in that effort.

Physical improvement, for a freediver, spearfisher or fin swimmer, is closely linked to the improvement of the following features:

- Aerobic capacity
- Lactic anaerobic capacity
- Strength in muscle areas involved
- Technical capacity, joint flexibility and muscle elasticity

Regularly performing physical training with these specific objectives in mind will help us perform at our best in freediving.

Bear in mind that our goal in freediving training is to be fit at the right moment. We do not have to become competitive athletes in swimming, running or cycling, but we can benefit from these sports, achieving a fitness level that will lead to better performance in freediving or spearfishing. After the intermediate-to-advanced level of the physical training period (swimming, running, weight-lifting, etc.), the freediver must go his own way – into the sea.

A freediver shifts most of his training from the land to the water by adapting the benefits of his physical preparation to the new environment. The freediver's com-

petitive period (we will deal with it in depth in our next book) corresponds with the period that focuses on improving performances in the pool, deep freediving or spearfishing performances.

Freediving causes particular body adaptations, so a well-trained freediver may not appear well-trained for running or other endurance and power-related activities.

2.3 Practical tips

It is important to bear in mind that physical preparation alone, especially in workload stages, does not lead to the best performance in freediving.

The later stages of physical preparation (running, cycling, weight-lifting, swimming) include **breath-holding exercises**. However, according to some theories, physical effort in freediving is more useful from a mental standpoint than from a physical one, because you do not face the same environmental conditions as in water. The freediver adapts by performing psychological training and getting used to the suffering caused by low O_2 and high CO_2 values.

Bear in mind: **The best training for freediving is holding your breath.**

It is almost impossible to re-create the required body adaptations during dry training because underwater our body undergoes changes that do not take place in air (pressure, blood shift, hypercapnia, bradycardia, diving reflex, etc.).

One important aspect of training is to keep a record of one's own training sessions.

A freediver or spearfisher who trains in any activity only twice a week is simply performing maintenance training. In sports, two training sessions per week cannot be defined as "training." At least three sessions per week are needed in order to advance and improve.

Type of Workout Performed	Sessions per Week
Maintenance	2 or less
Training	3 or more

The various disciplines in freediving are very different from one another, and each requires different skills. Therefore, choosing the right workout for your particular discipline can be difficult. In the next chapter, the various disciplines of freediving and spearfishing will be analyzed, and the skills and training needed for each will be outlined.

Here are 10 tips to follow in order to train correctly.

1. Set your ultimate goal, then work backward from there to design your training program.
2. Do not overdo, and do not leapfrog over important stages.
3. Always start with a light workload, and give your body time to adapt and get used to an increasingly heavier workload.

4. Do not overwork, and do not try to keep up with others who are ahead of you in the training program. Respect your method.
5. Follow your training schedule. If today is an off day, do not train, or if you must, perform only a light or alternative workout. If you miss a training session, do not make a fuss about it. Simply accept it and count it as an additional day off to recharge.
6. Consistency is essential for improvement. It is better to train three times a week for a whole month than to workout seven days the first week, one day the second, one day the third and three days the fourth. At the end of the month, the sum may still be 12, but mathematics is one thing and training is another.
7. Follow a diet that provides the fuel you need to face your more demanding days. Do not hesitate to consult a specialist if needed. Healthy eating habits are fundamental in sports and in ordinary life.
8. Drink, drink and drink (water), especially if you train indoors, or outdoors in hot weather. Understand the difference between weight loss and fluid loss.
9. Make the most of each training session. Remember you are not a professional athlete. (If you are, why are you reading this book?) Everything you do should make you feel good and satisfy you. If this is the case, the physical improvements you are seeking will come. It must be like in static apnea: train to improve well-being, not to increase pain.
10. Remember the five virtues that help make the most of your training and lead to results: persistence, willingness, resolution, competitiveness and enthusiasm.

If you have reached this point, you also have another virtue: dedication. You have read this book this far! You might as well continue reading!

Chapter 3
FREEDIVER AND ATHLETE

3.1 Analysis of freediving disciplines

In freediving there are many physical aspects to be trained. Each of them can vary in importance, depending on the specific discipline you are training for. That is why, in the following chapters, various freediving disciplines will be analyzed and the connected physical skills will be identified.

It is important to bear in mind that each individual training session does not rely on the silo approach. A dynamic apnea training session, for instance, can be beneficial to many other freediving disciplines. Trainer consultation and athlete feedback can help develop the best training routine for you.

3.2 Analysis of pure freediving disciplines

3.2.1 *Static apnea*

ATHLETIC GESTURE ANALYSIS

In static apnea, no technical or swimming skills are required. To perform it well, you need to be loose, relaxed and good at NOT doing something! Lots of amateur freedivers who are not particularly outstanding in other freediving disciplines have a natural talent for static apnea. Some trainees struggle to go beyond 50 meters in dynamic apnea, whereas in static apnea they can often get close to, or even beyond, 6 minutes of apnea.

In this discipline, the mental factor plays a fundamental role, especially in delivering a brilliant and replicable performance. Indeed, every freediver has his glorious day, when he performs at his best, but the real goal is to be consistently good. One of the best Italian freedivers in this discipline is Gaspare Battaglia. He is not only able to perform well but also able to repeat his consistently high level of performance. In the freediving world, he is the athlete everyone would want on their team because of his consistency.

Static apnea requires a huge amount of mental energy and awareness of one's own limits, but most of all, it requires the ability to spend a few minutes suffering in an uneasy condition.

AEROBIC CAPACITIES REQUIRED ****

In static freediving, aerobic training for muscle development does not play a big role, because you don't move. But aerobic training plays a leading role in strengthening the cardiovascular system. Aerobic training allows the freediver to better develop bradycardia and capillarization of peripheral blood vessels.

A well-functioning cardiovascular system enables the freediver to take full advantage of his potential when performing static apnea. During a performance, in a state of total relaxation and in a prone position, a bradycardic heart may drop below 35 beats per minute, using less oxygen and enabling a longer, more comfortable breath-holding period. Furthermore, aerobic training helps optimize the vascular system, and vessels are able to oxygenize cells more widely. A widespread cellular oxygenation enables the body to stock a larger quantity of oxygen in the tissues and the muscles. Bear in mind that static apnea depends not only on the volume of air retained in the lungs but also on how much our cells have been oxygenated during ventilation before a performance.

A detailed look at oxygenation and cellular respiration can be found in "*Breathing Techniques for Freediving,*" published by Magenes.

ANAEROBIC CAPACITIES REQUIRED *

During static apnea, the muscles are almost static, so they do not need to be trained for anaerobic effort. At the end of a static apnea session, we may perceive a muscular heaviness, caused by significant peripheral vasoconstriction. This perception is very important from a mental level and from the performance self-analysis point of view. Being aware of what your body is doing and evaluating it in a clear-headed way enables you to understand more precisely your breath-holding limits.

STRENGTH CAPACITIES REQUIRED *

As outlined above, static apnea is associated with immobility and abandon. Therefore strength skills are unnecessary.

TECHNICAL CAPACITIES REQUIRED *

Everyone is able to be still and do nothing, so static apnea does not require many technical or motor skills, but it calls for significant mental strength and bodily self-awareness. These two qualities can be obtained through training. Static apnea training requires a great deal of concentration, which must be part of a good training regimen.

Static apnea training sessions are sometimes considered to be "non-training," because the athlete does not perform a motor action. But, they are still a very important part of the training routine.

PHYSICAL ELASTICITY REQUIRED **

Even though there is no motor action involved in static apnea, body elasticity is extremely important, particularly in the chest, shoulders and shoulder blades.

Chest elasticity allows for maximum skeletal expansion and pulmonary filling during the final inhalation before static apnea. Chest mobility is also important when diaphragmatic contractions kick in, because if the rib cage and muscles involved are elastic, the contractions will be less violent. Having an elastic body means having a body that is easier to keep relaxed. Good elasticity is key to maintaining adequate relaxation before and during static apnea.

3.2.2 *Dynamic apnea with fins*

ANALYSIS OF THE ATHLETIC GESTURE

Dynamic apnea is the most physically strenuous discipline. It requires continuous movement in order to maintain the propulsion needed to keep moving forward. Continuous forward motion in water is strenuous, and the farther the distance, the heavier and more painful the legs become, sometimes resulting in muscular acidosis. In the past few years, athletes performing dynamic apnea have learned how neutral buoyancy can improve the ability to direct the fins and significantly reduce the effort required to swim forward.

Records speak clearly: In 2002 Stéphane Mifsud's world record was 174 meters. In 2010 Dave Mullins set a record of 265 meters. In 8 years, performances have improved by 91 meters. In dynamic apnea with fins, the finstroke is continuous, and the only stops are the turns at the end of each length.

Thanks to the monofin and use of the neck weight, freedivers are completely neutral in the water and use a propulsive and fragmented movement consisting in 2 or 3 fin kicks in dolphin-crawl style followed by a 2-to-3-second pause. At this stage, the

athlete continues to glide forward, thanks to his neutral buoyancy, without losing speed during the motor stop, thanks to his hydrodynamic position. This technique has helped sharply reduce effort and energy waste.

AEROBIC CAPACITIES REQUIRED ****

Swimming in dynamic apnea requires the "most energy-efficient finstroke." A speed that is too high leads freedivers to consume too much energy and increases the heart rate. This can negatively affect the performance of the freediver, who, after a short period of time, faces shortness of breath and cannot help but re-emerge to breathe. Meanwhile, a speed that is too slow, even though it may be moderate in pace, requires holding the breath for a longer period. Covering a distance of more than 150 meters, can take up to 3 minutes. It is difficult to cover such a long distance in such a short time. The most energy-efficient finstroke enables the freediver to exert the least amount of effort and intensity of movement.

The first stage of the dynamic apnea performance, when blood, tissues and muscles are still rich with oxygen, is an aerobic exercise. So, if an athlete is well trained from an aerobic point of view, his cardiovascular system will help him during freediving.

ANAEROBIC CAPACITIES REQUIRED ****

While the workout in the first stage of dynamic apnea is aerobic, the absence of air exchange in the lungs soon leads to a progressive decrease in oxygen in blood and an increase in carbon dioxide. The workout switches from aerobic to anaerobic, resulting in the release of lactate, and the freediver begins to experience muscle heaviness and pain. When covering a long distance, this painful feeling may be with the freediver for a long period, and dynamic apnea becomes tiring, not only physically but also mentally. Swimming underwater with muscle pain and the need to breathe is anything but pleasant.

Lengthened anaerobic training is necessary to help endure that feeling and to increase a physical and mental tolerance to lactate.

This will be discussed further in the chapters that follow.

STRENGTH CAPACITIES REQUIRED ***

As we have said, dynamic apnea requires moderate movement, but the explosive strength necessary to lift heavy loads is not needed in this discipline.

Proper training is important in order to effectively move the propulsive device (monofin or fins).

The training includes aerobic, anaerobic and strength-oriented sessions, avoiding muscular hypertrophy. A moderate and constant rhythm requires basic muscular strength that is able to support both aerobic and anaerobic training.

TECHNICAL CAPACITIES REQUIRED ****

Technical capacities are fundamental in every sport that requires athletic skill. Dynamic apnea is one of the most technical disciplines in the freediving panorama. Yet, in dynamic apnea, it is easy to obtain good results even without strong technical abilities, since the size of the fins or monofin causes significant movement of water, creating strong propulsion even if the kicking technique is not perfect.

Freedivers able to hold their breath for long periods obtained modest results, but if we the analyze the technique of record holders in this discipline, we see that it is flawless. Freedivers who are considered aliens in deep disciplines sometimes lose their edge in dynamic apnea because of rough technique. Athletes such as Alexey Molchanov, Ryuzo Shinomiya, Dave Mullins and Frédéric Sessa are clear examples of how good technique in this discipline is fundamental for achieving outstanding results.

PHYSICAL ELASTICITY REQUIRED ****

Good joint mobility enhances the beauty and effectiveness of the athletic gesture. The technique used with fins is easier and does not require particular joint mobility, but good chest elasticity ensures better pulmonary ventilation and cellular oxygenation. If one fin is used instead, mobility in several areas is fundamental. Lumbar tension or stiffness in the shoulders, shoulder blades or pelvis can compromise the technique needed for proper finning movement and hydrodynamic posture. To conclude, in dynamic apnea, especially when it is performed with one fin, physical elasticity is critical.

3.2.3 *Dynamic apnea without fins*

ANALYSIS OF THE ATHLETIC GESTURE

Dynamic apnea without fins is one of the most complex disciplines in the freediving panorama. It requires swimming the breaststroke underwater, and it entails all the physical difficulties involved in dynamic apnea, as well as strong technical skill. Without propulsive supports such as fins or a monofin, and without an excellent technique, the freediver must work harder to perform the movements, and more energy is used for propulsion. In dynamic apnea without fins, buoyancy is critical. Neutral buoyancy combined with the propulsion of limbs enables the freediver to swim and glide without wasting energy. The pursuit of neutral buoyancy has led athletes to use ballast distributed over two main parts of the body, such as the hips and the neck, using a weight belt and a neck weight.

Distributing the weight across two parts of the body results in better horizontalization and hydrodynamism. Nowadays, we often see athletes who use wetsuits in combination with ballast. Wetsuits ensure a more homogeneous floatation. A freediver wearing a bathing suit is negatively buoyant in the lower part of his body while floatation is completely borne by the chest. Athletes wearing wetsuits have three advantages:

1. Better thermal insulation ensures a higher level of relaxation and the ability to stay in water for a longer time. Training sessions become easier, even those over longer distances, which require longer recovery time.
2. Better distribution of buoyancy, since the legs float more easily and improve body alignment while swimming underwater.
3. Less resistance when athletes wear smooth neoprene wetsuits.

The underwater breaststroke used in dynamic apnea without fins is different from a surface breaststroke. Propulsive movement is fragmented and alternated with glide phases, while in a surface breaststroke the movement is continuous.

The underwater propulsion is less explosive than in a classic breaststroke, since the goal is not to swim as fast as possible but to swim with fluidity and continuity.

In dynamic apnea without fins, this can be described as follows:

- Breaststroke using arms
- Glide
- Breaststroke using legs with recovery of arms to swim forward
- Stretching and glide
- Breaststroke using arms

Even the breaststroke using legs is different from a surface breaststroke. In an underwater breaststroke, being close to the bottom of the pool allows for more streamlined swimming, but it leads the freediver to open his knees more than in the classic technique.

AEROBIC CAPACITIES REQUIRED *****

As in traditional dynamic apnea, aerobic capacities are important. At the beginning of a performance, the fragmented propulsion allows the muscles to work aerobically.

The better the technique, the greater the distance you will be able to cover without feeling heaviness and muscle pain.

If the movement is rough or the buoyancy is incorrect, moving forward will require more abrupt and powerful movements, using different muscle groups.

The ability to take full advantage of your aerobic capacities also depends on your technical skill. A trained athlete with good aerobic endurance will certainly have a cardiovascular system that makes it easy for him to work while holding his breath. Therefore, the aerobic endurance skills required for dynamic apnea without fins are very similar to those required for traditional dynamic apnea.

ANAEROBIC CAPACITIES REQUIRED ****

In the underwater breaststroke, the anaerobic lactic acid effect depends a lot on technique. A lack of technical skill often leads to more abrupt and unnecessarily powerful movements. With a proper technique, the arm and leg movements are alternated with breaks, which amount to short static apnea intervals. With this "fragmented" propulsion, the onset of muscle heaviness slows considerably.

When it does occur, however, it is best if the freediver tries to maintain his pace and fluidity, since sudden acceleration will make the athlete feel even more muscle pain.

In this discipline it is extremely important to train the anaerobic lactic acid capacities, because the lack of propulsion tools will make it even more difficult to endure muscular pain associated with air hunger.

STRENGTH CAPACITIES REQUIRED ***

Strength is involved in every athletic movement. In this case, however, there is no assistance from any tool for propulsion. You can only use your hands and feet to swim underwater, and a fluid and steady motion is needed to move smoothly.

Without a fin or fins moving large volumes of water, you will not need as much kicking strength, but you will need more endurance, since the cyclical and repetitive strokes and kicks move significantly lower volumes of water.

TECHNICAL CAPACITIES REQUIRED *****

As you can imagine, technique is a key factor in this discipline. If you compare freediving world records for traditional dynamic apnea with those for dynamic apnea without fins, you will not see much difference in terms of percentages. However, freedivers involved in this discipline who lack proper technique could find that the difference in distance covered will be much more.

A good yardstick is to determine how many strokes and kicks you need to swim the usual 25 or 50 meters. Leading athletes are able to easily swim 25 meters with three or four strokes.

That said, dynamic apnea without fins is one of the disciplines where the degree of technical training accounts for a great share of the final performance.

PHYSICAL ELASTICITY REQUIRED ****

Swimming the breaststroke, as we have said, is very technical. Therefore, it requires good joint mobility. The shoulders, shoulder blades, back and chest are involved in all the movements of the upper body, while the hips, knees and ankles work hard in breaststroke kicks.

Limited joint mobility and muscle imbalances can affect the swimmer's technique, leading to a less effective motion. So, in this discipline as well, body elasticity is essential.

3.2.4 *Constant weight with fins*

ANALYSIS OF THE ATHLETIC GESTURE

Constant weight with fins has always been considered the mother of all freediving disciplines, for both the pleasure of swimming in the sea and the physical and emotional complexity involved.

The athletic movement of a freediver who descends underwater in constant weight can be divided into several stages, each involving different muscle fibers. The intensity of movement changes depending on the stage of diving.

If we analyze a dive in detail, we can see how, during the first few meters, the freediver must kick in a rhythmic, fluid and intense fashion in order to counteract buoyancy.

At this stage, the freediver breaths until a few moments before, so his cells and lungs are full of oxygen. Although pulmonary ventilation stops, it is assumed that at this stage the body is still working aerobically.

Continuing his descent, the freediver approaches the point of neutral buoyancy, and the intensity of his finning will gradually decrease until, when the buoyancy becomes negative and the descent speed increases, he will stop kicking, and the passive phase of fall will begin.

At this point, his body has used up most of the cellular and lung oxygen, but luckily propulsion needs decrease, so energy consumption is gradually reduced until it becomes minimal during the fall.

The most demanding and difficult energy stage begins immediately after the turn at the bottom, when the freediver heads back toward the surface.

The bottom turn is a very intense effort, because negative buoyancy is pulling the freediver down, and he must counter this force with powerful and fast kicks.

This stage is classified as anaerobic, given its intensity and speed. Fortunately, as described in sport physiology books, for the first ten seconds of ascent, the body is able to use the alactic anaerobic system to access stocks of ATP located in the muscle tissue.

This mechanism allows the freediver to make use of special energy supplies and allows him to delay the feeling of heaviness and pain in his legs during the first stage of ascent.

After rising several meters, however, even if the kick becomes milder, the workout tends to be more of a lactate anaerobic workout.

This stage is the hardest part of the whole dive, both physically and emotionally. During dives to great depths (more than 80 meters), heaviness in muscles develops at about the halfway point, when the path is still long and the stocks of oxygen in the body are shrinking.

Only when the freediver reaches positive buoyancy can he stop kicking and begin the final phase of the ascent without any movement.

The analysis of energy pathways used during a dive in constant weight comes from the observations of professional freedivers. By examining their feelings, they tried to determine what was happening inside their bodies.

To date there is still no medical or scientific evidence for this, although more and more researchers are studying freediving with great interest.

It is likely that before long, medical journals and other scientific publications will be offering explanations for what until now has been studied only through the sensations described by top athletes.

AEROBIC CAPACITIES REQUIRED ****

A properly functioning aerobic system can be regarded as the driving force behind a good athlete.

An efficient cardiovascular system is an excellent base in all athletic disciplines, including freediving.

Also, strong aerobic training is important, particularly for those freedivers who do deep freediving.

ANAEROBIC CAPACITIES REQUIRED *****

In indoor disciplines, speed of propulsion can be mild and homogeneous throughout the performance. There are, of course, slight variations in speed that can be considered negligible, because they do not represent a real shot. In these disciplines, the switch from aerobic to anaerobic workout depends on the gradual decrease of oxygen available.

In constant weight, in addition to the decrease of oxygen because of the absence of pulmonary ventilation, there is also a moment when finning must become impetuous and powerful. This moment, which usually corresponds to the bottom turn, comes at the halfway point of the dive.

By combining muscular exertion with a low amount of remaining oxygen, you get a situation that leads us to say the anaerobic workout will be significant during the ascent phase.

Therefore, when training for deep freediving, it is essential to include a training stage focused on developing your anaerobic endurance. This preparation will make it possible to face the delicate ascent phase with greater awareness and peacefulness.

STRENGTH CAPACITIES REQUIRED *****

The types of strength to train for depend on the pace of your constant weight dive. We have already seen that during both descent and ascent, there are several changes in speed. This means that each muscle involved will be used in several different ways.

Indeed, in constant weight you will see both strength endurance and explosive strength involved. Therefore, both of them must be trained for and analyzed by the freediver who wants to try this wonderful discipline.

TECHNICAL CAPACITIES REQUIRED ****

Being able to perform a technical movement well is extremely important. The more precise the movement, the greater the energy savings.

Efficient kicking combined with good hydrodynamics enables the freediver not to waste energy with excessive effort.

This combined technique involves not only accurate kicking but also the proprioceptive feedback of the athlete.

In constant weight, several aspects must be coordinated and synchronized, such as the propulsive movement, the equalization frequency, the variation in kicking frequency depending on depth, and the management of rest during the descent. Good movement technique enables the freediver to do the right thing at the right moment and in the most economical way in terms of energy. As you can imagine, all this takes a lot of practice.

PHYSICAL ELASTICITY REQUIRED ****

Joint and muscle mobility, which can be trained for out of the water, can make it easier to learn proper technique, since an elastic body uses less energy.

A simple example highlights the importance of general training combined with other more specific training. Body elasticity allows for effective movement associated with hydrodynamic posture without a reduction in physical relaxation. This is essential in this discipline. If the muscles aren't relaxed, equalization problems may occur, and they can significantly jeopardize the performance of the freediver.

3.2.5 *Constant weight without fins*

ANALYSIS OF THE ATHLETIC GESTURE

This discipline became popular throughout the freediving world in early 2000. William Trubridge is responsible for fostering enthusiasm for this discipline, which embodies the essence of freediving.

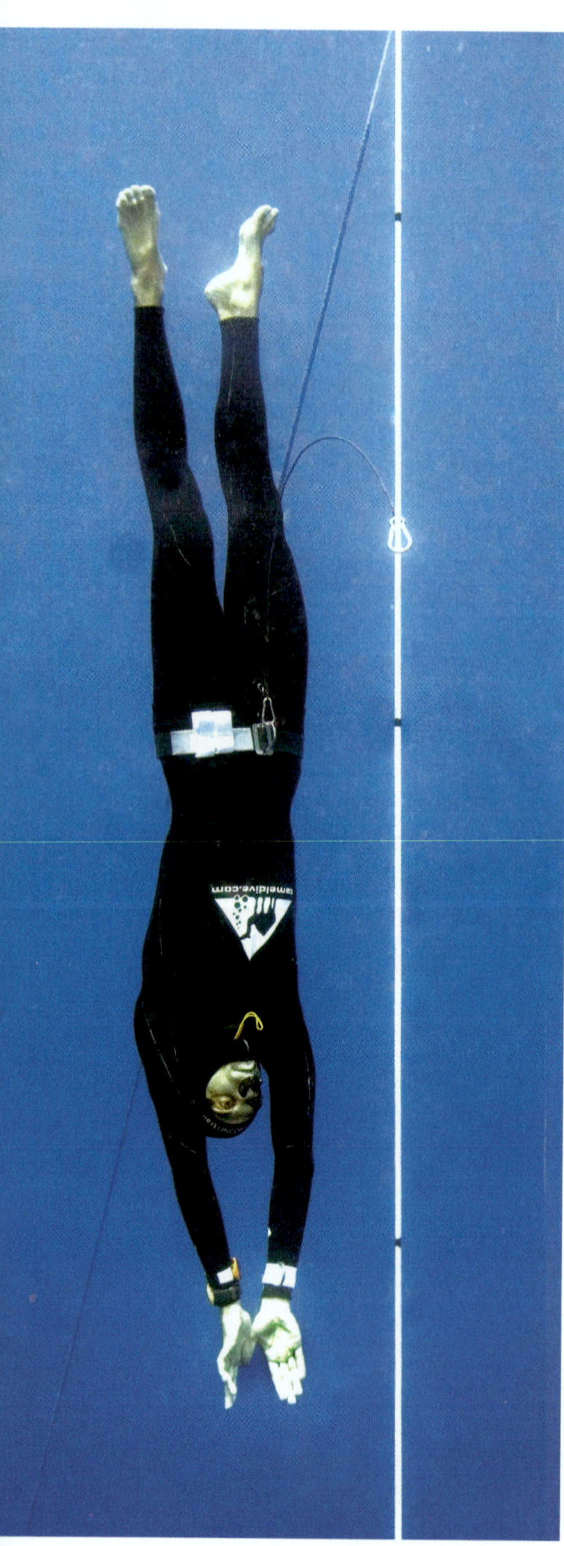

The descent in constant weight without fins is the purest freediving discipline you can imagine. There are no tools for propulsion, only the body.

We believe there is no discipline more technical or difficult than this one. Both descent and ascent are done by swimming the breaststroke underwater. The physical effort required in this sport is already perceived in the first few meters of descent, in which the freediver must overcome buoyancy using only the breaststroke.

The best freedivers can easily get to 30 meters in depth with less than 10 strokes. Then they can begin the relaxed descent stage. But the most difficult thing is the turn at the bottom. Without fins or a monofin, the athlete needs superhuman effort to move away from the bottom.

At abyssal depths, after you kick, you often do not feel any kind of progress. Only your inner calm, paired with perfect physical training, allows you to keep swimming until you grasp the momentum needed for the ascent.

In this discipline, weight must be calculated with extreme accuracy. In constant weight with fins, the strong propulsion of the fins allows a certain range of choice in the amount of ballast to use. In constant weight without fins, being slightly off on the amount of ballast used could make it impossible to successfully perform the first stage of the ascent.

AEROBIC CAPACITIES REQUIRED ****

In constant weight without fins, aerobic training is essential for good performance.

In this discipline, the athlete has to get used to working without excessive muscle loads. The lack of propulsion tools makes movement lighter, more frequent and steadier. Once again, aerobic training is important for freedivers who love no-fins disciplines.

ANAEROBIC CAPACITIES REQUIRED *****

As stated in the analysis of the movement, the best freedivers can easily reach 30 meters in depth in less than 10 strokes, then they start the descent stage.

This stage takes place early in the breath-holding period, when cells, blood and lungs are still full of oxygen. Therefore, the freediver's state is not yet considered to be anaerobic. After turning at the bottom, the freediver is likely to perform the whole ascent in a lactate anaerobic state.

This discipline is difficult, not so much because of the amount of water that must be moved, but because of the need to maintain a constant and regular swimming pace, even when the legs and arms are strained and painful, so as not to lose propulsion. A high lactate tolerance is crucial in these stages. Therefore, in this discipline it is even more important to focus training on lactate anaerobic endurance.

STRENGTH CAPACITIES REQUIRED *****

Unlike constant weight with fins or a monofin, the muscles are less involved in moving large volumes of water, Therefore, the amount of exercise associated with muscle load will be less intense when training for constant weight without fins.

Instead, training for strength endurance must be a primary focus in order to achieve outstanding performance in this discipline. In addition, the strength endurance associated with hypoxic conditions makes the freediver's task even harder.

TECHNICAL CAPACITIES REQUIRED *****

We have already said that this discipline is considered to be the most complex one. Lack of proper technique could make the descent and ascent effort substantial and could significantly reduce the freediver's level of performance.

Perfecting your technique should first be done in a pool, where you do not have to face the depth and you can work safely. Then you can begin to practice the descent by swimming the breaststroke underwater.

PHYSICAL ELASTICITY REQUIRED ****

Swimming the breaststroke requires good joint and muscle mobility. Hips, knees, ankles, shoulders and shoulder blades all need to be strong and flexible to perform a good breaststroke.

3.2.6 *Free immersion*

ANALYSIS OF THE ATHLETIC GESTURE

As in constant weight without fins, propulsion equipment cannot be used in free immersion. The freediver must dive only by pulling on a rope during descent and ascent.

Since free immersion does not require a special technique, it is one of the easiest disciplines to learn.

Also, energy consumption is lower than in the other deep freediving disciplines. In this discipline, legs are not used at all; propulsion depends on the arms only. Because muscle involvement is less, less energy will be consumed.

During the descent, the freediver pulls on the rope until his buoyancy becomes negative and he reaches a good falling speed.

Usually the falling stage begins deeper than it does in constant weight with or without fins. This is because, even if the depth is the same, the speed you reach is slower than in the other disciplines.

The ascent is performed by keeping strokes steady and regular along the entire length of the rope. There are no special changes in speed as in the other constant weight disciplines. In free immersion, the movement frequency is quite regular. Free immersion has many real advantages in terms of energy and technique, but the total dive time is very long, which is not good. As we have already said, the propulsion speed is slower than in other disciplines, therefore the freediver must hold his breath for a longer time.

Consider two world records achieved by Herbert Nitsch in 2010. Diving to 124 meters in constant weight took him about 4 minutes, whereas diving to 120 meters in free immersion took him about 4 minutes and 30 seconds. When both descent and ascent are considered, that's 30 seconds more to cover 8 meters less.

So, it is easy to see that in free immersion the ability to hold one's breath for a long time is crucial.

AEROBIC CAPACITIES REQUIRED ****

Free immersion has been awarded 4 stars since it is similar to the other deep freediving disciplines.

Aerobic training plays an important role in this discipline as well.

ANAEROBIC CAPACITIES REQUIRED *****

While there are similarities in terms of aerobic training, free immersion is different from the other disciplines in terms of anaerobic preparation.

In constant weight with or without fins, the first stage of the ascent involves an intense muscular effort, which relies on the anaerobic system. By comparison, free immersion is quite monotonous in terms of motion, since it does not require any special changes in pace.

But at the same time, the breath must be held longer, so the anaerobic system is triggered by the lack of air recharge.

The long breath-holding times in free immersion lead us to believe that there is a strong dependence on the anaerobic energy system.

STRENGTH CAPACITIES REQUIRED ****

The movement associated with free immersion is regular, smooth and not particularly fast, so the development of strength endurance is one of the main priorities for a freediver performing this discipline.

TECHNICAL CAPACITIES REQUIRED ***

The arm movements used in free immersion are really basic. That is why descent exercises using the arms are among the first exercises given to freediving beginners.

Learning how to properly move the arms does not require a lot of skill or a lot of physical preparation. Therefore, free immersion is the easiest discipline to learn.

PHYSICAL ELASTICITY REQUIRED ****

Physical elasticity is very important in free immersion, especially in deep freediving. By deep, we do not mean a specific distance. We are talking about the depth at which the pressure makes the freediver no longer able to stay relaxed.

Pulling on the rope while experiencing chest and lung squeeze might cause some traction problems, which may cause a pulmonary edema.

This traction does not depend only on the strength applied to strokes. It can also be affected by the sliding vertical movement of the rope caused by the waves.

In a rough sea, the wave energy may affect the freediver's body, especially his chest.

Freedivers have often seen blood traces in their saliva after unexpected underwater pulling movements.

Good physical elasticity and good chest mobility reduce the possibility of trauma caused by the movements induced by the rope.

That is why in this discipline, which does not require any particular motor capacity, physical elasticity, especially chest elasticity, plays a key role in preventing trauma such as pulmonary edema.

Table 3.1 Comparative Table of Freediving Disciplines

	STAT	DYN	DNF	CWT	CNF	FIM
Aerobic system	★★★★	★★★★★	★★★★★	★★★★	★★★★	★★★★
Anaerobic system	★	★★★★	★★★★	★★★★	★★★★★	★★★★★
Strength	★	★★★	★★★	★★★★★	★★★★★	★★★★
Technique	★	★★★★	★★★★★	★★★★	★★★★★	★★★
Elasticity	★★	★★★★	★★★★	★★★★	★★★★	★★★★

3.3 Analysis of freediving spearfishing techniques

Although spearfishing involves breath-holding techniques, it is very different from freediving, both in terms of training and in its approach to the apnea itself.

The first big difference is that many spearfishers approach the world of fishing as a hobby, and they are often self-taught or taught by friends, rather than being taught by professional spearfishing instructors. While many freediving schools have included spearfishing courses for several decades, the first official and regulated spearfishing course dates back only to 2010.

Many courses organized by spearfishing champions or experts, although they may be fruitful, do not necessarily use standard teaching methods that lead to homogeneously and consistently throughout the discipline.

There is often a certain degree of customization of freediving techniques, which are often adjusted according to the person and the fishing site.

These variables makes the approach to this discipline very subjective, and the beginner who starts fishing without any freediving experience is likely to find it staggering.

Just as you should know how to drive before taking a road-racing class, we believe it is best to learn the basic techniques of freediving before learning to spearfish.

Other differences between freediving and spearfishing are listed below.

BALLAST

Usually the spearfisher dives with more weights than the freediver, because his needs are different. He must silently fall while finning less vigorously than a freediver.

With heavier ballast, the spearfisher will expend less energy during the descent, but more intense muscular work will be needed during the ascent.

This approach is not in line with the natural availability of oxygen, since the less demanding stage occurs when the freediver is enjoying the maximal oxygen intake, while the final effort takes place when the oxygen supply has been mostly consumed.

This is why choosing the right amount of ballast is extremely important.

BREATH-HOLDING TIME

In pure freediving, the forward speed is usually about 1 meter per second and does not include any stop at the bottom (unless we are dealing with special exercises). This means that for a dive to 25 meters, about 50 seconds will be required; for a dive to 37 meters, about 1 minute and 14 seconds; and so on.

Spearfishers move more slowly so as not to startle the fish. Therefore, the duration of the dive becomes longer.

In addition to the slower speed, there is the time spent waiting for the fish (waiting at depth) and the horizontal dynamic moves aimed at surprising and ambushing the fish (ambush). All this further increases the necessary breath-holding time. Therefore, spearfishing may be risky for reckless or imprudent spearfishers.

Spearfishing champions reassure us by saying that a fishing action at a depth of about 25 meters should last no longer than 1 minute and 40 seconds. They also remind us that it is useless to keep holding one's breath any longer, because if the fish is going to show up, it will do so within this time frame.

Because spearfishing is very different from pure freediving, the following sections will deal in detail with the most popular spearfishing techniques.

3.3.1 *Ambush spearfishing*

ANALYSIS OF THE ATHLETIC GESTURE

This technique involves stopping at a certain depth and waiting for a predatory fish. Temperate waters are perfect for this kind of spearfishing, because the spearfisher can descend to depths that would be out of reach (for many people) in colder water.

During the descent, the spearfisher dives the first meters to counteract the buoyancy. Once he reaches negative buoyancy, the glide – a period of mostly oblique falling – begins. This is necessary so as not to gather too much speed (that would scare the fish) and to explore the surrounding area to identify the potential prey and to find a place to wait. During the glide, the dive slows down and the total time of descent increases.

Once he reaches the bottom, the spearfisher lies down and waits motionlessly for prey to appear within his range. In this phase, ambush spearfishing can be compared to static apnea, since energy consumption is close to the baseline.

After shooting, or after deciding that the fish is not in range, the ascent phase begins. As we have said, the spearfisher uses more weights than the freediver, so the ascent phase is more difficult and demanding. This is why it is essential to be cautious and not go beyond one's limits.

The most challenging phase of the ascent, in terms of kicking, is the first one. As you head back toward the surface, meter by meter, the finstroke is less demanding in terms of frequency and power.

Once the spearfisher reaches positive buoyancy, he can stop kicking until he reaches the surface.

AEROBIC CAPACITIES REQUIRED *****

The spearfisher needs an efficient muscular and cardiovascular system, even more so than the freediver.

In addition to holding his breath under water, the spearfisher must also swim along the surface looking for the best hunting area. This is usually done while finning, going far out and coming back to the shore, sometimes swimming against the tide or upstream. Therefore, good aerobic capacities are fundamental in spearfishing.

ANAEROBIC CAPACITIES REQUIRED *****

The spearfisher needs good anaerobic preparation in order to hold his breath for long periods of time, which means an increased consumption of oxygen supplies, and to execute a bottom turn with ballast that is heavier than that of the freediver.

STRENGTH CAPACITIES REQUIRED *****

Strength endurance is definitely important for the spearfisher who loves fishing for several hours, which involves doing a lot of finning. Explosive or maximal strength also plays an important role. In the first phase of the ascent, the muscles will have to work at high speed, supplying a great amount of power. So, having well trained legs is definitely a benefit for the spearfisher.

TECHNICAL CAPACITIES REQUIRED ****

The better the technique, the lower the energy expenditure during the descent and the ascent.

Among professional freedivers, there are many excellent spearfishers using special, customized techniques. At the same time, many top spearfishers are using technical skills that come from the world of freediving. We believe that a good freediving technique is a good starting point if you want to become a good spearfisher.

PHYSICAL ELASTICITY REQUIRED ****

Muscle and joint elasticity is essential, since good flexibility allows for a smoother motion. In addition, it may sometimes be necessary to wait for a fish to appear while you are in a position that is not particularly comfortable. Good flexibility enables you to maintain an uncomfortable position more easily. If you are not flexible, the contraction of certain muscles may significantly reduce your ability to stay relaxed and hold your breath in a comfortable and safe way.

3.3.2 *Stealth hunting*

ANALYSIS OF THE ATHLETIC GESTURE

Stealth hunting and ambush spearfishing are very similar in the descent and ascent phases. Stealth hunting is different from ambush spearfishing in that, once he gets close to the bottom, the stealth spearfisher does not stop. Instead, he swims along the bottom, sheltered by boulders and other projections. In this way, he can get close to the prey without the prey seeing him, and once the prey is in range, he shoots his spear.

Slow, fluid movement is essential to stealth hunting. Quick movements cause water disturbances that are easily perceived by the fish. If they realize we are there, they will quickly leave our fishing area. The spearfisher finds his prey mainly through the sense of sight, while a fish can sense a threat without seeing it.

A slow approach, often employing mimicry, is crucial for a successful hunt. There are many different styles of mimicry proposed by companies and by artisans of wetsuits, but it is important to learn the proper movements for a good approach technique.

Certainly, the finning style usually used in freediving is disturbing to the fish, but good freediving training allows you to understand how to adjust your technique to fit the new requirements.

In stealth hunting, energy is consumed during dynamic moves on the sea floor, but usually the depths are shallower than in ambush spearfishing.

However, remember that ambush spearfishing and stealth hunting are not that different from one another. Many features of ambush spearfishing also apply to stealth hunting, and vice versa. The capacities required are therefore very similar in both disciplines.

AEROBIC CAPACITIES REQUIRED *****

As explained in the previous section, even in stealth hunting the spearfisher needs great aerobic capacities. Stealth hunting usually entails long sessions, during which the movements with fins can be considerable. In addition, there will be several dives to stalk the fish.

The aerobic capacities associated with this technique must therefore be trained to a high level.

ANAEROBIC CAPACITIES REQUIRED *****

Anaerobiosis in stealth hunting results from staying under water for a long time without ventilation while moving almost constantly, albeit slowly.

Once the approach phase and of the potential catch phase are over, there is still the difficult phase of ascent, which is athletically challenging and primarily anaerobic.

In addition, if you catch a big prey, you will add to the ascent phase the resistance of the fish, which will be opposing your efforts by trying to get back to the bottom and into its den.

This stress is added to the other anaerobic-lactic acid activities the diver must face.

STRENGTH CAPACITIES REQUIRED *****

Once again, strength endurance supports long movements on the surface and slow movements under the water.

Explosive strength is used less often, but it kicks in during the bottom turn or when you need to catch up to a big prey.

These are two conditions a spearfisher should consider and train for.

TECHNICAL CAPACITIES REQUIRED ***

The technical capacities required are not so different from those needed in ambush spearfishing. It's the movements on the bottom that require specific technical ability. You often see newcomers to spearfishing moving in a clumsy way. Those classified as "those who plow the bottom" often suffer from their excessively heavy ballast. This makes the moves along the bottom challenging and makes it easy for the spearfisher to hit rocks with his fins, legs or ballast. The resulting noise can put fish on high alert. Therefore, good technique involves not only good kicking but also a good choice of equipment and weights. Proper ballast can allow you to move along the bottom without using your fins. All that's needed are small arm motions.

PHYSICAL ELASTICITY REQUIRED ****

Even in stealth hunting, it may be necessary to lie in wait in uncomfortable positions or to move in an awkward fashion. Good body elasticity enables you to creep like a snake in tight surroundings without suffering significantly. Please remember that an easily performed action uses much less energy than an action that causes muscle or joint tension and contraction.

3.3.3 *Spearfishing in shallow waters*

ANALYSIS OF THE ATHLETIC GESTURE

Practiced most often during the winter, spearfishing in shallow waters aims to catch fish that run around in shallow water or in the foam produced by breaking waves, or fish that sit quietly in their dens. This type of fishing often requires a succession of dives associated with short ambush sessions or short stealth hunting sessions. The spearfisher may also be looking for fish in their dens by inspecting every hole, crack or split that could indicate the presence of prey.

The main feature of this type of fishing is frequency. Breath-holding periods are not as long, but they come in rapid succession. Short recovery periods and repetitive breath-holding make shallow-water spearfishing very intense.

AEROBIC CAPACITIES REQUIRED *****

Strong cardiovascular and muscular systems ensure good fishing sessions. Basically, the spearfisher is constantly moving, alternating periods of breathing with periods of freediving. A well-trained cardiovascular system allows a faster recovery and a greater capacity to store oxygen in the blood and in the tissues.

Outstanding aerobic capacities are therefore essential for successful spearfishing as well as freediving.

ANAEROBIC CAPACITIES REQUIRED ****

In this discipline, it is difficult to define how much the lactate anaerobic system is involved, since long breath-holding time and great muscle strain are usually not required.

Surely, if the pace is high and the recoveries are short, it might result in a hypercapnia. Another component, which may lead to special muscle strain, is the fact that in shallow waters the backwash is often strong. Even a spearfisher with a quite heavy ballast must cling to something or wedge himself in to stay on the bottom. This effort is definitely huge.

STRENGTH CAPACITIES REQUIRED ***

This sport does not require great effort for the descent and ascent, therefore the main efforts are those relating to movement (strength endurance) and those needed to cling firmly to the bottom, which often require isometric contractions.

TECHNICAL CAPACITIES REQUIRED ***

In this type of fishing, there is not a lot of emphasis on special kicking techniques. Kicking is used mainly for propulsion in horizontal displacements. When spearfishing in shallow waters, the descent is simplified by heavy ballast, so you need just a few kicks to get to a point of negative buoyancy. Also the ascent is not as challenging, so you need just a few fin strokes to emerge smoothly.

PHYSICAL ELASTICITY REQUIRED ****

The body elasticity needed in this discipline is related to the ability to creep into spaces that can ensure good stability despite the backwash. The smaller the spaces, the more points of support there will be. Of course, comfort is not the main characteristic of this discipline, but it can produce a wealth of fish.

This long analysis of the various disciplines reveals that there are common features in many of the abovementioned sports. It also shows that a good athlete can more easily become a good freediver.

This section is designed to help you understand which features are necessary for a freediver to focus on when preparing a training program.

Later, we will focus on training and workouts that will help develop the characteristics described above.

Table 3.2 Comparative Table of Fishing Techniques Table

	Ambush	Stealth Hunting	In Shallow Waters
Aerobic system	★★★★★	★★★★★	★★★★★
Anaerobic system	★★★★★	★★★★★	★★★★
Strength	★★★★★	★★★★★	★★★
Technique	★★★★	★★★	★★★
Elasticity	★★★★	★★★★	★★★★

Chapter 4
MENTAL TRAINING

In order to be successful in freediving, it is important to train not only your body but also your mind.

Self-listening is a fundamental skill for the evolution of a freediver. A self-aware freediver may prove to be a more successful athlete than one who is merely physically gifted. It is not just by chance that the strongest freediving athletes all over the world are not extremely young. Many are more than 30 years old and have had more time to develop this essential self-awareness.

Training one's mental capacities is crucial, since they are a very important part of freediving. By training those capacities in a conscious way, even during physical preparation, the athlete will get used to taking a conscious approach to each discipline he practices.

4.1 The learning process

Learning is the cornerstone of any improvement in sports. There are several mental characteristics involved in the learning process. In this chapter, we will discuss these characteristics to help you figure out which ones you need to work on. To improve those characteristics, a freediver may choose to work on them consciously, but improvement can take place unconsciously as well. The evolution of motor skills associated with exercise depends on a continuous subconscious analysis of the athletic gesture. If the athlete combines this with a conscious mental evaluation of his progress, learning will be faster and more profitable.

It is not our intention to write an essay on motor control. Many comprehensive texts have already been written that discuss the motor evolution of athletes and non-athletes as well.

4.2 Motor learning

It is important for any sportsman, including the freediver, to understand the variables involved in motor learning.

An athlete who is aware of his body and his emotions is able to make the most of his workouts and training. Knowing what is happening to your body and your mind during your workout helps you stay more focused on the acquisition of new motor capacities.

Broadly speaking, motor learning can be divided in three phases:

- cognitive phase
- associative phase
- autonomous phase

The **cognitive phase** and the **associative phase** are the first two stages of motor learning. The cognitive phase is the period when a person is new to the motor activity to be performed and tests his action through a sequence of basic movements. The associative phase comes next, merging individual movements together to create a single, smooth action.

These two phases are essential for the novice, but they are not important to focus on here. The average reader of this book will be an athlete who has already acquired the basic motor skills and needs only to maximize them.

For the athlete, it's the third phase – the **autonomous phase** – that plays a key role. In most cases, the motor capacities have already been acquired, but the autonomous phase can help maximize them, leading to a smoother, faster, energy-saving motor sequence.

The word "autonomous" conveys the idea of how automatic the motor skill should become. If the athlete needs to think about how to perform a movement or how to control it, he will waste a lot of physical and mental energy, which in turn will decrease the level of his performance. Only through repetition is it possible for the athlete to reach a point where he can move in an automatic way.

In addition, repetition helps build a strong and enduring muscular system. When your body is trained to resist fatigue, it is easier to train it to accomplish new tasks.

4.3 The importance of repetition

As was just mentioned, repetition is the best way to acquire new motor skills. Training is nothing more than an organized repetition of those skills that, through the learning process, leads to improvement in the skill themselves and consequently to improvement in the athlete's overall performance. That is why training has to take place frequently and on a regular schedule.

Repetition is important, but the degree of attention placed on the training session is just as important.

When you train, it is important to pay utmost attention to the specific task you are performing and to the overall goal of that training session.

It is much better to train for 45 minutes every day in an intense and concentrated way than to train 2 hours a day in a mild, distracted manner.

One of the first things that will let you know if your training session is properly adjusted to your level of ability is how much "mental digression" you experience during training. If during your workout you are able to spend time fantasizing or thinking about things other than your exercises, then your workout is too easy – either physically or technically or both. (This does not apply to warm-up and cool-down periods, of course.) If your workout involves a high level of exercise and technical complexity, then you will stay focused on the task at hand.

Getting back to repetition, a training stimulus is most efficient if you workout at least three times a week. An irregular or less frequent repetition of the task is less likely to effectively trigger the mechanisms of physical, motor, physiological and memory adaptation that are essential to learning.

4.4 Visualization

In addition to practicing a skill you are trying to perfect, it is important to visualize it. The visual system is an important support system for kinesthetic perception; the human body processes up to 90% of all sensory input through sight.

A new motor skill can be learned more efficiently if the athlete not only feels it but also "sees" it.

Being able to picture your body in your mind and "watch" it go through its movements enables you to reach your motor capacity faster and more successfully.

Many athletes use visualization as part of their training process. Visualization helps prepare the body for action, allowing it to be quicker, more reactive and less stressed when it has to carry out the real task.

A positive visualization – one where the athlete visualizes a perfect exercise performance over and over again – creates psychomotor reinforcement that helps the athlete carry out the task.

The visualization should be consistent and realistic, adjusted to the skills and abilities of the athlete who is using it. Visualizations of amazing performances way beyond our abilities are not visualizations; they are just dreams!

THE USE OF VISUALIZATION

Here is an exercise that can help you better understand how to use visualization:

- Take about 10 minutes. Sit down in a comfortable, quiet place and start breathing slowly.
- Imagine you are performing a training session, and try to analyze the variables it involves (physical sensations, surrounding environment, equipment used, people who are usually around, etc.)
- Are you visualizing the exercise as if you were experiencing it first-hand within yourself? Or, are you acting as a spectator, watching yourself perform?

Either way is fine. Perceiving yourself as a third person is known as dissociative visualization. Seeing and feeling the action first-hand is known as associative visualization. Both types of visualization can be beneficial to the learning process.

ASSOCIATIVE VISUALIZATION

During associative visualization, the athlete is deeply involved, both in terms of perception and in terms of emotion, so it can be very useful for bringing out the good feelings induced by an athletic performance.

During this type of visualization, you may experience the sense of calm you feel during a yoga session, for example.

If visualizing a run or a biking session, you may imagine a beautiful landscape running through your mind. During a swimming visualization, you may sense the cool water as you glide smoothly through the sea.

All these positive perceptions can contribute to a more enjoyable and effective performance. Vividly recalling pleasant sensations can increase your desire to train and your motivation to perform well. But unfortunately there can be a counterproductive affect to visualization if the athlete envisions a poor performance or a negative situation that leads to failure. In this case, the athlete will find himself experiencing and reinforcing negative feelings about his athletic performance.

Associative visualization is a very strong tool, which can be used either positively or negatively. It can recall very strong feelings and moods that can get in the way of making an objective assessment of your performance. It can stimulate the senses and amplify the emotions associated with a performance. Therefore, the athlete must learn how to benefit from associative visualization, focusing on its positive effects and avoiding visualization of troubles or failure.

If an athlete carries the idea of potential failure in his mind, it can lead to visualizations that reinforce the potential for a catastrophic outcome. Each of us has certainly experienced how one's state of mind can affect an athletic performance.

DISSOCIATIVE VISUALIZATION

Dissociative visualization allows the athlete to step outside himself and analyze the most mechanical and objective aspects of his performance. He sees himself from the outside, like a spectator trying to learn by watching his performance.

This less emotional type of visualization still may evoke strong feelings, but it also engages the intellect in identifying essential moves and fine-tuning athletic technique.

This method of visualization is useful in helping to erase, or overwrite, negative memories. For example, if a training session has gone badly, instead of playing the bad performance over and over in your head, force yourself to have a dissociative visualization that maintains a neutral view of the event and can help you analyze and understand what led to failure.

Every athlete has his own way of reliving the past, as well as his own way of projecting himself into the future. With these tools borrowed from neurolinguistic programming (NLP), a freediver will be able to draw benefits from each kind of visualization. The first step is to determine which type of visualization is most natural for you. Then, learn to understand which sense or senses your mental projections are based upon – sight, hearing, or kinesthetics. Finally, learn how to use associative visualization to motivate and inspire, while using dissociative visualization to help hold back unpleasant memories and emotions.

4.5 The mental management of physical stress

The athlete who trains frequently must deal with the physical and mental consequences arising from his workload.

In the Western view, the lone athlete (who is not constantly followed by a trainer) is often a victim of the "must do, do and still do" syndrome.

Unfortunately, the freediver is often a lone athlete. He is rarely followed by a trainer. If he decides to physically train by performing activities such as running, cycling or going to the gym, he often finds himself surrounded by people who have goals completely different from his own. In this environment, it is easy to lose sight of the final goal and focus instead on the training itself.

The concept of "the more I train, the more I am trained" can lead to overloads that you may pay for both physically and mentally.

Excessive work, or work that is not properly planned, can be a major source of stress for the athlete, and despite his great effort, he's not likely to see much improvement.

It is important to learn how to plan training sessions, followed by adequate recovery periods. While undertraining will not help you achieve your goals, overtraining may be both physically and mentally harmful.

Therefore, be thorough, be careful and recognize the possible clues to an excessive workload. Being irritable and nervous, experiencing depletion of the immune system, having trouble sleeping, or waking up in the morning with tachycardia may be warning signals of overtraining.

If you experience any of the above symptoms, you should consult with a skilled trainer who, after assessing your training regimen, can advise you on the best way to restore physical and physiological balance in your life.

4.6 Recording a training session

During the learning process, one thing that can improve your state of consciousness and the training session itself is analysis of the training session.

Assessing the feelings you have at the end of a workout is an important way to understand how your body and mind are reacting to the training. It is important to record these feelings while they are fresh and clear in the hours immediately after the session. Otherwise, they tend to sink into oblivion.

Keeping good workout records can contribute to the growth of the athlete in two fundamental ways:

- Writing about your feelings is not easy because it requires mental processing of your emotions. It can be difficult at first and may seem meaningless. You will find it easier to write about key reactions to your workout if you get used to doing it regularly. It will soon become simpler and more straightforward;
- By recording your training achievements after each workout, you can compare the results obtained from various sessions. This is fundamental to determining whether you are improving your performance or not. Many good freedivers find it difficult because they are not used to recording their training sessions. At the end of the day, they make assessments such as, "Today it went well", or "Today there was something wrong".

Such statements are of no help if you do not record specific results that were achieved during your workout. Without this essential information, you can't analyze your training session or compare it with others. You will have no way to figure out which aspects may be positively or negatively affecting your training.

ANECDOTE OF THE TRAINING SESSION THE DAY BEFORE THE COMPETITION

By Federico Mana

To further stress what has been said above, I would like to share with you how I made a significant change in the way I face an important competition thanks to recording. At the end of 2007, I was training with the aim of setting a world record in constant weight without fins during the AIDA World Championship. Over the weeks before the event, I was training myself by simulating the competition phase. 24 hours before the supposed competition, as is normal, I had a recovery day, as I have always seen doing by high-level freedivers.

One day, while I was talking to Giusy, my swimming coach, and consulting with her on recordings of training sessions performed in the previous months, she pointed out to me that during my first day of training after recovering, as a mathematic rule, I have always recorded a greater perception of stiffness in the movements I made associated with a lesser relaxation, if compared to the second day of the training session. Therefore, Giusy suggested scheduling a workout the day before the competition and we both decided to implement this approach.

The results were amazing: I found out that I was able to dive in a looser and more self-confident way just because I had changed my program.

When, during the Championship, the other athletes saw me going out in the open sea to train myself the day before the competition, I was asked why I was doing so and I explained the reasons that had driven me to this approach. At the same time, I asked them why they should have rested and I found out that many of them did so because they saw that many others were resting; they finally confided to me they had never examined so carefully their approach.

4.6.1 *A running session record*

Running Session Record

NAME:

DATE ______________________
PLACE ______________________
TIME ________ TEMP______°C

Weather conditions

Sunny ☐ Cloudy ☐
Rain ☐ Snow ☐

HYDRATION AND NUTRITION BEFORE AND DURING THE SESSION:
How long before the session: ______________________
Meal description: ______________________
Integration: Before ____________ During____________ After____________

Training goal:

- ☐ FR (Fast Run)
- ☐ SR (Slow Run)
- ☐ ER (Easy Run)
- ☐ MR (Medium Run)
- ☐ RPM (Running Pace per Minute)
- ☐ IT (Interval Training)
- ☐ LSD (Long Slow Distance)

WARM-UP	YES	NO	DURATION
COOL-DOWN	YES	NO	DURATION

Description of the Training Session:

Description of Physical Sensations

Technical Description
Km Covered Pace
Heart Rate
N. of Trials
Recovery min.
Recovery dist.

Other Notes
SHOES KM
BODY WEIGHT BEFORE AFTER

4.6.2 *A cycling session record*

Cycling Session Record

NAME:

DATE ____________________
PLACE ____________________
TIME ________ TEMP______°C

Weather conditions
Sunny ☐ Cloudy ☐
Rain ☐ Snow ☐

HYDRATION AND NUTRITION BEFORE AND DURING THE SESSION:
How long before the session: ____________________
Meal description: ____________________
Integration: Before ____________ During____________ After____________

Training goal:

- ☐ LD (Long Distance Cycling)
- ☐ MD (Medium Distance Cycling)
- ☐ FPC (Fast-Paced Cycling)
- ☐ MR (Medium Run)
- ☐ CPM (Cycling Pace per Minute)
- ☐ IT (Interval Training)
- ☐ LSD (Long Slow Distance)

WARM-UP	YES	NO	DURATION
COOL-DOWN	YES	NO	DURATION

Description of the Training Session:

Description of Physical Sensations

Technical Description
Km Covered
Cycling Pace
Heart Rate
N. of Trials
Recovery min.
Recovery dist.

Other Notes
BODY WEIGHT BEFORE AFTER

4.6.3 *A gym session record*

Gym Session Record

NAME:

DATE ______________________
PLACE ______________________
TIME ______________________

External temperature ______________
What you wear ______________
____

HYDRATION AND NUTRITION BEFORE AND DURING THE SESSION:
How long before the session: ______________________
Meal description: ______________________
Any mineral salts or drinks during the training: ______________

Training Goal:

- ☐ Strength
- ☐ Strength Endurance
- ☐ Interval Training
- ☐ Cardio Fitness
- ☐ Weight Lifting while Holding One's Breath

Description of the Table and/or Circuit

Description of Physical Sensations

Description of Technical Sensations

Other Notes

4.6.4 A swimming session record

Swimming Session Record

NAME:

DATE ______________________
PLACE ______________________
TIME ______________________

Water Temperature ______________________

HYDRATION AND NUTRITION BEFORE AND DURING THE SESSION:

How long before the session: ______________________

Meal description: ______________________

Any mineral salts or drinks during the training: ______________________

Training goal:

- ☐ A1
- ☐ A2
- ☐ B1
- ☐ B2
- ☐ C1
- ☐ Technique
- ☐ Fins

Description of the Training Session:

Description of Physical Sensations

Description of Technical Sensations

Other Notes

4.6.5 A yoga session record

Yoga Session Record

NAME:

DATE ______________________
PLACE ______________________
TIME ______________________

External temperature ______________
What you wear ______________
____

HYDRATION AND NUTRITION BEFORE AND DURING THE SESSION:
How long before the session: ______________________
Meal description: ______________________
Any mineral salts or drinks during the training: ______________________

Training Goal:

- ☐ Hathayoga
- ☐ Pranayama
- ☐ Joint Elasticity
- ☐ Muscle Elasticity
- ☐ Mobility of Shoulders and Shoulder Blades
- ☐ Mobility of the Back
- ☐ Mobility of Hips and Pelvis
- ☐ Mobility of Tibiotarsal Joint
- ☐ ______________________
- ☐ ______________________

Brief Description of the Training Session:

Description of Physical Sensations

Description of Technical Sensations

Other Notes

Chapter 5

RUNNING

Running is one of the easiest exercises for most humans, regardless of age. We all know how to run. We've been doing it since we were children, when we ran to play, to escape from the others, or just for fun. We run for a variety of reasons: for recreation, to support other sports (such as football and basketball), or simply to help improve our performance in other disciplines where running is not involved, such as freediving.

By combining our efforts and relying on three qualities – method, perseverance and dedication – we can get the sought-after results from running. Whether we want to lose weight, improve our freediving skills, or test ourselves in a half marathon, running can help us reach our goals. Your individual levels of perseverance and dedication are up to you, but running as a method of training is definitely a topic to be explored.

Running can bring about positive changes in our body, ranging from the reduction of cholesterol and triglycerides in the blood to increases of respiratory efficiency and lung volume – features that are so dear to us freedivers. Just as important as the physical benefits of running are the numerous psychological benefits. But training for running in an inappropriate way may not bring improvement. In fact, illnesses and injuries might occur, causing damage rather than benefit.

So remember: method, perseverance and dedication. Repeat these words like a mantra to get the results you want to achieve.

Rule number one: Appropriate shoes are required!

Inadequate footwear can cause injuries to the joints of the lower limbs: knee, ankle and hips joints. Such injuries can affect our daily life as well as our athletic training.

To preserve our feet, as well as our back and joints, we must go to a specialized shop where an experienced salesperson can advise us and help us find the right shoes. Please forgive me if the following question seems a bit stupid, but we choose our fins with care and attention. Why don't we do the same with running shoes?

Next, we must design our running routine. Most training parameters for running are based upon the working heart rates. We train to achieve specific heart-rate targets.

In running, acronyms abound. ER, SR, FR, TR, FR, RPM and IT are codes used to identify specific paces and types of training sessions. For those who don't practice running as their primary sport, it is sufficient to know simply SR (slow running), TR (tempo running), IT (interval training) and FRK (fartlek).

The goal of slow running is to keep the HR at between 70% and 80% of the max HR (maximal heart rate). This stimulates the use of fatty acids for energy, and therefore contributes to weight control. It is also used as a basis for acquiring adaptations and important skills needed to perform more difficult running work.

1
THE NORTH FACE
THE NORTH FACE
THE NORTH FACE
THE NORTH FACE

THE
NORTH
FACE

The most interesting training sessions for a freediver are those using tempo running, which aims to improve aerobic power (VO_2max). The goal of TR is to keep the HR between 80% and 85% of max HR, while IT is performed with peaks of HR close to the aerobic threshold.

Now, we will describe the various paces and how to interpret them.

• LONG-DISTANCE RUNNING

Long-distance running involves covering a long distance while running continuously for more than an hour. It requires developing various organic, muscular and mental adaptations to ensure that you can maintain your level of effort over a previously established period of time. For those who want to devote themselves to running with perseverance and regularity, this kind of aerobic training is fundamental. By covering a long distance at a steady pace, you can improve your running technique while burning "fats," which is an added benefit for most everyone.

• SLOW RUNNING

Slow running involves a specific training period – usually less than an hour – with adequate recovery time between training sessions.

• MEDIUM-DISTANCE RUNNING

Medium-distance running is performed at a steady, uniform pace throughout the entire training session. The session is shorter than a slow running session, because more effort is required. The heart rate ranges from 80% to 85% of the aerobic threshold rate. Medium-distance running acts as a link between endurance training sessions and training sessions aimed at developing greater intensity.

• FAST RUNNING

Fast running can range from 20 minutes to 50 minutes for top runners. This kind of training involves a cardiovascular effort close to the anaerobic threshold; with the heart rate ranging from 95% to 100% of the max HR.

Another category of running to consider incorporates pace variations using the following paces:

• FARTLEK, OR "SPEED PLAY"

Fartlek was launched in the 1950s by Swedish runners, who lead the way in outdoor endurance running.

During that time, top European runners performed their training sessions in a small Swedish town in the middle of nowhere called Vålådalen.

Fartlek training was introduced as a way to deal with a really rough and rugged terrain.

This practise began to catch on and became popular with many athletes, who found it to be an irreplaceable addition to their standard training schedules.

With its the evolution came a variety of different methods, which distorted the true nature of fartlek training, depriving it of its spontaneity, which was one of its original assets. A training session may be marked by long-lasting pace variations, during which the threshold speed is increased and the muscles' ability to use oxygen improved, or it can be marked by short pace variations. The goal of short pace variation is to rapidly increase the heart rate, then allow it to slow down during recovery time, then increase it again, all for the benefit of the heart itself.

- **PROGRESSIVE**

As you can guess from the word itself, the progressive method involves a gradual increase in pace, starting out with slow and medium running, then switching to fast running in the last phase of the training session. This enables us to employ as many muscle fibers as we can. This method may include medium and long repetitions close to the aerobic threshold, endurance repetitions, uphill running and more. We will not analyse this topic in depth, since there are many books dealing with it (listed in the bibliography).

5.1 Running technique

Like any athletic activity, running requires a specific technique. A perfect technique ensures energy savings and improvement in terms of performance. Those who run correctly waste less energy and work less hard.

In order to run properly, it is necessary to examine the following:

- **Trunk:** We often see runners leaning forward. This not only makes running more difficult but also significantly stresses back and trunk muscles. Keeping one's gaze fixed straight ahead helps maintain a proper upright posture, thus ensuring better overall balance, which leads to lower energy consumption (sequence 2).

- **Feet:** When we talk about feet, we are specifically talking about the ankle joint, which is significantly stressed with every stride. When the feet are in contact with the ground, the ankle joint is subjected to many negative forces, which can damage the joint, forcing the athlete to slow down.

The first goal of any runner is to reduce contact with the ground to a minimum. This can be done with a "horizontally developed run," which enables the athlete to run using a straighter movement, rather than a vertical one. In addition, the toes should be higher than the heel when the foot hits the ground. This technique is called "heel-toe" (sequence 3).

What if we don't have these skills? As far as trunk posture is concerned, it is necessary to strengthen the abdominals and the erector spinæ muscles in order to make the upper part of the body more sound. This should be combined with adequate stretching of the back muscles. To develop and effective heel-toe movement, we can perform a set of exercises that stimulate foot sensitivity. For example, you can do exercises that involve running or walking on your heels (sequence 4 in the following pages) or exercises to train reactivity, such as jumps and leaps (sequence 5 in the following pages).

5.2 Reasons for running

Freedrivers can run several months per year, stopping only in the weeks before competitions. Taking a break from running before competitions ensures that trauma caused by the feet's impact with the ground does not negatively affect the musculoskeletal system during a time when it needs to be at its best.

In addition, during the break period, our metabolism slows down and restores itself in order to ensure adequate energy for consumption during competition.

Running can be used as a simple warm-up, as a cool-down or as a training session all its own. When we plan our training sessions, we must take our goals into account.

4
THE NORTH FACE

5
THE NORTH FACE

Are we running for general exercise, to reduce body weight, or to improve our aerobic and anaerobic capacities? Or perhaps we are running as part of the recovery stage after the competitive season has ended, or after a holiday or an injury. In any case, running rebuilds and increases our fitness level, which is always lower after any period of rest.

We can use the most enjoyable form of running – slow running – to obtain:

- Increase in general endurance or training capacity.
- Regeneration after a training session or other physical exercise. (Imagine a regenerating run in a park or in the woods, treading on leaves and pine needles. This is a wonderful change of scene for our brain and our body.)

Needless to say, we can use running, ranging from slow to fast, any time we want to achieve improvement in our aerobic capacities.

5.3 Starting test for running

COOPER TEST

Drawn up by Kenneth H. Cooper, a NASA physician, this test measures the distance a runner can cover in 12 minutes. It is performed on a standard 400-meter track. The following table ranks the runner's level of performance.

Table 5.1 Table of valorisation for athletes (KUNZE, 1977-BOSCO, 1990)

Distance Covered	Category of Performance
Up to 2.000 meters	Insufficient
Up to 2.400 meters	Mediocre
Up to 2.800 meters	Good
Up to 3.200 meters	Very good
More than 3.200 meters	Excellent

In February 2000, during the Italian Spearfishing, Freediving and Underwater Shooting Championship held at the Italian National Olympic Committee's Olympic Training Center in Tirrenia, freedivers performed better than athletes from other disciplines. Ten athletes covered distances ranging from 2.130 meters to 3.123 meters. This test can be applied in cycling as well, but distances and related evaluations will be different.

CONCONI TEST

The Conconi Test is an incremental maximal test launched in 1982 and later modified by its inventor, Professor Francesco Conconi.

The Conconi Test is used to determine the aerobic maximal speed and the anaerobic threshold. It is performed on level ground with markers every 50 o 100 meters. A

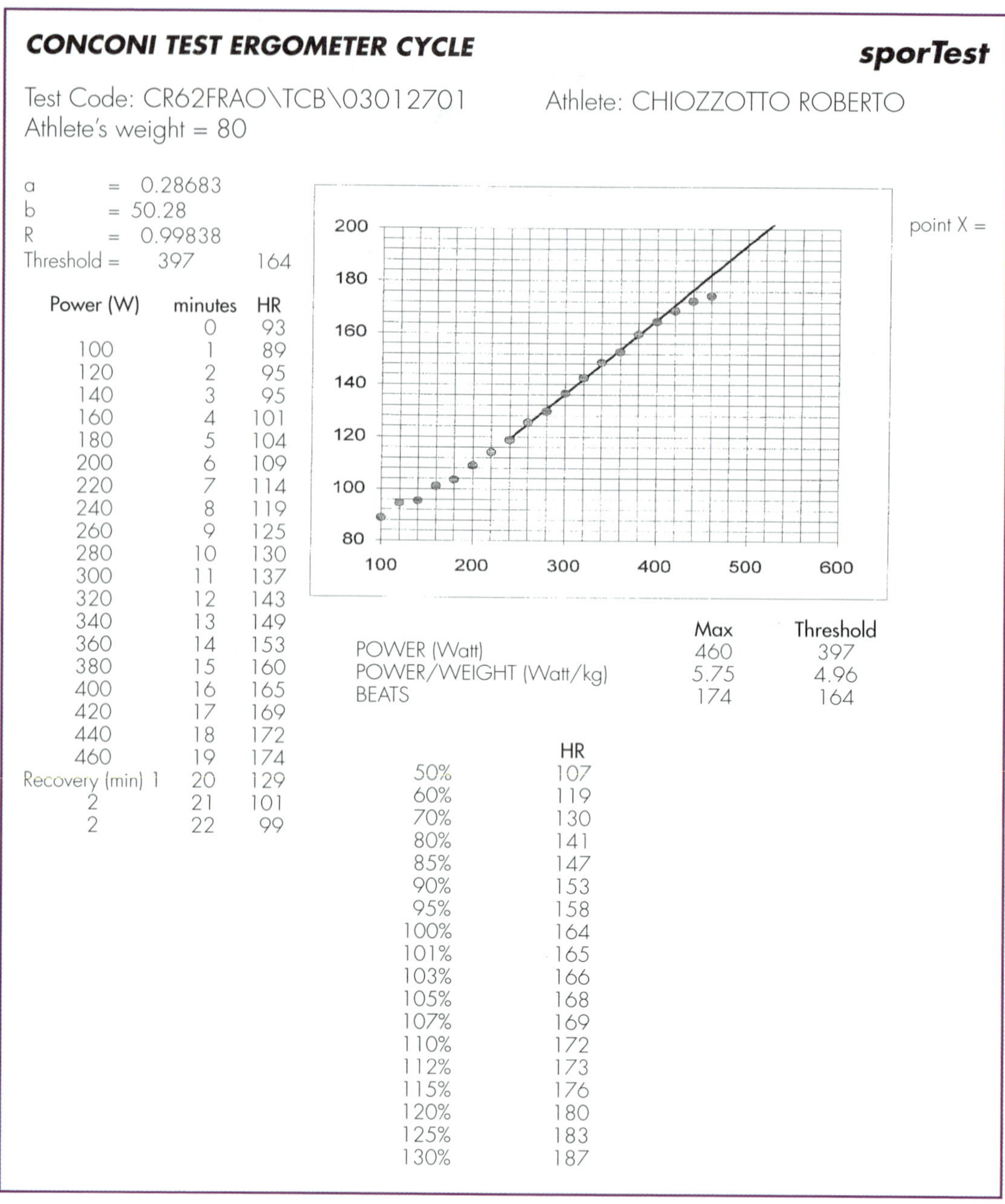

CONCONI TEST ERGOMETER CYCLE **sporTest**

Test Code: CR62FRAO\TCB\03012701 Athlete: CHIOZZOTTO ROBERTO

Athlete's weight = 80

a = 0.28683
b = 50.28
R = 0.99838
Threshold = 397 164

point X =

Power (W)	minutes	HR
	0	93
100	1	89
120	2	95
140	3	95
160	4	101
180	5	104
200	6	109
220	7	114
240	8	119
260	9	125
280	10	130
300	11	137
320	12	143
340	13	149
360	14	153
380	15	160
400	16	165
420	17	169
440	18	172
460	19	174
Recovery (min) 1	20	129
2	21	101
2	22	99

	Max	Threshold
POWER (Watt)	460	397
POWER/WEIGHT (Watt/kg)	5.75	4.96
BEATS	174	164

	HR
50%	107
60%	119
70%	130
80%	141
85%	147
90%	153
95%	158
100%	164
101%	165
103%	166
105%	168
107%	169
110%	172
112%	173
115%	176
120%	180
125%	183
130%	187

heart rate monitor and a chronometer are the tools required. Athletes start running at slow speed and are given signals to speed up at regular intervals until they reach their maximal effort. Every 30 seconds, the timekeeper blows a whistle, signaling a speed increase. In this test, a good perception of speed is necessary. The speed increases should be performed in a way that makes it possible to record an increase in heart beats lower than 8 units per minute of training. In order to avoid excessive speed increases, which can invalidate the test, freedivers who want to participate in this test can be followed and guided by more skilled runners, who are more familiar with the pace variations and the speed progressions. This will help ensure that the speed increases are correct so that the test will be valid.

The chart shows the recorded data (heart rate and running speed) and highlights the point when the heart-rate/speed ratio turns from linear to curvilinear. This is called the deflection point. Also known as the anaerobic threshold, it is the point where the level of lactate in the blood increases. This test can also be used for cyclists and swimmers by adapting the heart rate and the pace variations.

There are, of course, many tests that measure coordination, endurance, strength and speed. More than 20 tests can be used to measure endurance. The ones we mention are the ones used most often because they are simple to perform and easy to interpret.

5.4 Basic running program

Whether you want to lose weight, increase your fitness level or feel more competitive, running is and exercise that's good for your health and makes you feel better.

To ensure that this good feeling does not turn to suffering and lack of motivation, those just starting out should approach running slowly and cautiously.

Beginners can follow the table below:

Table 5.2

Week	Session 1	Session 2	Session 3
1	Run for 2 minutes and walk for 1 minute. Repeat 10 times for a total of 30 minutes.	Run for 3 minutes and walk for 1 minute. Repeat 8 times for a total of 32 minutes.	Run for 4 minutes and walk for 1 minute. Repeat 7 times for a total of 35 minutes.
2	Run for 4 minutes and walk for 2 minutes. Repeat 6 times for a total of 36 minutes.	Run for 6 minutes and walk for 2 minutes. Repeat 6 times for a total of 48 minutes.	Run for 8 minutes and walk for 2 minutes. Repeat 5 times for a total of 50 minutes.
3	Run for 10 minutes and walk for 2 minutes. Repeat 3 times for a total of 36 minutes.	Run for 12 minutes and walk for 1 minute. Repeat 3 times for a total of 39 minutes.	Run for 15 minutes and walk for 1 minute. Repeat 3 times for a total of 48 minutes.
4	Run for 20 minutes and walk for 3 minutes. Repeat twice for a total of 46 minutes.	Run for 30 minutes continuously.	Run for 40/45 minutes continuously.

5.5 Advanced running program

Here, we will analyse a possible micro-cycle, taking into account concepts previously described concerning specific periods of training, recovery periods and the overall training program.

In a 3-week training program, we would devote 2 sessions to slow running and 1 session to medium-speed running or IT. If we added a fourth session, it would be repetition training (for example, 6 × 300 and 5 × 400) or training in pace progression. This would start at a warm-up pace, then progress to a slow run, a medium-speed run and finally a fast run.

The following example is a training table used when running was employed as a part of training for freediving.

It goes without saying that the pace must be appropriate to the person's physical condition. Therefore, this program would not be undertaken by a beginner.

Table 5.2

Week	Session 1	Session 2	Session 3	Session 4
1	SR for 45 minutes.	TR for 15 minutes, SR for 5 minutes as recovery time. Repeat twice.	SR for 45 minutes during the repetitions.	Pyramidal IT 4'-3'-2'-1'-2'-3'-4'. Recovery time 2 minutes between reps.
2	SR for 50 minutes.	TR for 15 minutes, SR for 3 minutes as recovery time. Repeat twice.	SR for 50 minutes + sprints during the repetitions.	Pyramidal IT 4'-3'-2'-1'-2'-3'-4'. Recovery time 1 minute between reps.
3	SR for 50 minutes + final sprints.	TR for 25/30 minutes.	Pyramidal IT for 50 minutes + sprints between repetitions.	Pyramidal IT 5'-4'-3'-2'-3'-4'-5'. Recovery time 2 minutes between reps.
4	SR for 50 minutes + final sprints during tests.	Repeat 6/8 times 600 meters. Recovery 2 minutes between reps.	SR 50 minutes + sprints.	10 km race

5.6 Running indoors

For many of us, running indoors on treadmill is just a fallback. For others, it is a necessity. For some, it is simply entertainment. But one thing is certain: Running indoors allows us to train year round, even in bad weather. There are many good reasons for running indoors if you have a treadmill or access to a gym:

1. It makes running possible in cold or rainy weather.

DIADORA
ITALIA

2. The computer does everything for you. All you have to do is set it and push "Start."
3. You can train your leg muscles for trail running even if you live in Milan.
4. You can run any time of day or night.
5. You do not have to dress warmly; a T-shirt and shorts are enough.
6. If you are recovering from an injury, a treadmill is more inviting than hard ground.
7. If you think running is boring, you can read a book or watch TV, and training time will pass quickly.

Here are a few tips for getting the most from training on a treadmill:

- Learn how to regulate your run. An exact comparison between running outdoors and running on a treadmill does not exist. However, it is common to increase the inclination by 1 or 2 points to simulate as much as possible the inclination of the ground.
- Shorten your pace. The rolling movement of the treadmill surface will force you to have a shorter pace. The harder the surface, the more power it can generate. So, if you have difficulty keeping the pace you would usually maintain on a paved road, slow down.
- Wear more rigid shoes. This counteracts the bouncing effect of the treadmill.
- Drink a lot of water, particularly if you plan to run for a long time. When training indoors, you usually sweat more than when you're running outside.

5.7 Running holding one's breath

When we learned about a famous middle-distance runner, Emil Zátopek, running while holding his breath during training, we were very surprised, to put it mildly. He was a runner, not a freediver. This took place in the mid-'50s when freediving was almost unknown, and yet he performed such weird training. It is undoubtedly useful, and freedivers can benefit from this approach. Zátopek held his breath while running in order to accustom his body to running in the absence of oxygen. Breath-holding is undoubtedly effective for situations where you face high levels of carbon dioxide. In a test we carried out many years ago at Mapei Training Center in Castellanza, the results showed an unusual ability to bear a high value of carbon dioxide. In that period, we realized through our many notes that running while holding one's breath was a constant. Running while holding your breath should be included in your training. Or, at least it should be a path to consider.

Of course, time and distance cannot be taken into account, since this exercise is more about total distance covered than it is about speed.

This method can be applied starting with taking control of your breath (for example, 5 steps inhaling, 10 steps exhaling), then progressing to a more difficult breathing pattern while running at the same pace (5 steps inhaling, 5 steps holding your breath and 5 steps exhaling). Variations are almost limitless; you can increase the number of steps taken while holding your breath, decrease the number taken while inhaling or double the number taken while exhaling. You can give free rein to your fantasy, but be careful of workloads.

However, from experience, we suggest that you practice this for no more than 30 minutes at a time.

5.8 Running as a way to strengthen muscles

A toned musculature and good muscle strength allow you to more easily handle any kind of training. We will explain how to strengthen muscles in the weight room in the following chapter. However, for those who prefer a more natural form of training and are lucky enough to have slopes around their neighborhoods, an uphill run can be an effective way to provide an optimum training stimulus for your muscles.

Among the various types of strength we focus on, muscular strength is particularly important. It provides our bodies with the ability to oppose and overcome external resistance force.

Maximum strength, reactive strength, speed strength, static and elastic strength are all critical, but the most important of all is strength endurance, the capacity to make all these other types of strength last as long as possible without losing their effectiveness. If we don't have adequate strength endurance, for example, when we ascend to the surface with fins, the "driving force" of our legs begins to run out. We can incorporate an uphill run into any period of our training program, but it is better to do less uphill running during the specific and competitive period. Running can be done along slopes of different length and incline. During the initial period, we can run along a path with small ups and downs, then we can progress to medium-distance slopes (1 km) with 4%-6% inclines. Once our muscles have built up more strength and endurance, we can run along rises ranging from 2 km to 6 km with inclines of less than 6%. This

training will improve strength endurance. Other kinds of endurance training include sprints on 150-meter to 200-meter hills with higher inclines to improve VO_2max.

Remember that the longer the rise is, the lower the incline should be, and vice versa, in order to adapt our cardiovascular systems and achieve our goals.

When performing repetitions, recovery training between repetitions can be performed by going back down the hill to the starting point. When you run downhill, the muscles work in eccentric ways, so you need to be careful to avoid traumas. Before having a look at the following table, you had better conclude your workout with a stretching session to give your legs relief and to reset your muscle elasticity.

Kind of Training	Distance	Inclination	Repetitions	Recovery
Continuous running	6 km	4/6%	only one	—
Medium repetitions	1 km	6/8%	from 2 to 4	running downhill
Short repetitions	150/200 m	8/10%	from 6 to 10	running downhill
Steps	15/30 rungs		from 2 to 6	running downhill

Chapter 6

THE BICYCLE

For a multitude of reasons, the bicycle is an extraordinarily invention. Whether the bicycle is being used for transportation, recreation or, as in our case, a tool for optimising one's training regimen, it is easy to see why it is a valuable resource for many people. However, this chapter is not intended as a homage to the bicycle. In order to remain faithful to the goal of this book, we will simply state that from an organic point of view, cycling provides many of the same benefits as running, but with less trauma to the body. This is one reason why some of the most successful marathonersas well as athletes from various other disciplines, use cycling as a preferred method of recovery. This method is commonly referred to as *cross training*.

Cycling has been shown to be one of the most effective activities for helping people lose weight. It can be performed for extended periods of time without placing undue stress on the tendons and the muscles of those who are overweight and/or untrained. The after-effect consists of a relatively minimal feeling of fatigue lasting for a short period of time, thereby enabling a person to start again with enthusiasm. Perhaps the only conceivable downside to cycling is that its ease, its effectiveness and simply how enjoyable it is can lead to cycling being relied on more than other, more strenuous training activities.

Motivation for training can be measured according to your will, and the daunting uphill battle can be easily conquered with the aid of a bicycle's modern technology. Despite the fact that many of us prefer cycling to running, there is one obvious detail we cannot overlook ... the bicycle! Not everyone has a bicycle, and while they can be relatively inexpensive, a bike still costs considerably more than a pair of running shoes.

Running scores yet another point when you consider that in order to ensure significant results, bicycle training requires a more sustained effort than running.

In other words, running for a specific period of time will yield more gain than cycling for the same period of time. Other potential impediments to cycling include the impracticality, or even danger, of dealing with traffic, as well as finding time to fit long bike rides into our busy schedules. This is why many of us reluctantly gave up the recreational Gran Fondo, a more-than-200-km cycle road race, which offered not only exercise but also the tranquillity of wonderful and fascinating panoramas. For some, it also resulted in injuries and illness. However, it is not necessary for us to train to the level of a professional cyclist, as we are simply using cycling as a means of effectively increasing our level of fitness. We will apply to our bicycle training regimen the same elements we employ in our traditional training sessions: repetitions, interval training, medium-distance run, slow run and heart rate monitoring. Bicycle training workouts, mostly on flat routes, will be included in the first stage program.

This will be followed by strength development training, where athletes perform workouts known as strength-endurance climbs (SFR). They ride up a hill with a 5% to 10% incline for a specified period of time ranging from 2 to 6 minutes, with a long ratio (50 × 13/17) and an effort ranging from 80% to 85% of their heart rate threshold. In order to perform this exercise effectively, it is necessary to maintain the correct posture, sitting on the saddle (picture 6.1) and keeping both hands on the handlebars, but taking care not to pull the handlebars toward the chest. They will facilitate the pedal thrust created by the movement of the legs. The next step will be to increase the threshold level by performing exercises approaching the limits of one's own threshold (picture 6.2). At the end of this third stage, if it has been performed well, we will be ready for the *Giro d'Italia* bike race!

In addition to the above mentioned exercises, there are others worth considering. The first is geared toward weight loss. It is a long-distance or very-long-distance cycling race at a steady pace, pedalling at a heart rate of 75% of our heart rate threshold for a time ranging from 3 to 6 hours. Through training sessions such as this, you can reach the goal of improving the use of fatty acids. The second exercise is similar to the first in terms of intensity and its physiological goal, which is muscular cool-down. Reaching this goal requires a slow run of 45 to 90 minutes. These exercises only differ in terms of pedalling pace: slower in the long-distance cycling, ranging from 80 to 90 RPM, and faster during the cool-down, ranging from 90 to 100 RPM. As you may rightfully suspect, these are the most enjoyable training sessions. We now go back to the concept of strength and its development, particularly the natural muscular hypertrophy caused by workout. Provided your effort is not excessive, hypertrophy will be transformed into flexible and firm muscles without sacrificing strength.

Now we need to focus on the use of gear ratios. It may seem like a banal topic, but it is actually very important. We often see cyclists who are breathless, trying to push by using a gear to make 10 meters of development! The first rule is to use gear ratios that enable us to make an easy and round pedal thrust. By doing so, we will avoid expending energy too quickly. In order to make an easy and round pedal thrust, we have to use the smallest front sprocket, and the rear gears should be adjusted in accordance to our capabilities.

Those who weigh more than 80 kg are likely to have difficulty in pedaling at 100 BPM (beats per minute), especially if their muscles are not extremely flexible. However, safeguarding our musculature by pedalling nimbly means, first of all, being sure we come back home on our own feet!

One final recommendation: Whether you plan to buy a bike or resurrect one that was abandoned long ago by your brother, it is of utmost importance that the bike fit your body. The Internet offers a variety of websites that allow you to simply enter your size and you will be told what size bike is suitable for you. This includes handlebars-saddle distance, height gap between them, length joint-handlebars, etc. An investment of very little time and effort will go a long way toward helping you avoid unnecessary injury. To conclude, it is important to say that cycling requires a prior medical assessment, regardless of whether you are an amateur or a professional performing at the competitive level. At minimum, the assessment should include a clinical examination, an ECG at rest, a cardiac stress test and a urine test.

Picture 6.1

Picture 6.2

6.1 Cycling techniques

You might think that cycling techniques could be a particularly tedious subject. However, what can be achieved by adopting effective cycling techniques is cause for excitement. Anyone reading this can travel back to when he was a child learning to ride a bicycle for the first time, first with training wheels, then without them. Riding a bike is easy. Nonetheless, riding down to the corner store for ice cream is a far cry from riding at high speed among other cyclists along a steep downhill stretch.

Maybe you will not become a top cyclist, but just a few tips can help prevent falls and injuries that will force you to stop training. Cycling is generally considered to be a summer activity. Just imagine how terrible a fall in the middle of the summer would be. It could mean not going in the water for a while, which is very bad for a freediver.

First of all, it is good to have a less aerodynamic but higher position when riding a bike, thus ensuring a wide view. In addition, the distance between the saddle and the handlebars must be minimal, with the handlebars rotated upward (picture 6.3).

If you are good at cycling and you want to improve cycling downhill, regardless of your size, move the saddle 1 cm back. This will cause your weight to fall on the rear part of the bicycle, improving the center of mass and helping prevent the rear wheel from slipping. Additionally, it will be more comfortable for long distances. (Pay attention to professionals' position during long tours.) When cycling downhill, brake with both hands and use the brakes only on straight roads. Never use the rear brake when

Picture 6.3

Picture 6.4

cornering, and release the brake mid-turn on hairpin turns. Regardless of the value of your bike, do not try to save money on pneumatic tires. Good tires are important in terms of comfort, performance and safety. Most falls that occur while cornering are caused by sharp-cornered, worn-out or low-quality tires.

With regard to tires, here are a few tips for keeping them in a good condition and preventing flats.

When you return from a cycling tour, deflate your tires immediately. Keeping them fully inflated for several days can cause tire dilatation and a change in the clamp shape, resulting in deflation of the inner tube. When you replace the inner tube, sprinkle talcum powder over it and inside the tire. This helps avoid early wear and prevents the valve from being subjected to twist during sudden braking. Secondly, both hands must be firm and stable on the handlebars. Do not ride with your phone in one hand and only two fingers on the handlebars. A hole, a sewer cover or a rough spot in the road is enough to make you lose your balance (picture 6.4).

Moreover, bear in mind that a group tour is as enjoyable as it is dangerous. It is important to understand whether the group is harmonious or not, whether there are well-established rules or whether it is a scratch team (the most dangerous). Mutual understanding is an important element that can help you avoid accidents. With a scratch team, however, pseudo-cyclists may join in on the way, and accidents are significantly more prevalent. We recommend not joining such groups, as the likelihood of accidents is greater. The most likely accident is wheel against wheel, when the front wheel collides with the rear wheel of the person ahead. A change of direction or a badly executed change-over (a maneuver performed to let someone pass) is enough to cause the wheels to collide. The nitty-gritty: Be highly skeptical of those who invite you on a Sunday cycling tour with the phrase "the more, the merrier." Choose your tour companions carefully to help make sure the adventure does not turn into a nightmare. The slogan "better alone than in bad company" has never been so appropriate.

6.2 Reasons for cycling

Cycling, like running, brings with it the physical and athletic improvements typical of all aerobic activities. Cycling can be a good alternative to running for those who are overweight or for those people who have certain injuries or support problems. Cycling causes no trauma to the body, so we can perform this activity at any point during the training season, and even during the competitive stage.

A bland pedal thrust with nimble gear ratios allows us to gain capillarization at a muscular level, to release oxygen to muscle areas, and to give muscles renewed energy for the next physical effort. We also receive a psychological benefit (particularly dear to freedivers) from a pedal thrust, particularly on a hill far away from the city. The more peaceful you are, the better your tour will be. Logic should prevail over instinct; we do not have to follow those who, without any "freediving goals," dart past us while they push for record speeds.

PINARELLO
TEAM GRANFONDO
PINARELLO
2843
1938

6.3 Starting test for cycling

We cannot stress enough that measuring our initial level of athletic skill and fitness is extremely important with respect to designing an appropriate training program. This is equally applicable to cyclists. There is no need for the cyclist to be subjected to specific tests of strength, endurance and speed. We can carry out a simple Conconi Test on an ergometer cycle to obtain the information we need to develop our training program. We have already introduced this test in the previous chapter.

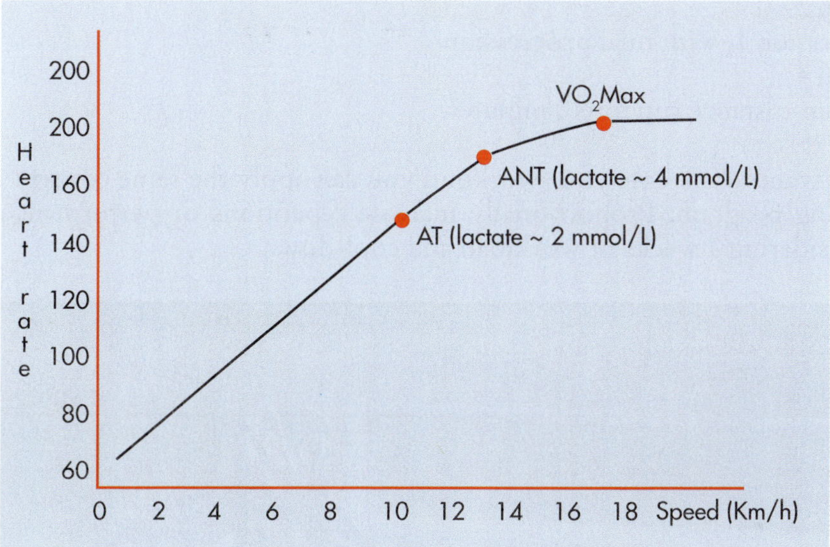

6.4 Basic cycling program

The first bike tours should aim at preparing the musculoskeletal system. We suggest that you start by covering short distances. This allows you to gradually become accustomed to the correct position on the racing bike. Your back must gradually adapt itself to the bending posture. Over-exerting yourself can lead to traumas that could force you to stop training. The correct position on a bike is the first thing to learn!

We suggest starting with 30-minute to 40-minute sessions, gradually increasing them to 100 or 120 minutes, thus ensuring a good basis to continue the training. If you like, you can include some pace variations, sprints and gentle climbs at a steady pace that will not require you to put your feet on the ground, which is so humiliating for any cyclist.

Remember to have the bike maintained by a good technician, and follow the tips suggested at the beginning of this chapter to ensure that the bike suits your size and the saddle/handlebars distance is well-balanced.

6.5 Advanced cycling program

Like running, once you have mastered and adapted to the bike, you can start working to improve your organic capacities. You can obtain these results by following the chart below.

- Session 1
  Agility 1 hour at long-distance slow run heart rate and RPM (cycling pace per minute) 100/110.
- Session 2
  Repetitions at aerobic threshold heart rate 7 × 3 minutes. Recovery 3 minutes.
- Session 3
  Like session 1, with final progression.
- Session 4
  Medium-distance run for 40 minutes.

If you want to increase your workout, you can apply the same concept as used in the running program: Proportionally increase repetitions or performance time, always considering 3 weeks of workload and cool-down.

Table 6.1

Week	Session 1	Session 2	Session 3	Session 4
1	Medium-distance run 20 minutes + 3 x 3 minutes repeated at threshold on flat with 3 minute-recovery.	Long/medium-distance run from 60 to 90 minutes.	Medium-distance run 15 minutes + 3 x 3 minutes repeated at threshold on inclination of 6/9% with 3 minute-recovery.	Custom running with increasing pace variations over the threshold.
2	Medium-distance run 20 minutes + 4 x 3 minutes repeated at threshold on flat with 3 minute-recovery.	Long/medium-distance run from 60 to 90 minutes.	Medium-distance run 15 minutes + 4 x 3 minutes repeated at threshold on inclination of 6/9% with 3 minute-recovery.	Custom running with increasing pace variations over the threshold.
3	Medium-distance run 20 minutes + 5 x 3 minutes repeated at threshold on flat with 3 minutes-recovery.	Long/medium-distance run from 75 to 105 minutes.	Medium-distance run 15 minutes + 5 x 3 minutes repeated at threshold inclination of 6/9% with 3 minute-recovery.	Custom running with increasing pace variations over the threshold.
4	Medium-distance run 20 minutes + 3 x 3 minutes repeated at threshold on flat with 3 minute-recovery.	Long/medium-distance run from 90 to 120 minutes.	Medium-distance run 15 minutes + 3 x 3 minutes repeated at threshold on inclination of 6/9% with 3 minute-recovery.	Custom running with increasing pace variations over the threshold.
		90/110 RPM frequency.	SFR 35/40RPM with the suitable gear ratio.	

6.6 Indoor cycling

During the past few years, many outdoor activities have been turned into indoor activities. As for running, treadmills allow you to run even on rainy and cold winter days. With the arrival of the stationary bike, cycling can now be included among the list of activities formerly thought to be exclusive to the outdoors. Even so, you often see cyclists wrapped up like Santa Claus challenging adverse weather conditions. If indoor cycling suits you (and trust us, even if it does not, give it serious consideration) covering thousands of miles is reasonable. Spinning is one of the most suitable indoor activities (the other is the treadmill). Imported from the U.S., spinning is an alternative to the stationary bike and it is, as a matter of fact, a cycling simulator. Furthermore, it enables you to cover the most varied and difficult tracks, despite working indoors. You can change resistance, speed, pedaling, positions and many other variables of road cycling. Spinning sessions range from 45 to 60 minutes. You can be coached by a good trainer, or you can just spin along to the music. The heart of this activity is the coach, who acts as a group motivator. You can perform any bike exercise, ranging from variations to progression repetitions, interval training, fartlek, etc. We suggest going to well-equipped gyms that enable you to perform the exercises we have selected for you. Bear in mind that it is very difficult, if not impossible, to perform customized exercises in a scheduled training program. For this reason, it is important to choose a good coach. Ask him or her to teach you about session scheduling, including technical contents, whether the workloads exceed the threshold, or whether the program includes threshold workload only. This is important in order to balance the sessions during micro-cycle training.

Chapter 7

THE GYM

Any high-level or medium-level athlete in any discipline must follow a comprehensive program of physical training, calisthenics and exercises with equipment.

A physical training program at the gym can help the athlete reach the best physical condition in order to obtain the best psychophysical response during breath-holding training. A proper schedule of general physical training sessions, together with specific training sessions, ensures that you will be able to reach your optimal performance level.

Weight lifting, on one hand, can provide a toned and strong musculature so that you can face training sessions in the best possible condition. On the other hand, weight lifting exposes us to traumas that can require long periods of rest. Therefore, in the weight room it is very important to be coached by an **instructor** or a **personal trainer** who is familiar with freediving. This person will not only advise you on which exercises to perform but also watch you perform them, making sure you are breathing correctly and using the weights properly. This is extremely important for all the exercises described here.

During training sessions, we do not use **maximum loads** because they increase muscle mass excessively, which is counterproductive to performance in the water.

The following **tables are purely indicative.** Obviously, they must be tailored to the person, to his physical features and to the time he can devote to training. The exercises described can be replaced with others that have the same effect on the same muscle areas.

At the end of each gym training session, it is fundamental to devote at least 15 minutes to **stretching**.

We will use some pictures to illustrate the most difficult exercises. We believe this is more useful than written descriptions.

If you perform two training sessions (weight lifting and breath-holding training) in the same day, we recommend scheduling the **weight lifting after breath-holding training**. This will help avoid stressing the muscles before breath-holding training. When you experience muscle hypoxia (in a set of dynamic apnea sessions, for example), it can lead to decompensations. The muscles involved in breath-holding training may be affected by the work in the gym, bringing the accessory muscles into play, and thus leading to anomalies.

7.1 Freediver at the gym

Here are the main advantages a freediver can obtain from training at the gym:

- **developing strength** to performance the specific gesture of any freediving discipline, **avoiding hypertrophic effects**.
- **maintaining muscle tone;** performing only water training, over time, may lead to muscle mass decrease.
- **improving endurance** through cardio fitness and strength-training circuits that help the respiratory and cardiovascular systems.
- **improving joint mobility**, especially shoulder joints, which are important to optimize the position of upwardly outstretched arms in hydrodynamic position. This allows us to maintain the right position more easily when performing dynamic apnea and constant weight. It also ensures smoother movement in disciplines such as variable weight and free immersion. Good scapula humeral mobility saves the athlete from having to exert excessive effort at shoulder and paravertebral levels in order to maintain the correct position.
- **maintaining/improving flexibility of the ribcage** to allow for better diaphragm expansion and contraction, thus optimizing deep breathing.
- **maintaining flexibility of the spine**, thereby reducing hypertonic development of the posterior kinetic chain of the body.

A freediver's training program must not be based only on weight lifting or cardio machines. It should be varied and comprehensive, and it should intersperse gym equipment with calisthenics to improve strength, joint mobility, muscle elasticity, agility and motor coordination. Many of these exercises will use smaller equipment such us rubber bands, medical balls, fit-balls, etc.

7.2 Starting test for physical preparation at the gym

The training programs are nothing more than a set of exercises divided into periods of time, which are designed to build up to a training optimum – the external load that produces the best possible training effect for the athlete.

Even so, programs must be personalized to fit the characteristics of each individual.

In order to determine the psychophysical aptitude and performance potential of the athlete, the physical trainer will analyse and test him, assessing his functional skills and evaluating his performance level in terms of strength, endurance, speed, coordination, joint mobility, flexibility and so on.

There are many initial tests the athlete may undergo at the gym. The trainer will choose which tests to administer depending on the person, the facility and equipment that might be used.

Some tests measure strength, while others analyse aerobic endurance and VO_2max. Still others measure the athlete's anaerobic capacities, balance, joint mobility and speed.

A professional trainer will test the athlete for each of the above-mentioned aspects. It is strongly recommended that you schedule the tests over the course of several days, so that the results of one test are not affected by the fatigue resulting from previous tests.

Such tests are essential in order to design a training program that provides a workload and intensity that is right for the individual.

7.3 Physical activity at the gym combined with seasonal competitive program

Structuring an annual training program at the gym designed to supplement preparation for a specific discipline is a very complex task.

With the same neuromuscular involvement, the athlete who has greater strength and endurance will experience less stress and less mental and physical effort than a weaker athlete. Therefore, he will deliver a more efficient performance and will finish his workout with more energy reserves and needing considerably shorter recovery times. The athlete with more strength and endurance can handle an annual training plan that includes more training units than the plan of a weaker athlete.

As the competitive freediving period draws near, training sessions at the gym should intensify to a higher training potential. If properly modulated with stops, this elevated program allows the athlete to benefit from a much higher training effect. This is the concept of supercompensation. In other words, if you are less tired, you recover faster, allowing you to train more and reach a higher level of performance.

A **gym workout program** needs to be structured over time, using the concept of periodization. This means that all the workout parameters should be designed as a succession of stages in order to gradually achieve the desired physical condition.

The season of training with weights can be split into three parts:

- **General preparatory period**: The ratio between training sessions at the gym and training sessions in the water should be 1:1. During this period, the athlete must be trained to tolerate a gradual increase in workload. It is therefore advisable to prepare, from the outset, a circuit training schedule, beginning with calisthenics, then adding free weights and weight machines with many repetitions, light loads and relatively short recovery intervals.
- **Special preparatory period**: The intensity of work should be carefully increased, focusing on strength capacity, strength endurance and speed strength endurance. Calisthenic exercises will still be included, but the use of dumbbells and barbells will significantly increase, as well as the use of weight machines. The development of speed strength endurance is achieved by performing from 10 to 20 repetitions with a load of 30% to 50% of the maximum weight load for 3 to 5 sets. The focus will be on working through lactate and alactic anaerobic pathways, therefore reps will decrease and recovery time will increase. At this stage, the ratio of training in

the water to training out of the water is 2:1. That is to say, the number of sessions at the gym will be half the number of sessions in the water.

- **Period of preparation for competing**: The competitive period for freediving is characterized by the attainment of the best possible physical condition. The athlete is subjected to a sudden decrease in physical loads, especially during the 8 weeks before the competition. The ratio of in-water workouts to out-of-water workouts is 3:1 or 4:1. That is, the number of sessions at the gym will be only one-third or one-fourth the number of sessions in the water. The physical training sessions are aimed at maintaining the levels of strength that has been achieved.

If the freediver decides to train at the gym throughout the entire year, at the end of the competition period – the period in which he should be at the top of his fitness for freediving – the athlete will enter a **transition period**. This period focuses on both physical and psychological recovery. The athlete will perform general training exercises interspersed with active recovery intervals. The overall volume of work will be about three times less than during the preparatory stage. Toward the end of the transition period, the load can be gradually increased by decreasing the active recovery intervals and increasing the number of general training exercises.

If full psychological recovery is the goal, we recommend stopping all training, including physical preparation, for at least the first 2 weeks of the transition period. During this period, the only recommended exercises are those dealing with muscle flexibility and stretching, and the athlete should get a change of scene by exercising in places other than where he trains the rest of the year.

Please remember that each training session is split three phases:

- **warm-up**
- **main part**
- **cool-down and stretching**

7.4 Training with schedules

Purely as examples, we show you two typical schedules of exercises to be performed in the weight room. The first one may be used for initial training for freedivers who begin their season of physical training at the gym. It is designed for the general preparatory period, so it includes exercises involving large muscle groups and is not strictly focused on improving the technical skill of the freediver.

Table 7.1 Basic Training (2 or 3 times a week)

	Exercises	Sets	Reps	Break
1	Dumbbell shrugs	4	12	45"
	Pectorals and chest			
2	• pull over	2-4	10	1'
3	• pectoral machine	4	10-12	1'
	Back			
4	• behind neck lat pull down	4	10-12	1'
	Triceps			
5	• bent over barbell triceps kickback	4	12	45"
	After 2-3 weeks you can add:			
6	• dumbbell kick back	4	10	1'
	Shoulders			
7	• dumbbell lateral raise	4	10	45"
	After 2-3 weeks you can add:			
8	• dumbbell front raise	4	4	45"
9	Legs			
	• (alternate) leg extension	4	10	1'
	After 1-2 weeks you can add:			
10	• 45 degree leg press	4	8-10	1'
11	• leg curl	2-4	8-10	1'
12	Abs			
	• crunch	4	8-10	1'

- The number of reps initially has to be completed easily and smoothly.
- As you progress, try to complete each set with a level of fatigue higher than the previous one.
- If the workload volume is correct, you will not need to perform more than two or three reps compared to the agreed set.
- As you progress, you can decrease the time of breaks and/or recovery periods.
- Do not increase the load at the expense of proper form.

1 DUMBBELL SHRUGS

Sets	4
Reps	12
Break	45"

Sequence 1 p. 161

2 PECTORALS AND CHEST

- pull over

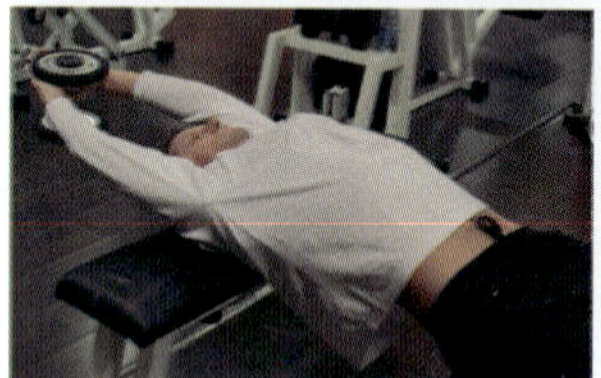
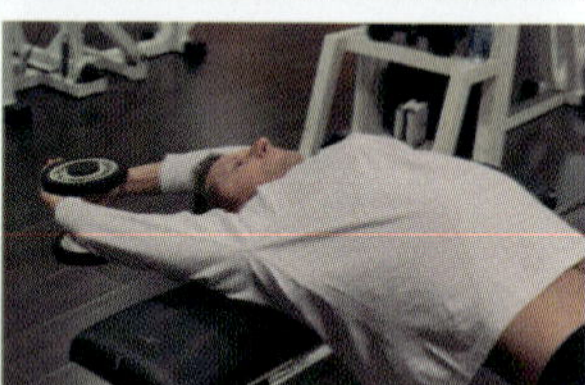

Sets	2-4
Reps	10
Break	1'

Sequence 2 p. 161

3 PECTORALS AND CHEST

- exercises with pectoral machine

Sets	4
Reps	10-12
Break	1'

Sequence 3 p. 162

4 BACK

- behind neck lat pull down

Sets	4
Reps	10-12
Break	1'

Sequence 4 p. 162

5 TRICEPS

- bent over barbell triceps kickback

Sets	4
Reps	12
Break	45"

Sequence 5 p. 162

6 DUMBBELL KICK BACK

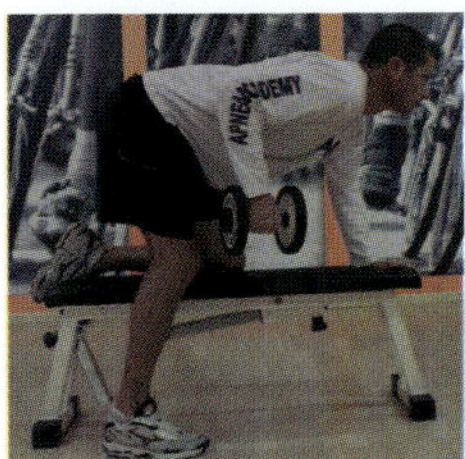
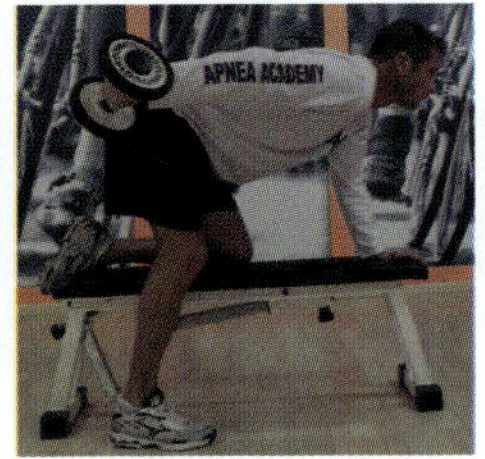

Sets	4
Reps	10
Break	1'

Sequence 6 p. 163

7 SHOULDERS

- dumbbell lateral raise

Sets	4
Reps	10
Break	45"

Sequence 7 p. 163

8 DUMBBELL FRONT RAISE

Sets	4
Reps	4
Break	45"

Sequence 8 p. 164

9 LEGS

- (alternate) leg extension

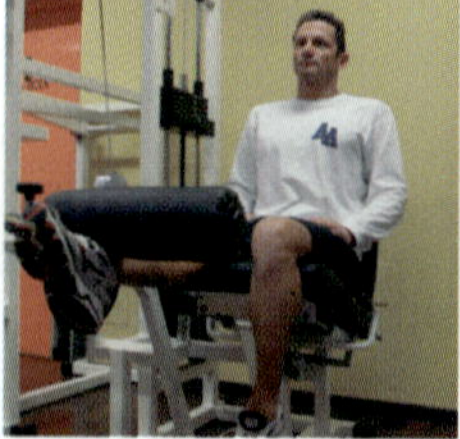

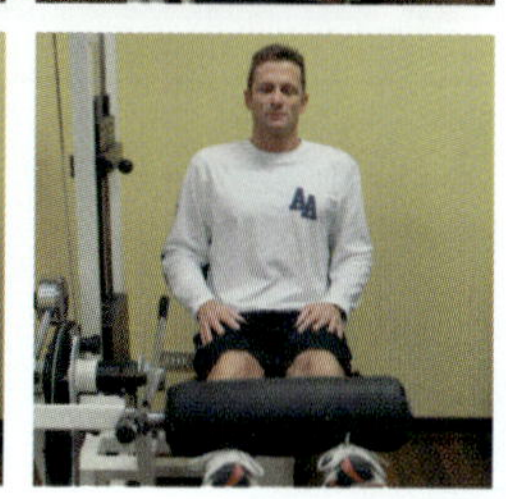

Sets	4
Reps	10
Break	1'
Sequence 10 p. 164	

10 LEGS

- 45 degree leg press

Sets	4
Reps	8-10
Break	1'
Sequence 9 p. 164	

11 LEGS

- leg curl

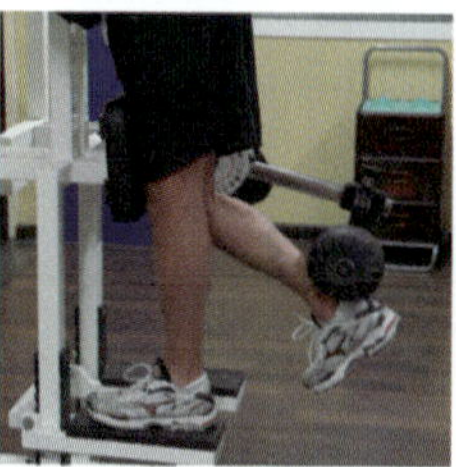
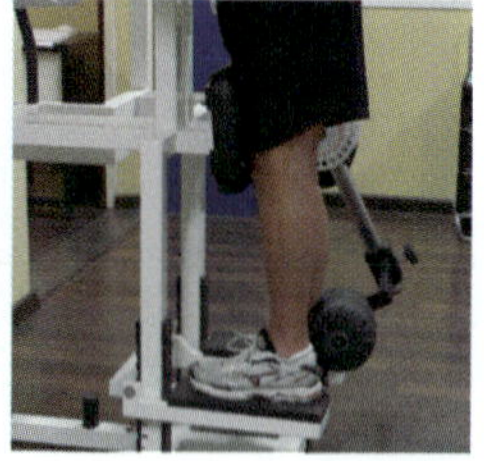

Sets	2-4
Reps	8-10
Break	1'
Sequence 11 p. 165	

12 ABS

- crunch

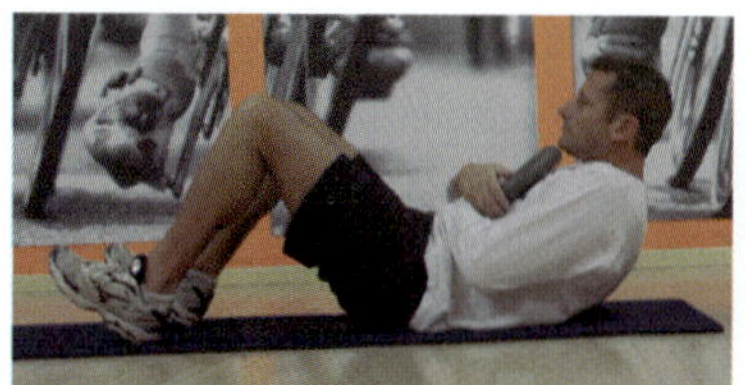

Sets	4
Reps	8-10
Break	1'
Sequence 12 p. 165	

Table 7.2 Advanced Training (3/4 times a week)

	Muscles/Exercises	Sets	Reps	Break
	Pectorals I			
1	• Pectoral machine	2	10	1'
2	• Barbell bench press	4 × 10-8-6-4		1'30"
3	• Cable crossover	2	15	30"
	Pectorals II			
4	• Inclined dumbbell fly		8	
	Superset	2-3		1'30"
5	• Push-ups		till exhaustion	
	Upper Back I			
6	• Lat machine	2	12	45"
7	• Vertical row	4	8	1'15"
8	• Low pulley	4	6-8	1'30"
	Upper Back II			
9	• Dorsy bar		6-8	
	Superset	2-3		1'30"
10	• Barbell bent over row		8-10	
	Lower Back			
11	• Good morning	4	15	30"
12	• Lower back bench extension	4	till exhaustion	30"
	Quadriceps			
13	• Leg extension	2	18	30"
14	• Squat	4	6	2'
	Hamstrings I			
15	• Stiff-legged barbell deadlift		6-8	
	Superset	2-3		1'30"
16	• Leg curl		8-10	
	Hamstrings II			
17	• One-legged cable kickback	4	till exhaustion	45"
18	• Leg curl	2+2	8	
	Shoulders I			
19	• Standing barbell shoulder press	2	6	1'
20	• Dumbbell lateral raise	4	8	45"
21	• Incline bench reverse fly	4	12	30"
	Shoulders II			
22	• Dumbbell front raise		8	
	Superset	2-3		1'30"
23	• Dumbbell shrugs		8	

	Muscles/Exercises	Sets	Reps	Break
	Biceps			
24	• Barbell curl		8	
	Superset	2		1'
25	• Dumbbell alternate curl		8	
	Triceps			
26	• Kneeling cable triceps extension		8	
	Superset	3		1'
27	• Dumbbell kick back		12	

PLEASE NOTE:

Superset means performing two series or sets one after the other, including exercises that involve agonist-antagonist muscle pairs, such as:

- pectorals and latissimus dorsi (lats)
- triceps and biceps
- quadriceps and hamstrings

Or, it may be two sets or series including exercises with the same purpose.

1 PECTORALS I

- Pectoral machine

Sets	2
Reps	10
Break	1'
Sequence 3 p. 162	

2 PECTORALS I

- Barbell bench press

Sets	4 x 10-8-6-4
Break	1'30"
Sequence 13 p. 166	

3 PECTORALS I

- Cable crossover

Sets	2
Reps	15
Break	30"
Sequence 14 p. 166	

4 PECTORALS II

- Inclined dumbbell fly

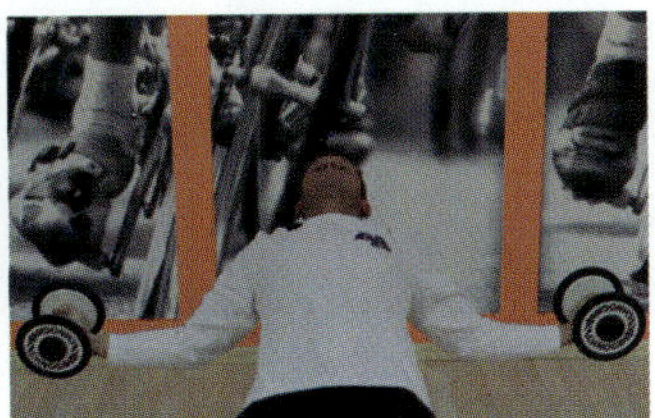

Reps	8
Sequence 15 p. 167	

4/5 SUPERSET

Sets	2-3
Break	1'30"

5 PECTORALS II

- Push-ups

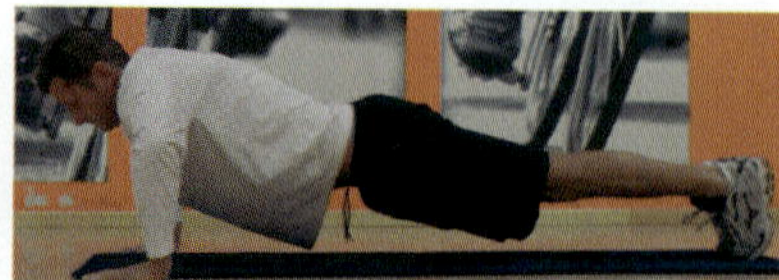

Reps	till exhaustion
Sequence 16 p. 167	

6 UPPER BACK I

- Lat machine

Sets	2
Reps	12
Break	45"
Sequence 4 p. 162	

7 UPPER BACK I

- Vertical row

Sets	4
Reps	8
Break	1'15"
Sequence 17 p. 167	

8 UPPER BACK I

- Low pulley

Sets	4
Reps	6-8
Break	1'30"
Sequence 18 p. 168	

9 UPPER BACK II

- Dorsy bar

Reps	6-8
Sequence 19 p. 168	

9/10 SUPERSET

Sets	2-3
Break	1'30"

10 UPPER BACK II

- Barbell bent over row

Reps	8-10
Sequence 20 p. 168	

11 LOWER BACK

- Good morning

Sets	4
Reps	15
Break	30"
Sequence 21 p. 169	

12 LOWER BACK

- Lower back bench extension

Sets	4
Reps	till exhaustion
Break	30"
Sequence 22 p. 169	

13 QUADRICEPS

- Leg extension

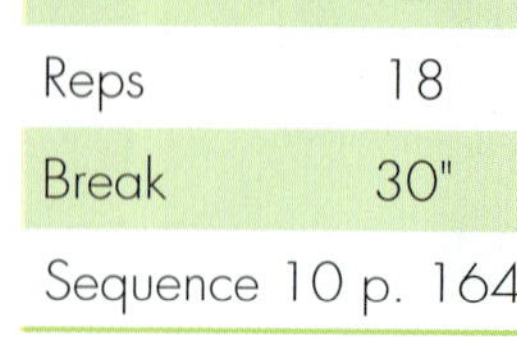

Sets	2
Reps	18
Break	30"
Sequence 10 p. 164	

14 QUADRICEPS

- Squat

Sets	4
Reps	6
Break	2'
Sequence 23 p. 169	

15 HAMSTRINGS I

- Stiff-legged barbell deadlift

Reps	12
Sequence 24 p. 170	

15/16 SUPERSET

Sets	2-3
Break	45"

16 HAMSTRINGS I

- Leg curl

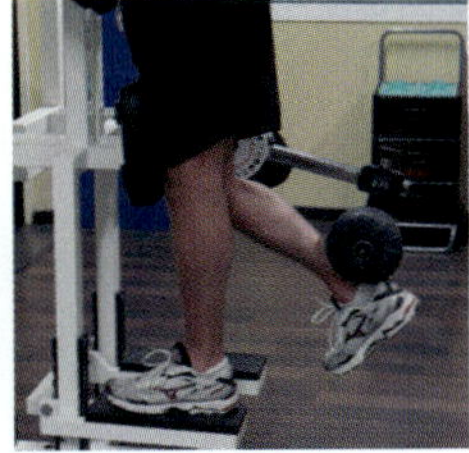
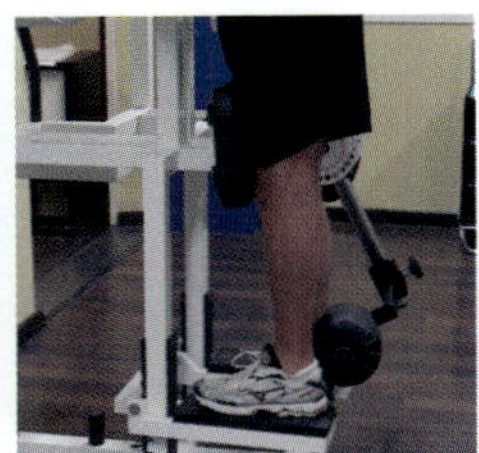

Reps	8
Sequence 11 p. 165	

17 HAMSTRINGS II

- One-legged cable kickback

Sets	4
Reps	till exhaustion
Break	45"
Sequence 25 p. 170	

18 HAMSTRINGS II

- Leg curl

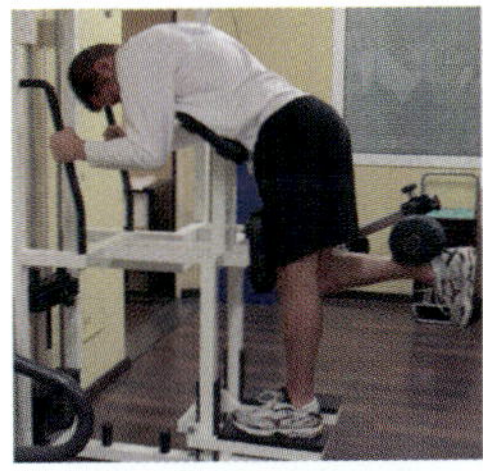
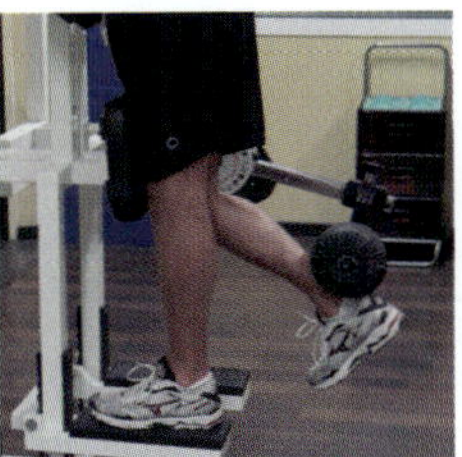
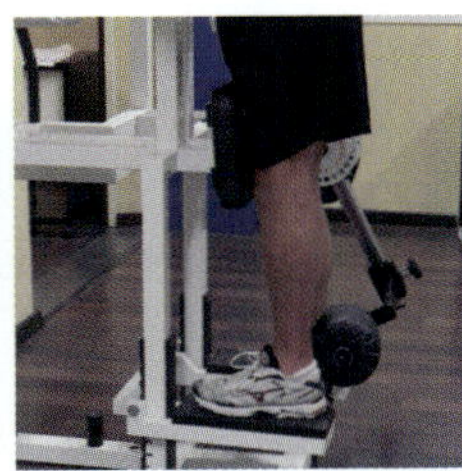

Sets	2 + 2
Reps	18
Sequence 11 p. 165	

19 SHOULDERS I

- Standing barbell shoulder press

Sets	2
Reps	6
Break	1'
Sequence 26 p. 170	

20 SHOULDERS II

- Dumbbell lateral raise

Sets	4
Reps	8
Break	45"

Sequence 7 p. 163

21 SHOULDERS I

- Incline bench reverse fly

Sets	4
Reps	12
Break	30"

Sequence 27 p. 171

22 SHOULDERS II

- Dumbbell front raise

Reps	8

Sequence 28 p. 171

22/23 SUPERSET

Sets	2-3
Break	1'30"

23 SHOULDERS II

- Dumbbell shrugs

Reps	8

Sequence 29 p. 171

24 BICEPS

- Barbell curl

Reps	8
Sequence 30 p. 172	

24/25 SUPERSET

Sets	2
Break	1'

25 BICEPS

- Dumbbell alternate curl

Reps	12
Sequence 31 p. 172	

26 TRICEPS

- Kneeling cable triceps extension

Reps	8
Sequence 32 p. 172	

26/27 SUPERSET

Sets	2
Break	1'

27 TRICEPS

- Dumbbell kick back

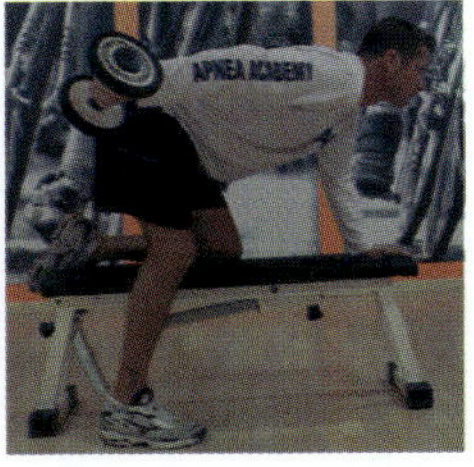

Reps	12
Sequence 6 p. 163	

7.5 Circuit training

The training should include a variety of circuits in order to make the training schedule less monotonous and more enjoyable for the freediver (who loves being in the water more than in a gym!).

Circuits at the gym **may include** doing gymnastic exercises while employing **breath-holding techniques and change or control of the respiratory rhythm**, provided that the workload is moderate.

These circuits can be performed while breathing, holding one's breath, in dyspnoea, and even in the hypoxic phase. In addition, during those exercises, you can use breathing techniques, such as triangular and **square** breathing.

The athlete will have to be assisted by a trainer when he does exercises involving effort in the hypoxic phase.

Circuit training involves a station workout where each exercise is repeated at least twice. The circuit can vary from 6 to 12 stations and may be continuous or have breaks between stations.

Circuits can be divided into:

- circuits aimed at strengthening the muscles, using weight machines, calisthenics and bodyweight exercises
- circuits aimed at training the cardiovascular system, using aerobic machines (biking, rowing, treadmill, etc.) or bodyweight exercises (running, skipping, jumping rope, etc.)
- mixed circuits, which mix exercises for the neuromuscular system with exercises for the cardiovascular system. They may mix aerobic stations with weight machine stations, calisthenics and bodyweight exercises, as well as stations with exercises designed for the athlete's specific discipline.

Only for examples, we show below some circuit training tables. They are designed to be used during the specific preparatory period, so there are exercises that, one by one, involve most all of the muscles used by the freediver.

Table 7.3 Circuit Schedule

	Muscles/Exercises	Reps	Speed	Time
1	Kinetic-postural chain • Walking with weights on the treadmill		6 km/h	20'
2	Quadriceps • Leg extension (Either normal or alternate)	20		
3	Biceps femoris • Leg curl	20		
4	Kinetic-postural chain • Walking with weights on the treadmill		7 km/h	15'
5	Rectus abdominis • Hanging knee raise	30		
6	Lower back muscles • Lower back bench extension	20		
7	Kinetic-postural chain • Walking on the treadmill		8 km/h	10'
8	Pectorals • Combined exercises on the bench: dumbbell bench press + dumbbell fly	30		
9	Upper back muscles • Lat machine pull down	30		
10	Legs • Bike		increasing speed 3' each minute	

1 KINETIC-POSTURAL CHAIN

- Walking with weights on the treadmill

Speed	6 km/h
Time	20'

2 QUADRICEPS

- Leg extension (Either normal or alternate)

Reps	20
Sequence	10 p. 164

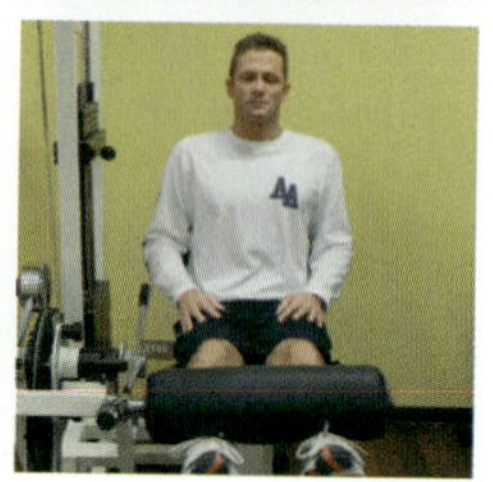

3 BICEPS FEMORIS

- Leg curl

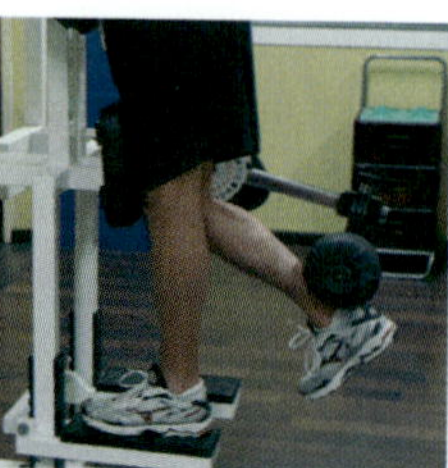
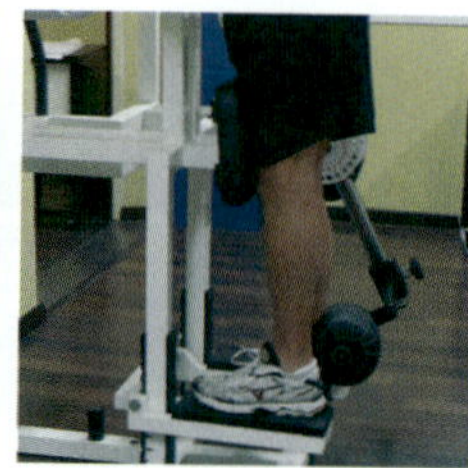

Reps	20
Sequence	11 p. 165

4 KINETIC-POSTURAL CHAIN

- Walking with weights on the treadmill

Speed	7 km/h
Time	15'

5 RECTUS ABDOMINIS

- Hanging knee raise

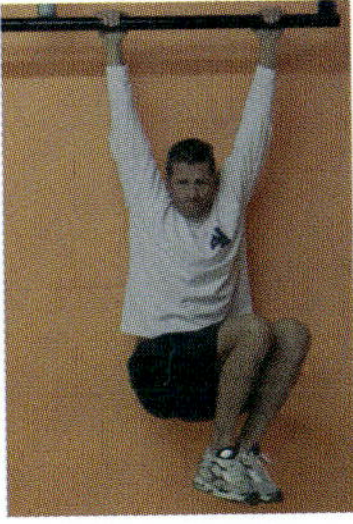

Reps	30
Sequence 33 p. 173	

6 LOWER BACK MUSCLES

- Lower back bench

Reps	20
Sequence 22 p. 169	

7 KINETIC-POSTURAL CHAIN

- Walking with weights on the treadmill

Speed	8 km/h
Time	10'

8 PECTORALS

- Combined exercises on the bench: bench press + dumbbell fly

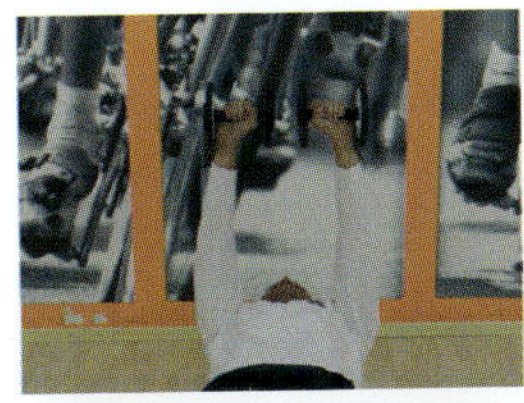
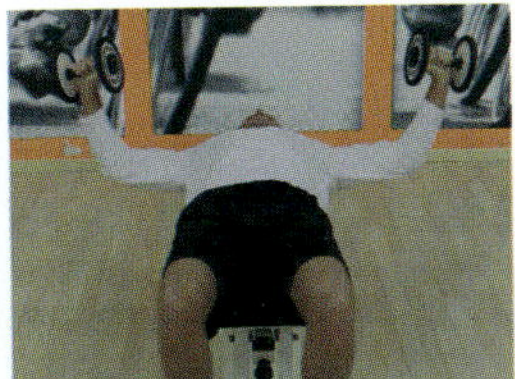

Reps	30
Sequence 34 p. 173	

9 UPPER BACK MUSCLES

- Lat machine pull down

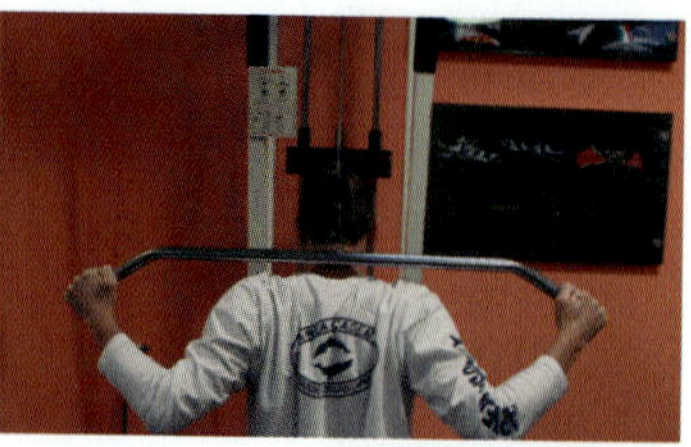

Reps	30
Sequence 4 p. 162	

10 LEGS

- Bike

Speed	increasing speed 3' each minute

The following schedule is for a split circuit workout. The first section involves strengthening of the upper body, while the second section involves leg training. In this schedule, the work on the lower part of the body includes aerobic activity.

Table 7.4 Split Circuit Schedule

	Muscles/Exercises	Reps	Speed	Time
1	Rectus abdominis • Decline crunch	30		
2	Front kinetic chain • Abdominal roller	20		
3	Pectorals, shoulders, triceps • Fitness pump	30		
4	Biceps, shoulders • Special combined exercises: curl + dumbbell shoulder press + slow dumbbell lateral raise + dumbbell upright rowing	15		
5	Kinetic-postural chain • Treadmill		7 km/h 6 km/h 8 km/h	10' 10' 10'

1 RECTUS ABDOMINIS

- Decline crunch

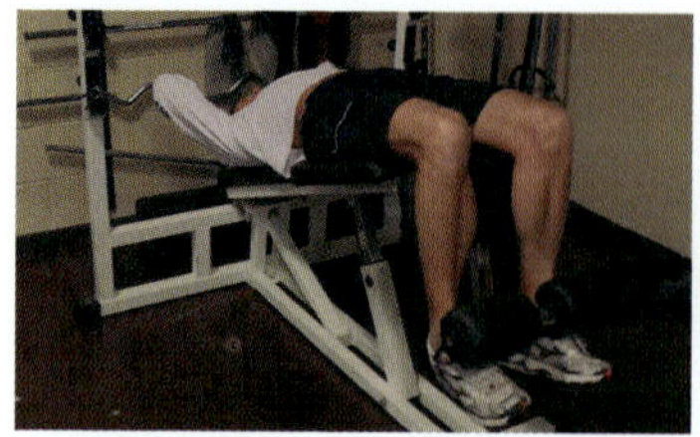
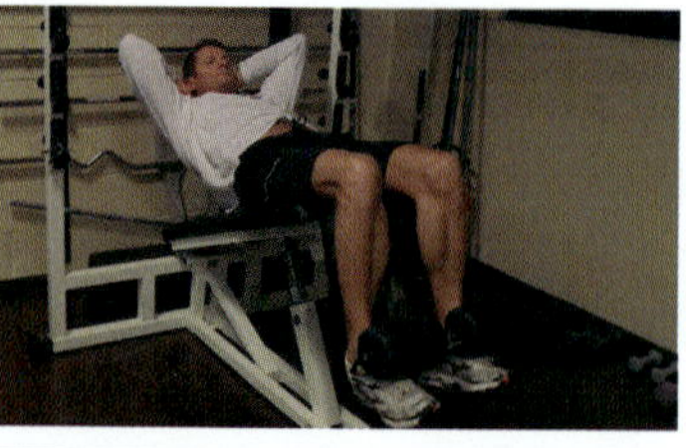

Reps	30
Sequence 35 p. 174	

2 FRONT KINETIC CHAIN

- Abdominal roller

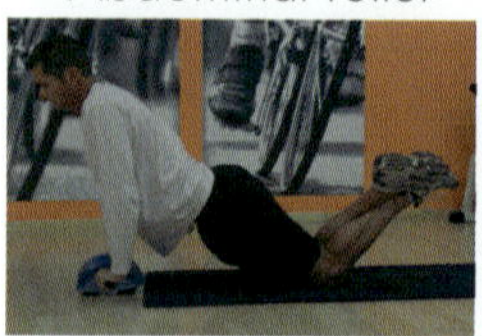

Reps	20
Sequence 36 p. 174	

3 PECTORALS, SHOULDERS, TRICEPS

- Fitness pump

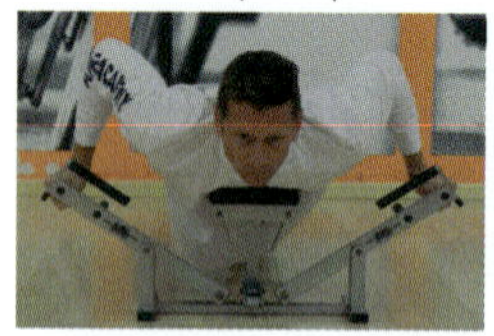

Reps	30
Sequence 37 p. 175	

4 BICEPS, SHOULDERS

- Special combined exercises: curl + bench press + open arm shoulder press + barbell upright rowing

Reps	15
Sequence 38 p. 175	

5 KINETIC-POSTURAL CHAIN

- Treadmill

Speed	7 km/h
Time	10'

Speed	6 km/h
Time	10'

Speed	8 km/h
Time	10'

7.6 Fitness circuit training

Fitness circuits can be used as an alternative to standard schedules. Using these exercises, the freediver can work mainly on aerobic endurance and power (VO_2max), as well as the lactate anaerobic system. These circuits are recommended during the basic preparatory period and/or during general training. However, they can also be integrated into the schedules of each specific period, thanks to their prevailing aerobic characteristics. Those recommended are:

- the aerobic cardio circuit
- the power aerobic circuit
- cardio fit training
- the anaerobic-aerobic circuit
- the spot reduction circuit
- peripheral heart action
- high intensity interval training

7.6.1 Aerobic cardio circuit

This circuit uses aerobic machines and involves aerobic intensity only. While training, the heart rate should be kept low, and you should not take breaks between one exercise and the next.

Table 7.5 Aerobic cardio circuit

Exercises	Time
Bike	10'
Treadmill	5'
Step	5'
Rowing machine	5'
Bike	10'

7.6.2 Power aerobic circuit

This circuit also uses aerobic machines only, but it includes sudden changes of intensity. The goal is to increase cardiovascular endurance in regard to the intensity, volume and density.

Table 7.6 Aerobic cardio circuit

Exercises	Max HR	Time
Bike	70%	10'
Treadmill	85%	5'

Exercises	Max HR	Time
Step	80%	5'
Rowing machine	80%	5'
Bike	75%	10'

7.6.3 Cardio fit training

This involves alternating exercises using aerobic machines with exercises using weights or weight machines. You should not take breaks. The weight workout should be performed at high intensity, while the workout with the aerobic machines should be performed at low intensity. The schedule must be set so that the time between aerobic exercises does not exceed 3 minutes. The workout can be intensified by increasing the loads, by increasing the time at each aerobic station or by eliminating recovery intervals between stations.

Table 7.7 Cardio fit training

	Exercises	Reps	Time
1	Bike		5'
2	Lat machine	15-20	
3	Shoulder press	15-20	
4	Rowing machine		3'
5	Crunch	20-30	
6	Leg press	12-15	
7	Pectoral machine	15-20	
8	Step		3'
9	Reverse crunch	15-20	
10	Lower back bench extension	15-20	
11	Treadmill		3'

1 BIKE

Time	5'

2 LAT MACHINE

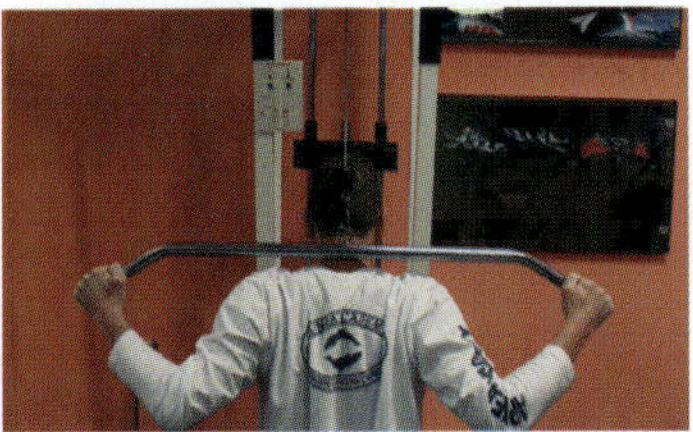

Reps	15-20

Sequence 4 p. 162

3 SHOULDER PRESS

Reps	15-20

Sequence 39 p. 176

4 ROWING MACHINE

Time	3'

5 CRUNCH

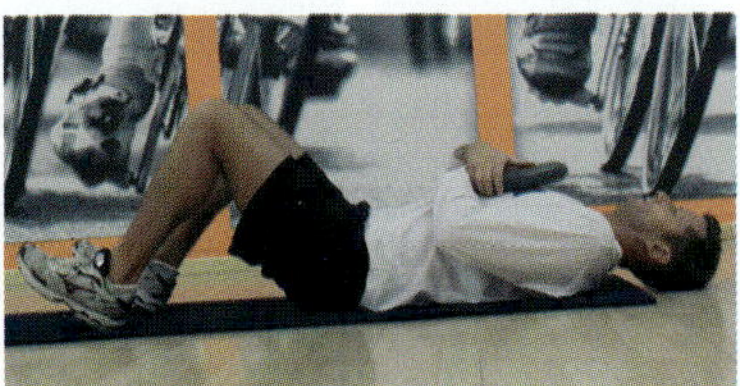

Reps	20-30

Sequence 12 p. 165

6 LEG PRESS

Reps	12-15

Sequence 9 p. 164

7 PECTORAL MACHINE

Reps	15-20
Sequence 3 p. 162	

8 STEP

Time	3'

9 LOWER BACK BENCH EXTENSION

Reps	15-20
Sequence 40 p. 177	

10 REVERSE CRUNCH

Reps	15-20
Sequence 22 p. 169	

11 TREADMIL

Time	3'

7.6.4 Anaerobic-aerobic circuit

This circuit is divided into two parts. The first part involves weight training only and is aimed at toning the muscles. The second part involves aerobic machines interspersed with muscle-strengthening exercises. There are no recovery intervals. The focus is on endurance and strength endurance.

Table 7.8 Anaerobic-aerobic circuit

	Exercises	Sets	Reps	Break	Time
1	Chest press	2-3	10-12	1'	
2	Pectorals pull over	2-3	12-15	1'	
3	Back lat machine	2-3	10-12	1'	
4	Shoulder press	2-3	10-12	1'	
5	Biceps machine	2	10-12	1'	
6	Triceps with dumbbells	2	10-12	1'	
7	Bike				5'
8	Leg press		12-15		
9	Abs crunch		15-20		
10	Step				3'
11	Reverse crunch		15-20		
12	Lower back bench extension		15-20		
13	Rowing machine				5'
14	Bike				3'

1 CHEST PRESS

Sets	2-3
Reps	10-12
Break	1"

Sequence 41 p. 177

2 PECTORALS PULL OVER

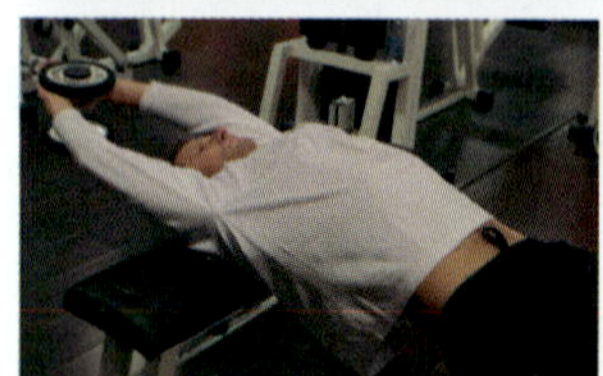
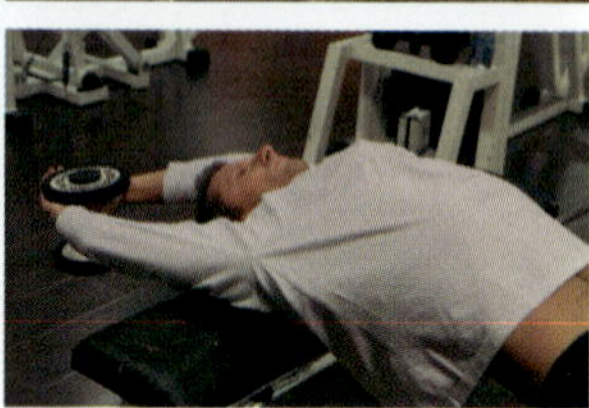

Sets	2-3
Reps	12-15
Break	1'

Sequence 2 p. 161

3 BACK LAT MACHINE

Sets	2-3
Reps	10-12
Break	1'

Sequence 4 p. 162

4 SHOULDER PRESS

Sets	2-3
Reps	10-12
Break	1'

Sequence 39 p. 176

5 BICEPS MACHINE

Sets	2
Reps	10-12
Break	1'

Sequence 42 p. 178

6 TRICEPS WITH DUMBBELLS

Sets	2
Reps	10-12
Break	1'

Sequence 43 p. 178

7 BIKE

Time	5'

8 LEG PRESS

Reps	12-15

Sequence 9 p. 164

8 ABS CRUNCH

Reps	15-20

Sequence 12 p. 165

10 STEP

Time	3'

11 REVERSE CRUNCH

Reps	15-20

Sequence 40 p. 177

12 LOWER BACK BENCH EXTENSION

Reps	15-20

Sequence 22 p. 169

13 ROWING MACHINE

Time	5'

14 BIKE

Time	3'

7.6.5 Sport reduction circuit

This circuit combines a traditional workout for the upper body (including sets with rest intervals) with an aerobic workout for the legs. The goal is to focus training on the parts of the body that need the most work and on muscles that need to be strengthened.

Table 7.9 Sport reduction circuit

	Exercises	Sets	Reps	Break	Time	Max HR
1	Treadmill				10'	70-80%
2	Crunch	2	20	20'		
3	Bike				6'	70%
4	Reverse crunch	2	20	20'		
5	Step				6'	80%
6	Treadmill				5'	70-80%
7	Crunch	2	20	20'		
8	Bike				6'	70%
9	Reverse crunch	2	20	20'		

1 TREADMIL

Time	10'	Max HR	70-80%

2 ABS CRUNCH

Sets	2
Reps	20
Break	20'
Sequence 12 p. 165	

3 BIKE

Time	6'	Max HR	70%

4 REVERSE CRUNCH

Sets	2
Reps	20
Break	20'
Sequence 40 p. 177	

5 STEP

Time	6'	Max HR	80%

6 TREADMIL

Time	5'	Max HR	70-80%

7 ABS CRUNCH

Sets	2
Reps	20
Break	20'
Sequence 12 p. 165	

8 BIKE

Time	6'	Max HR	70%

9 REVERSE CRUNCH

Sets	2
Reps	20
Break	20'
Sequence 40 p. 177	

7.6.6 Peripheral heart action

This circuit uses weight machines or free weights and is aimed at stimulating and improving blood circulation.

Table 7.10 Peripheral heart action

	Muscles/Exercises	Reps	Load
1	Trapezius, deltoid muscles • Barbell upright rowing	1st set: 20 2nd set: 6 3rd set: till exhaustion	60% 80% 30%
2	Calf • Calf machine	same as above	same as above
3	Pectorals • Barbell bench press	same as above	same as above
4	Quadriceps • Leg extension (sequence 4)	same as above	same as above
5	Rectus abdominis • Pull down cable crunch with lat machine	same as above	same as above
6	Biceps femoris, gluteus muscles, lower back • From 90-degree angle leg raise	3 sets made up of 15/20 reps	bodyweight exercise

N.B. This circuit must be repeated three times, and the athlete must perform one set for each exercise:

- first set, endurance: 20 reps, load 50%-60%;
- second set, strength: 4-6 reps, load 80%;
- third set: reps till exhaustion without barbells or any weights at high speed. No Breaks.

1 TRAPEZIUS, DELTOIDS

- Barbell upright rowing

Reps	Load
1st set: 20	60%
2nd set: 6	80%
3rd set: till exhaustion	30%

Sequence 44 p. 179

2 CALF

- Calf machine

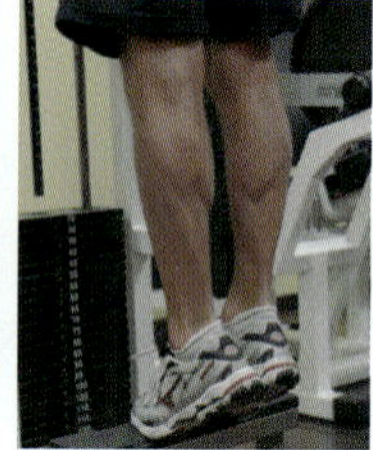

Reps	Load
1st set: 20	60%
2nd set: 6	80%
3rd set: till exhaustion	30%

Sequence 45 p. 179

3 PECTORALS

- Barbell bench press

Reps	Load
1st set: 20	60%
2nd set: 6	80%
3rd set: till exhaustion	30%

Sequence 13 p. 166

4 QUADRICEPS

- Leg extension

Reps	Load
1st set: 20	60%
2nd set: 6	80%
3rd set: till exhaustion	30%

Sequence 10 p. 164

4 QUADRICEPS (*to be continued*)

5 RECTUS ABDOMINIS

- Pull down cable crunch with lat machine

Reps	Load
1st set: 20	60%
2nd set: 6	80%
3rd set: till exhaustion	30%

Sequence 46 p. 180

6 BICEPS FEMORIS, GLUTEUS MUSCLES, LOWER BACK

- From 90-degree angle leg raise

Reps	Load
3 sets made up of 15/20 reps	bodyweight exercise

Sequence 47 p. 180

7.6.7 High intensity interval training

This circuit includes high- and low-intensity workouts for a period of no more than 20 minutes. The main goal is to improve resistance at high workload intensity and lactate concentration.

Table 7.11 Peripheral heart action

	Exercises	Reps	Pace	Speed	Time	Load
1	Abdominals • Leg raise as in candle pose + lateral twists	30	slow			bodyweight exercise
2	Treadmill			8 km/h 10 km/h 12 km/h	5' 3' 1'	increasing
3	Pectorals • Barbell bench press	12-8-4	fast			increasing 40% 60% 80%
4	Jumping squat	10-6-3	steady			increasing

1 ABDOMINALS

- Leg raise as in candle pose + lateral twists

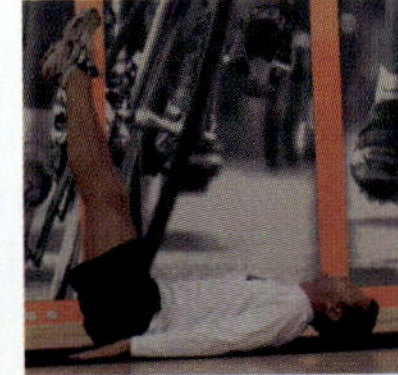

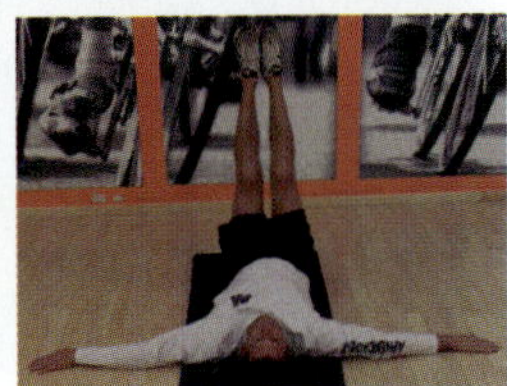

Reps	30
Pace	slow
Load	bodyweight exercise

Sequence 48 p. 181

2 TREADMIL

Speed	8 km/h 10 km/h 12 km/h

Time	5' 3' 1'

Load	increasing

3 PECTORALS

- Barbell bench press

Reps	12-8-4
Pace	fast
Load	crescente 40%-60%-80%

Sequence 13 p. 166

4 JUMPING SQUAT

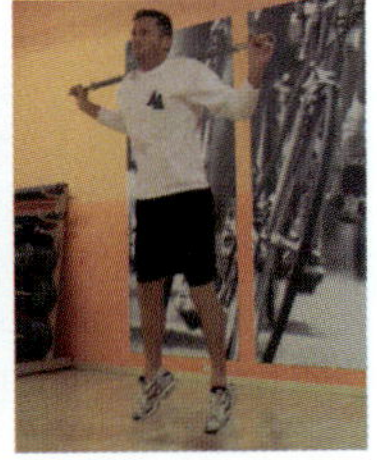

Reps	10-6-3
Pace	steady
Load	increasing

Sequence 49 p. 182

7.7 Circuit schedules for training underwater breastroke

These circuits are used to train for dynamic apnea and constant weight without fins. The leg exercises help train the muscles used in the breaststroke kick. The first three schedules are suitable for the period of specific training. The fourth one, where most of the exercises employ (out of the water) specific movements that the freediver normally performs in the water, is recommended during the training period before competition.

Table 7.12 Bodyweight circuit flexibility and joint mobility exercises

	Muscles and Joints	Exercises	Reps	Pace
1	Neck muscles, cervical region, spine	flexion, extension, lateral bending, rotation, circumduction of the head	3	slow
2	Shoulders, lateral muscles of the trunk (latissimus dorsi, triceps), glenohumeral joint	grasp the elbow upwards with the other hand and pull it behind the head	3-5 each side	slow
3	Shoulders, lateral muscles of the trunk (latissimus dorsi, triceps), glenohumeral joint	extend the arms on the front and upward over the head with the palms turned upward (ballistic stretching)	10-15	steady
4	Shoulders, lateral muscles of the trunk (latissimus dorsi, triceps), glenohumeral joint	forward and backward circumduction of arms outstretched	15-20 each direction	from slow to fast
5	Front and lateral muscles of the hip and acetabulofemoral joint	hip circumduction	8-10 each direction	slow
6	Knee joint	knee circumduction	10-15 each direction	slow
7	Lower back, inguen, acetabulofemoral joint, knee, ankles	squat with legs wide apart	8-10	fast going up, medium during kneebending + 6-8" in squat
8	Inguen, acetabulofemoral joint	bend knees on the floor wide open and bend elbows to the floor	25-30"	

	Muscles and Joints	Exercises	Reps	Pace
9	Calf, anterior tibial muscle, tibiotarsal joint	flexion, extension, circumduction of ankles, standing or seated	10-15 flexion extension and circumduction	medium/ slow

N.B. The exercises can be performed with different breathing techniques.

1. normal breathing;
2. diaphragmatic breathing (clavicular, chest, abdominal breathing);
3. triangular breathing, ratio 1:2-1:3, for example inhalation 2 seconds, exhalation 4 seconds;
4. square breathing, for example inhalation 2 seconds and breath-holding 3 seconds, exhalation 4 seconds and dyspnoea 3 seconds.

- 1st set: passive stretching (you naturally let the muscles slowly relax);
- 2nd set: assisted passive stretching (the partner intervenes to increase the effectiveness of the stretching);
- 3rd set: PNF stretching (involves a shortening contraction of the opposing muscle, thanks to the action of the partner, to stretch place the target muscle using the assisted passive stretching method).

1 NECK MUSCLES, CERVICAL REGION, SPINE

- Flexion, extension, lateral bending, rotation, circumduction of the head

Reps	3
Pace	slow
Sequence 50 p. 182	

2 SHOULDERS, LATERAL MUSCLES OF THE TRUNK (LATISSIMUS DORSI, TRICEP), SHOULDER JOINT

- Grasp the elbow upwards with the other hand and pull it behind the head

Reps	3-5 each side
Pace	slow
Sequence 51 p. 183	

3 SHOULDERS, LATERAL MUSCLES OF THE TRUNK (LATISSIMUS DORSI, TRICEPS), SHOULDER JOINT

- Extend the arms on the front and upward over the head with the palms turned upward (ballistic stretching)

Reps	10-15
Pace	steady
Sequence 52 p. 183	

4 SHOULDERS, LATERAL MUSCLES OF THE TRUNK (LATISSIMUS DORSI, TRICEPS), SHOULDER JOINT

- Forward and backward circumduction of arms outstretched

Reps	15-20 each direction
Pace	from slow to fast
Sequence 54 p. 184	

5 FRONT AND LATERAL MUSCLES OF THE HIP AND ACETABULOFEMORAL JOINT

- Hip circumduction

Reps	8-10 each direction
Pace	slow
Sequence 56 p. 185	

6 KNEE JOINTS

- Knee circumduction

Reps	10-15 each direction
Pace	slow
Sequence 53 p. 184	

7 LOWER BACK, INGUEN, ACETABULOFEMORAL JOINT, KNEE, ANKLES

- Squat with legs wide apart

Reps	8-10
Pace	fast going up, medium during kneebending + 6-8" in squat
Sequence 55 p. 185	

8 INGUEN, ACETABULOFEMORAL JOINT

- Bend knees on the floor wide open and bend elbows to the floor

Reps	25-30"
Sequence 57 p. 186	

9 CALF, ANTERIOR TIBIAL MUSCLE, TIBIOTARSAL JOINT

- Flexion extension, circumduction of ankles standing or seated

Reps	10-15 flexion extension and circumduction
Pace	medium/slow
Sequence 58 p. 187	

Table 7.13 Bodyweight strengthening circuit training with split method combination of arm and leg exercises in one single schedule

	Muscles and Joints	Exercises	Reps	Pace
1	Anterior deltoid, triceps, pectorals, shoulder, elbows and wrists joints	Push-ups arms wide apart on knees or with body straight	1st set: 10-15 2nd set: 15-20 3rd set: till exhaustion	increasing
2	Latissimus dorsi, shoulders, shoulder joints	Chin-ups with arms wide open and palms facing down	1st set: 5-6 2nd set: 8-10 3rd set: till exhaustion	increasing
3	Triceps, shoulder and elbows joints	Triceps dips with legs suspended	1st set: 8-10 2nd set: 10-15 3rd set: till exhaustion	increasing
4	Gluteus muscles, acetabulofemoral joint	Quadruped abduction + extension with legs outstretched	1st set: 10-15 2nd set: 15-20 3rd set: till exhaustion	increasing
5	Gluteus muscles, adductors, acetabulofemoral joint	Sidelying leg raises	1st set: 10-12 2nd set: 15-20 3rd set: till exhaustion	increasing
6	Gluteus muscles, thighs, adductors, hip, knee and ankle joint	Lateral wide lunge and then return to your standing position	1st set: 4-6 each side 2nd set: 6-8 each side 3rd set: till exhaustion	increasing

N.B. Those exercises can be performed while breathing in three ways:

1. inhaling during the concentric phase, exhaling during the eccentric phase and vice versa;
2. holding your breath during the concentric or eccentric phase;
3. dyspnoea.

1 ANTERIOR DELTOID, TRICEPS, PECTORALS, SHOULDER, ELBOWS AND WRISTS JOINTS

- Push-up arms wide apart on knees or with body straight

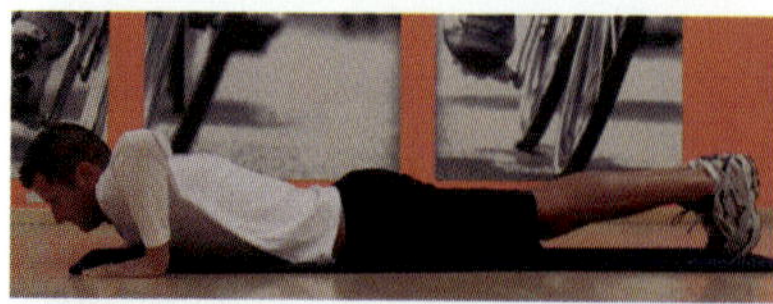

Reps	1st set: 10-15 2nd set: 15-20 3rd set: till exhaustion
Pace	increasing

Sequence 16 p. 167

2 LATISSIMUS DORSI, SHOULDERS, SHOULDER JOINTS

- Chin-ups with arms wide open and palms facing down

Reps	1st set: 5-6 2nd set: 8-10 3rd set: till exhaustion
Pace	increasing

Sequence 59 p. 188

3 TRICEPS, SHOULDERS AND ELBOWS JOINTS

- Triceps dips with legs suspended

Reps	1st set: 8-10 2nd set: 10-15 3rd set: till exhaustion
Pace	increasing

Sequence 60 p. 188

4 GLUTEUS MUSCLES, ACETABULOFEMORAL JOINT

- Quadruped abduction + extension with legs outstretched

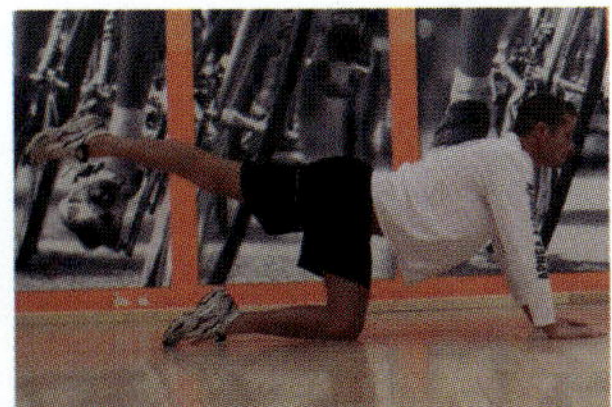

Reps	1st set: 10-15 2nd set: 15-20 3rd set: till exhaustion
Pace	increasing

Sequence 61 p. 189

5 GLUTEUS MUSCLES, ADDUCTORS, ACETABULOFEMORAL JOINT

- Sidelying leg raises

Reps	1st set: 10-12 2nd set: 15-20 3rd set: till exhaustion
Pace	increasing

Sequence 62 p. 189

6 GLUTEUS MUSCLES, THIGHS, ADDUCTORS, HIP, KNEE AND ANKLE JOINT

- Lateral wide lunge and then return to your standing position

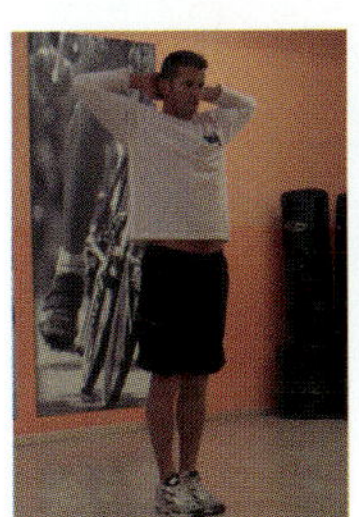

Reps	1st set: 4-6 each side 2nd set: 6-8 each side 3rd set: till exhaustion
Pace	increasing

Sequence 63 p. 190

Strengthening circuit training with split method (arms and legs in two separate schedules with equipment, weights, weight machines and cables)

These two circuit schedules can be combined in the following way:

A *Monday-Thursday*
B *Tuesday-Friday*
A + B *Saturday*

Table 7.14 Strengthening circuit training with split method - Table A

	Muscles and Joints	Exercises	Reps	Load
1	Triceps	Triceps cable pushdowns	1st set: 12-15 2nd set: 15-20 3rd set: till exhaustion	70% 60% 50%
2	Triceps, pectorals, anconeus muscle	Triceps dips between two benches	1st set: 10-12 2nd set: 12-15 3rd set: till exhaustion	body-weight exercise
3	Back, teres major muscle, latissimus dorsi, triceps long head	Cable straight arm pulldowns	1st set: 10-12 2nd set: 12-15 3rd set: till exhaustion	70% 60% 50%
4	Flexor and extensor muscles of the arm, humeral adductors, stabilizer muscles	Standing cable crossover	1st set: 10-12 2nd set: 12-15 3rd set: till exhaustion	70% 60% 50%
5	Lower back muscles, gluteus maximus, femoris muscles	Lower back extension	1st set: 8-10 2nd set: 10-12 3rd set: 12-15	body-weight exercise
6	**Abdominals:** oblique muscles, rectus abdominis **Legs:** quadriceps, femoris muscles, tensor fasciae latae	Hanging knee raises	1st set: 10-12 2nd set: 12-15 3rd set: till exhaustion	body-weight exercise

1 TRICEPS

- Triceps cable pushdowns

Reps	1st set: 12-15 2nd set: 15-20 3rd set: till exhaustion
Load	70% 60% 50%

Sequence 65 p. 191

2 TRICEPS, PECTORALS, ANCONEUS MUSCLE

- Triceps dips between two benches

Reps	1st set: 10-12 2nd set: 12-15 3rd set: till exhaustion
Load	bodyweight exercise

Sequence 64 p. 190

3 BACK, TERES MAJOR MUSCLE, LATISSIMUS DORSI, TRICEPS LONG HEAD

- Cable straight arm pulldowns

Reps	1st set: 12-15 2nd set: 15-20 3rd set: till exhaustion
Load	70% 60% 50%

Sequence 66 p. 191

4 FLEXOR AND EXTENSOR MUSCLES OF THE ARM, HUMERAL ADDUCTORS, STABILIZERS MUSCLES

- Standing cable crossover

Reps	1st set: 10-12 2nd set: 12-15 3rd set: till exhaustion
Load	70% 60% 50%

Sequence 67 p. 192

5 LOWER BACK, GLUTEUS MAXIMUS, FEMORIS MUSCLES

- Lower back extension

Reps	1st set: 8-10 2nd set: 10-12 3rd set: 12-15
Load	bodyweight exercise

Sequence 22 p. 169

6 ABDOMINALS: OBLIQUE MUSCLES, RECTUS ABDOMINIS. LEGS: QUADRICEPS, FEMORIS MUSCLE, TENSOR FASCIAE LATAE

- Hanging knee raises

Reps	1st set: 10-12 2nd set: 12-15 3rd set: till exhaustion
Load	bodyweight exercise

Sequence 68 p. 192

Table 7.15 Strengthening circuit training with split method - Table B

Muscles and Joints	Exercises	Reps	Load
1 Abdominals rectus and oblique muscles	Super combination: leg raise as in candle + lateral twists	1st set: 20 2nd set: 15 3rd set: 10	bodyweight exercise ankle weights: 1-2 kg each side ankle weights: 1 kg each leg
2 Arms: biceps, shoulders, latissimus dorsi	Super combination: curl + bench press + open arm shoulder press + barbell upright rowing	1st set: 15 2nd set: 10 3rd set: 6-8	70% dumbbells 80% 90%
3 Legs: adductors magnus, brevis and longus, quadriceps	Straight legs circumductions with ankle weights	1st set: 20 2nd set: 20 3rd set: 20	bodyweight exercise - ankle weights steady weight: 1 kg each leg
4 Arms: adductor pectoral, girdle, rhomboid major and minor, pectoralis major and minor, triceps brachii muscle	Simulation breaststroke arm movement at cable machine	1st set: 15 2nd set: 10 3rd set: 6-8	70% cables 80% 90%
5 Legs: quadriceps, hamstring adductors	Simulation breaststroke leg movement at cable machine	1st set: 15 2nd set: 10 3rd set: 6-8	50% cables 60% 70%
6 Kinetic postural chain	Running on the treadmill 15 minutes at 7-8 km/h		bodyweight exercise

N.B. This circuit is characterized by a pyramidal method (decreasing in reps and increasing in load). The movements should be wide and fast to make sure that there is no hypertrophic effect, even though the load does not exceed 70% of the maximum bearable load. The recovery time is the time required to change the station and the exercise. Between one circuit and the next, a break of at least 2 or 3 minutes is required.

1 ABDOMINALS: RECTUS AND ABDOMINAL OBLIQUE MUSCLES

- Super combination: leg raise as in candle pose + lateral twists

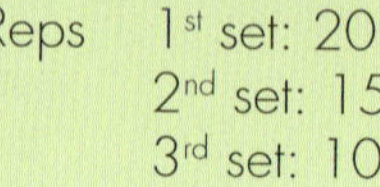

Reps	1st set: 20 2nd set: 15 3rd set: 10
Load	bodyweight exercise ankle weights: 1-2 kg each side ankle weights: 1 kg each leg

Sequence 48 p. 181

2 ARMS: BICEPS, SHOULDERS, BACK MUSCLES

- Super combination: curl + bench press + open arm shoulder press + barbell upright rowing

Reps	1st set: 15 2nd set: 10 3rd set: 6-8
Load	70% dumbbells 80% 90%

Sequence 70 p. 193

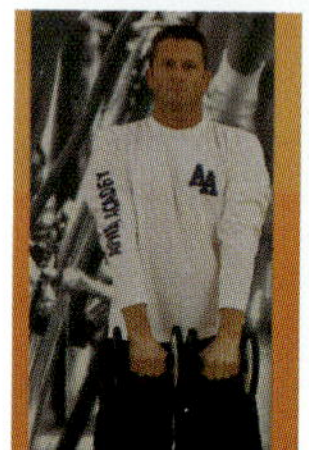
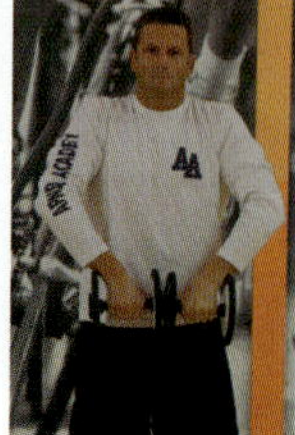

3 LEGS: ADDUCTOR MAGNUS, LONGUS AND BREVIS, QUADRICEPS

- Straight legs circumductions with ankle weights

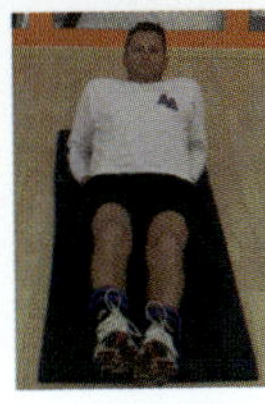

Reps	1st set: 20 2nd set: 20 3rd set: 20
Load	bodyweight exercise - ankle weights steady weight: 1 kg each leg

Sequence 71 p. 194

4 ARMS: ADDUCTOR PECTORAL GIRDLE, RHOMBOID MAJOR AND MINOR, PECTORALIS MAJOR AND MINOR, TRICEPS BRACHII MUSCLE

- Simulation breaststroke arm movement at cable machine

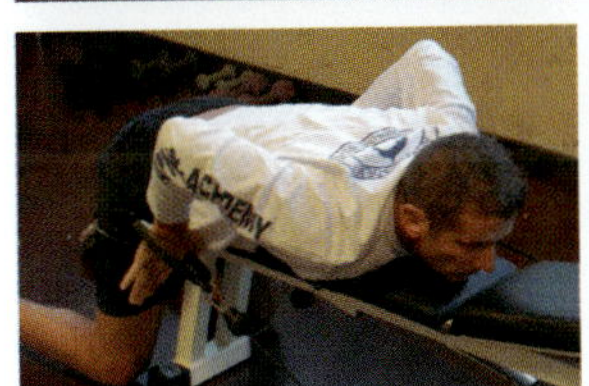

Reps	1st set: 15 2nd set: 10 3rd set: 6-8
Load	70% cables 80% 90%

Sequence 72 p. 194

5 LEGS: QUADRICEPS, HAMSTRINGS, ADDUCTORS

- Simulation breaststroke leg movement at cable machine

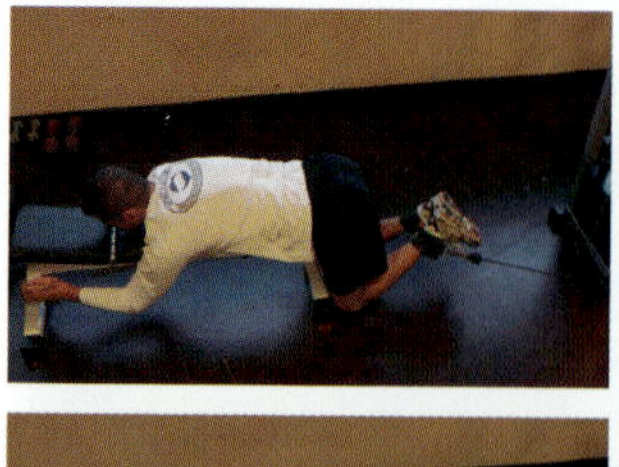

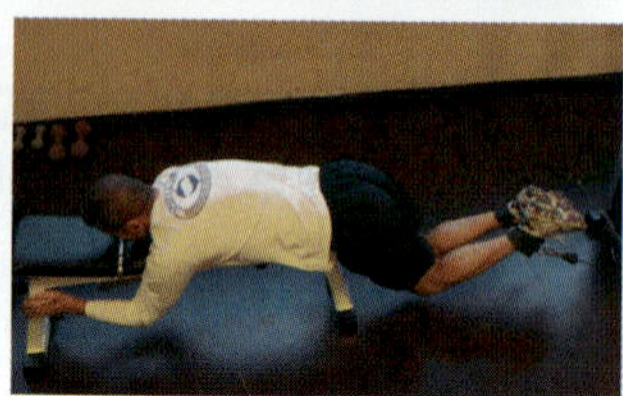

Reps	1st set: 15 2nd set: 10 3rd set: 6-8
Load	50% cables 60% 70%

Sequence 73 p. 195

6 KINETIC POSTURAL CHAIN

- Running on the treadmill 15 minutes at 7-8 km/h - bodyweight exercise

Table 7.16 Circuit training for high-level athletes to be performed during periods of maximum workload

	Muscles and Joints	Exercises	Reps	Load
1	Legs, adductors, gluteus muscles, acetabulofemoral joint, knee	Barbell sissy squat	1st set: 10-12 2nd set: 12-15 3rd set: till exhaustion	70% 60% 50%
2	Quadriceps: rectus femoris, vastus medialis, intermedius and lateralis, gluteus maximus, acetabulofemoral joint, knee, ankle	Horizontal leg press	1st set: 10-12 2nd set: 12-15 3rd set: till exhaustion	70% 60% 50%
3	Adductors: pectineus, adductor longus, adductor magnus, gracilis, acetabulofemoral joint	Adductor machine	1st set: 10-12 2nd set: 12-15 3rd set: till exhaustion	70% 60% 50%
4	Adductors: pectineus, adductor longus, adductor magnus, gracilis, acetabulofemoral joint	Standing cable hip abduction	1st set: 10-12 2nd set: 12-15 3rd set: till exhaustion	70% 60% 50%
5	Gluteus maximus, semitendinosus, semimembranosus, biceps femoris short and long head, acetabulofemoral joint	Good morning exercise	1st set: 8-10 2nd set: 10-12 3rd set: 12-15	70% 60% 50%

N.B. This circuit is characterized by a pyramidal method (decreasing in reps and increasing in load). The movements should be wide and fast to make sure that there is no hypertrophic effect, even though the load does not exceed 70% of the maximum bearable load. The recovery time is the time required to change the station and the exercise. Between one circuit and the next, a break of at least 2 or 3 minutes is required. The circuit can be performed in two ways:

1. by clocking the time it takes to make the circuit and keeping the number of reps unchanged. The increased strength of the athlete is shown by the decreased amount of time he takes to perform the circuit.

2. by keeping the workout time steady for each station and counting the number of reps the athlete is able to perform during that time. The improvement in strength is shown by the increase in the number of reps that can be done in the same amount of time.

1 BARBELL SISSY SQUAT

- Barbell sissy squat

Reps	1st set: 10-12 2nd set: 12-15 3rd set: till exhaustion
Load	70% 60% 50%

Sequence 74 p. 195

2 HORIZONTAL LEG PRESS

- Horizontal leg press

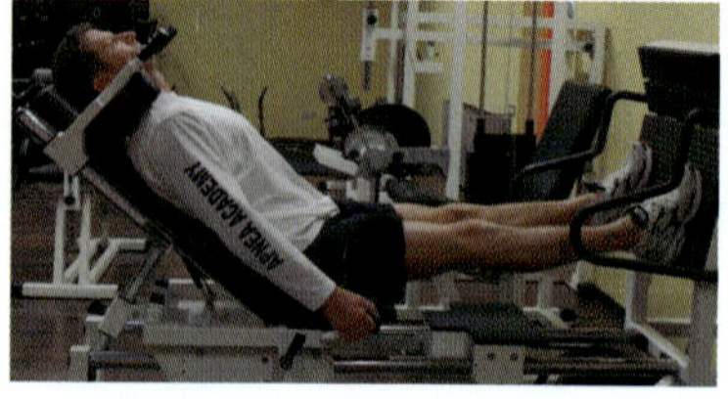

Reps	1st set: 10-12 2nd set: 12-15 3rd set: till exhaustion
Load	70% 60% 50%

Sequence 9 p. 164

3 ADDUCTOR MACHINE

- Adductor machine

Reps	1st set: 10-12 2nd set: 12-15 3rd set: till exhaustion
Load	70% 60% 50%

Sequence 75 p. 196

4 STANDING CABLE HIP ABDUCTION

- Standing cable hip abduction

Reps	1st set: 10-12 2nd set: 12-15 3rd set: till exhaustion
Load	70% 60% 50%

Sequence 76 p. 196

5 GOOD MORNING EXERCISE

- Good morning exercise

Reps	1st set: 8-10 2nd set: 10-12 3rd set: 12-15
Load	70% 60% 50%

Sequence 21 p. 169

7.8 Circuit schedules for training the finstroke

These schedules are useful for training athletes using traditional fins or the monofin (for dynamic apnea and constant weight). Leg exercises train the muscle groups involved in the finstroke. The first 3 schedules are recommended during the special preparatory training period. The fourth one re-creates (outside the pool) specific movements the freediver will perform in the water. It is recommended during the training period before competition.

Table 7.17 Bodyweight circuit training consisting of exercises for joint flexibility and mobility

	Muscles and Joints	Exercises	Reps	Performance time
1	Neck: sternocleidomastoid, Trapezius, joint of cervical region	Fexion, extension, lateral bending, rotation, circumduction of the head	Slow	As required
2	Pectoral girdle area, triceps, latissimus dorsi, glenohumeral joint, vertebral column	Grasp the elbow upwards with the other hand and pull it behind the head	Slow	15-20" each side
3	Trunk lateral muscles, glenohumeral joint	Extend the arms on the front and upward over the head with palms turned upward	Fast	As required
4	Trunk lateral muscles, latissimus dorsi, triceps, lower back muscles, hamstrings, glenohumeral joint	Standing half forward bend keeping the back flat	Slow	10-15" each rep
5	Anterior muscles - upper limbs of shoulders and trunk: pectorals, anterior deltoids, biceps brachii, flexor muscles of the arms, glenohumeral joint	Behind the back stretch with hands at the gymnastic ladder		10-15" each side
6	Anterior muscles - upper limbs of shoulders and trunk: pectoral, anterior deltoids, biceps brachii, flexor muscles of the arms, glenohumeral joint	Bent arm pectoral stretch		10-15" each side
7	Thoracic muscles, shoulders, glenohumeral joint	Forward and backward circumduction of the arms with the stick	Increasing	10" each rep

	Muscles and Joints	Exercises	Reps	Performance time
8	Anterior and lateral thoracic and abdomen muscles glenohumeral joint vertebral column from lumbar region to cervical region	Cobra pose		10-15" each rep
9	Posterior kinetic chain, joints of vertebral column, pelvis	Hamstring stretch standing or seated		10-15" each rep
10	Posterior kinetic chain, joints of vertebral column, pelvis	Plow pose - lift your legs off the floor each rep behind your head with torso perpendicular to the floor		10-15" each rep
11	Anterior and posterior muscles of the legs: calf and tibialis anterior, ankle joint	Flexion, extension, circumduction of ankles standing up or seated	Slow	As required

N.B. These exercises can be performed with different breathing techniques.

1. normal breathing;
2. diaphragmatic breathing (clavicular, chest, abdominal breathing);
3. triangular breathing, ratio 1:2-1:3, for example inhalation two seconds, exhalation 4 seconds;
4. square breathing, for example inhalation 2 seconds and holding breath 3 seconds, exhalation 4 seconds and dyspnoea 3 seconds.

It is recommended to perform the circuit at least 3 times, in the following ways:

- 1st set: passive stretching (you naturally let the muscles slowly relax);
- 2nd set: assisted passive stretching (the partner intervenes to increase the effectiveness of the stretching);
- 3rd set: PNF stretching (involves a shortening contraction of the opposing muscle, thanks to the action of the partner, to stretch the target muscle through the assisted passive stretching method).

1 NECK: STERNOCLEIDOMASTOID, TRAPEZIUS, JOINT OF CERVICAL REGION

- Fexion, extension, lateral bending, rotation, circumduction of the head

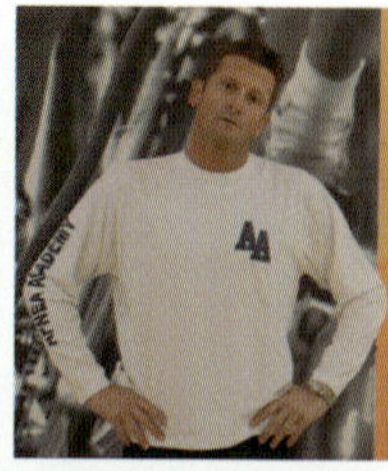

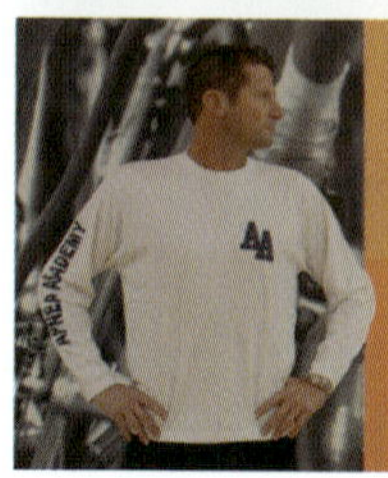

Reps	slow
Performance time	as required
Sequence 50 p. 182	

2 PECTORAL GIRDLE AREA, TRICEPS, LATISSIMUS DORSI, GLENOHUMERAL JOINT, VERTEBRAL COLUMN

- Grasp the elbow upwards with the other hand and pull it behind the head

Reps	slow
Performance time	15-20" each side
Sequence 51 p. 183	

3 TRUNK LATERAL MUSCLES, GLENOHUMERAL JOINT

- Extend the arms on the front and upward over the head with palms turned upward

Reps	fast
Performance time	as required
Sequence 52 p. 183	

4 TRUNK LATERAL MUSCLES, LATISSIMUS DORSI, TRICEPS, LOWER BACK MUSCLES, HAMSTRINGS, GLENOHUMERAL JOINT

- Standing half forward bend keeping the back flat

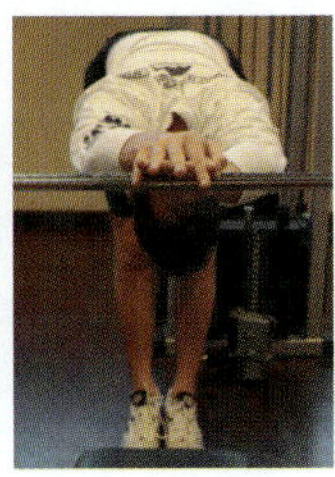

Reps	slow
Performance time	10-15" each rep

Sequence 69 p. 192

5 ANTERIOR MUSCLES - UPPER LIMBS OF SHOULDERS AND TRUNK: PECTORALS, ANTERIOR DELTOIDS, BICEPS BRACHII, FLEXOR MUSCLES OF THE ARMS, GLENOHUMERAL JOINT

- Behind the back stretch with hands at the gymnastic ladder

Performance time	10-15" each side

Sequence 78 p. 197

6 ANTERIOR MUSCLES - UPPER LIMBS OF SHOULDERS AND TRUNK: PECTORAL, ANTERIOR DELTOIDS, BICEPS BRACHII, FLEXOR MUSCLES OF THE ARMS, GLENOHUMERAL JOINT

- Bent arm pectoral stretch

Performance time	10-15" each side

Sequence 77 p. 197

7 THORACIC MUSCLES, SHOULDERS, GLENOHUMERAL JOINT

- Forward and backward circumduction of the arms with the stick

Reps	increasing

Sequence 79 p. 197

8 ANTERIOR AND LATERAL THORACIC AND ABDOMEN MUSCLES GLENOHUMERAL JOINT VERTEBRAL COLUMN FROM LUMBAR REGION TO CERVICAL REGION

- Cobra pose

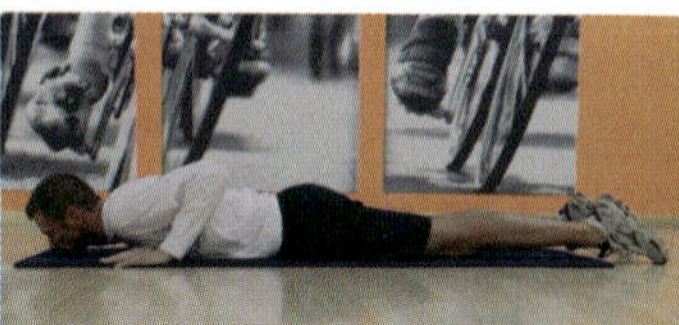

Performance time	10-15" each rep

Sequence 80 p. 198

9 POSTERIOR KINETIC CHAIN, JOINTS OF VERTEBRAL COLUMN, PELVIS

- Hamstring stretch, standing or seated

Performance time	10-15" each rep

Sequence 81 p. 198

10 POSTERIOR KINETIC CHAIN, JOINTS OF VERTEBRAL COLUMN, PELVIS

- Plow pose - lift your legs off the floor behind your head with torso perpendicular to the floor

Performance time	10-15" each rep

Sequence 82 p. 198

11 ANTERIOR AND POSTERIOR MUSCLES OF THE LEGS: CALF AND TIBIALIS ANTERIOR, ANKLE JOINT

- Flexion, extension, circumduction of ankles, standing or seated

Reps	slow
Performance time	as required

Sequence 58 p. 187

Table 7.18 Bodyweight strengthening circuit training

	Muscles and Joints	Exercises	Reps	Pace
1	Anterior kinetic chain, pelvis joints, vertebral column	Lift your legs to form a 180 angle, leg raise as in candle pose	1st set: 12-15 2nd set: 15-20 3rd set: till exhaustion	increasing between one set and the next one
2	Abdomen, ileopsoas, quadriceps, pelvis joints, vertebral column	Extension and raises of the trunk while seated on the partner's knees vertebral column	1st set: 12-15 2nd set: 15-20 3rd set: till exhaustion	1st-2nd set: very slow; 3rd set: fast
3	Low back muscles, gluteus muscles, joints of vertebral column lumbar region	Back extension with legs straight held by your partner-prone	1st set: 10-12 2nd set: 12-15 3rd set: 15-20	fast
4	Upper back muscles, lumbar region, gluteus muscles region biceps femoris, joints of vertebral column	Leg raises with the partner pushing them - supine	1st set: 10-12 2nd set: 12-15 3rd set: 15-20	medium-fast
5	Abdomen and thighs muscles, stabilizing action of postural static chain, knee joints	Flexion and extension of thighs on the legs with trunk straight	1st set: 10-12 2nd set: 12-15 3rd set: till exhaustion	fast
6	Gluteus muscles, biceps femoris, quadriceps, knee joints	Flexion and extension of legs on thighs in prone position, with partner pushing in the opposite direction	1st set: 10-12 2nd set: 10-12 3rd set: 10-12	1 medium

1 ANTERIOR KINETIC CHAIN, PELVIS JOINTS, VERTEBRAL COLUMN

- Lift your legs to form a 180 angle, leg raise as in candle pose

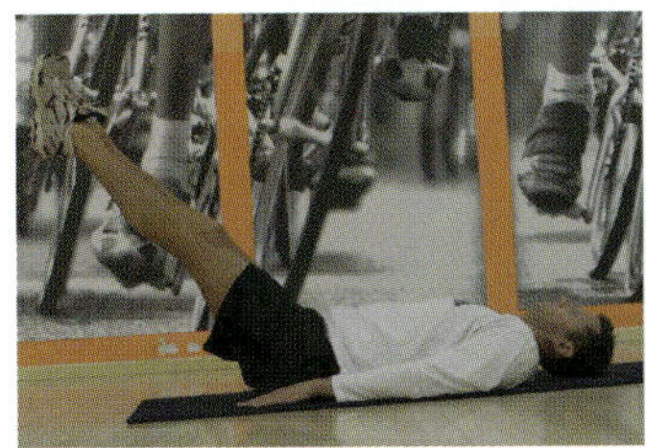

Reps 1st set: 12-15
2nd set: 15-20
3rd set: till exhaustion

Pace increasing between one set and the next one

Sequence 83 p. 199

2 ABDOMEN, ILEOPSOAS, QUADRICEPS, PELVIS JOINTS, VERTEBRAL COLUMN

- Extension and raises of the trunk while seated on the partner's knees

Reps 1st set: 12-15
2nd set: 15-20
3rd set: till exhaustion

Pace 1st-2nd set: very slow; 3rd set: fast

Sequence 84 p. 199

3 LOW BACK MUSCLES, GLUTEUS MUSCLES, JOINTS OF VERTEBRAL COLUMN LUMBAR REGION

- Back extension with legs straight held by your partner-prone

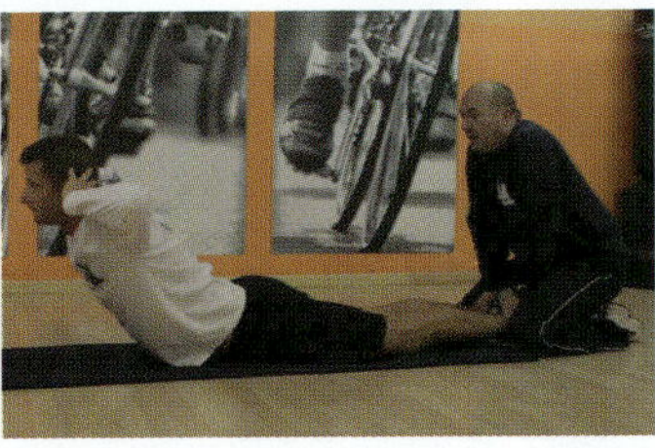

Reps 1st set: 10-12
2nd set: 12-15
3rd set: 15-20

Pace fast

Sequence 85 p. 199

4 UPPER BACK MUSCLES, LUMBAR REGION, GLUTEUS MUSCLES REGION BICEPS FEMORIS, JOINTS OF VERTEBRAL COLUMN

- Leg raises with the partner pushing them - supine

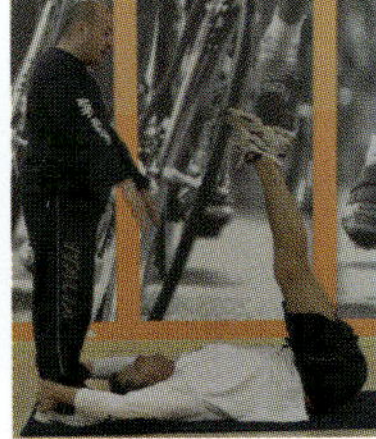

Reps 1st set: 10-12
2nd set: 12-15
3rd set: 15-20

Pace medium-fast

Sequence 86 p. 200

5 ABDOMEN AND THIGHS MUSCLES, STABILIZING ACTION OF POSTURAL STATIC CHAIN, KNEE JOINTS

- Flexion and extension of thighs on the legs with trunk straight

Reps 1st set: 10-12
2nd set: 12-15
3rd set: till exhaustion

Pace fast

Sequence 87 p. 200

6 GLUTEUS MUSCLES, BICEPS FEMORIS, QUADRICEPS, KNEE JOINTS

- Flexion and extension of legs on thighs in prone position, with partner pushing in the opposite direction

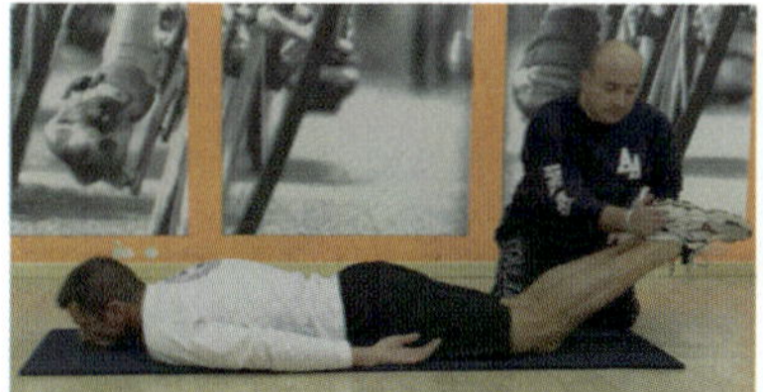
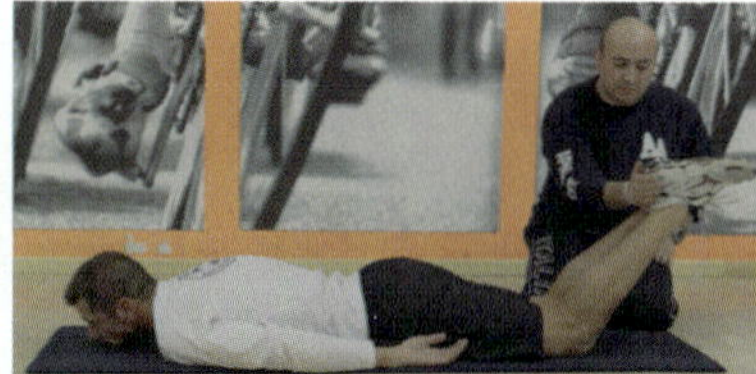

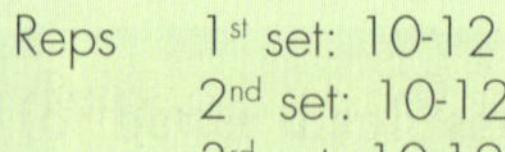
Reps 1st set: 10-12
2nd set: 10-12
3rd set: 10-12

Pace 1 medium

Sequence 88 p. 200

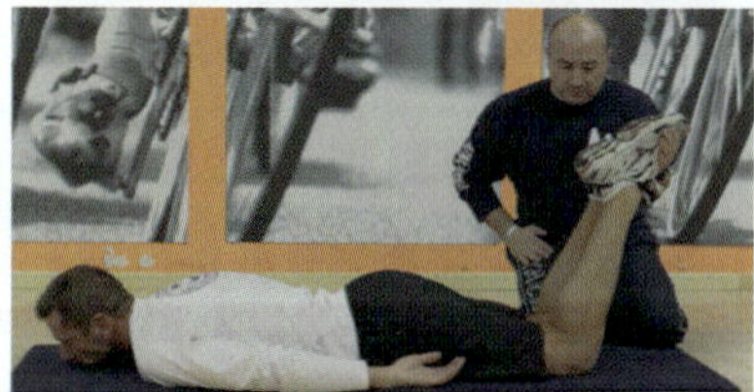
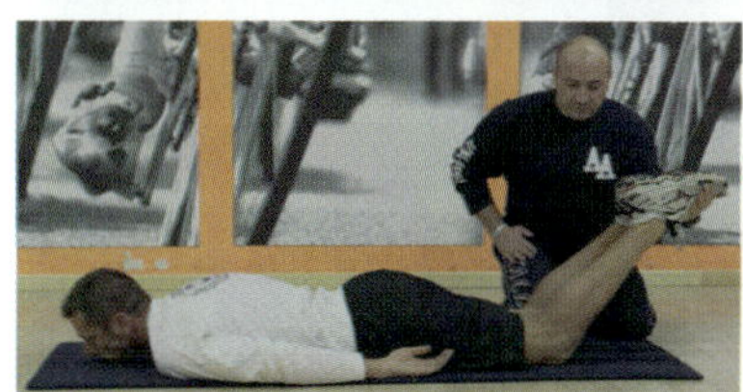
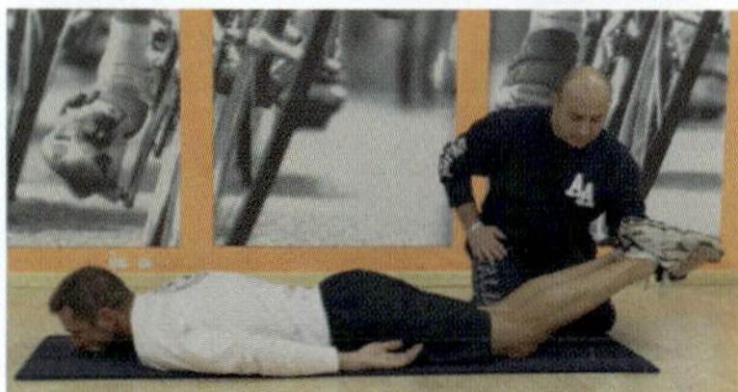

Table 7.19 Strengthening circuit training with equipment, weights, weight machines and cable machines

	Muscles and Joints	Exercises	Reps	Load	Pace
1	Abdominals: rectus abdominis, oblique muscles	Pull down cable crunch	1st set: 12-15 2nd set: 15-20 3rd set: till exhaustion	70% 60% 50%	Progressive, increasing between one set and the next one
2	Oblique muscles, rectus femoris, tensor fasciae latae	Hanging ab straps, lateral twist	1st set: 10-12 2nd set: 12-15 3rd set: till exhaustion	bodyweight exercise	steady, fast
3	Quadriceps	Leg extension	1st set: 10-12 2nd set: 12-15 3rd set: till exhaustion	50% 50% 50%	increasing
4	Gluteus muscles, biceps femoris	Good morning exercise with a light barbell	1st set: 10-12 2nd set: 10-12 3rd set: 10-12	50% 50% 50%	fast
5	Calves	Standing calf raise	1st set: 15-20 2nd set: 15-20 3rd set: 15-20	50% 50% 50%	steady

N.B. Since this circuit is made up of only 5 stations, it has to be performed 1 or 2 times more than longer circuits.
It is characterized by a pyramidal method (decreasing in reps and increasing in load); the movements must be wide and fast to make sure that there is no hypertrophic effect, even though the load does not exceed 70% of the maximum bearable load. The recovery is the time required to change stations and exercises. Between one circuit and the next, a break of at least 2 or 3 minutes is required.

1 RECTUS ABDOMINIS, OBLIQUE MUSCLES

- Pull down cable crunch

Reps	1st set: 12-15 2nd set: 15-20 3rd set: till exhaustion
Load	70% - 60% - 50%
Pace	Progressive, increasing between one set and the next one

Sequence 46 p. 180

2 OBLIQUE MUSCLES, RECTUS FEMORIS, TENSOR FASCIAE LATAE

- Hanging ab straps, lateral twist

Reps	1st set: 12-15 2nd set: 15-20 3rd set: till exhaustion
Load	bodyweight exercise
Pace	steady, fast

Sequence 33 p. 173

3 QUADRICEPS

- Leg extension

Reps	1st set: 10-12 2nd set: 12-15 3rd set: till exhaustion
Load	50% - 50% - 50%
Pace	increasing

Sequence 10 p. 164

3 QUADRICEPS (*to be continued*)

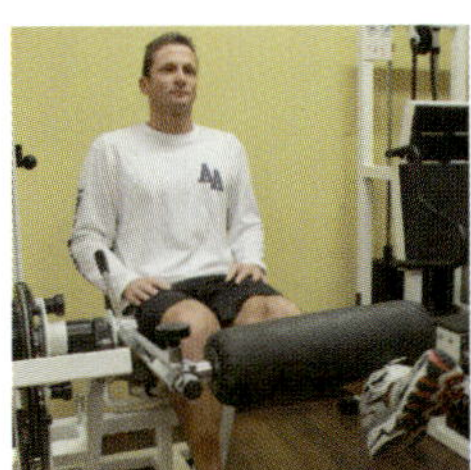

4 GLUTEUS MUSCLES, BICEPS FEMORIS

- Good morning exercise with a light barbell

Reps	1st set: 10-12 2nd set: 10-12 3rd set: 10-12
Load	50% - 50% - 50%
Pace	fast

Sequence 21 p. 169

5 CALVES

- Standing calf raise

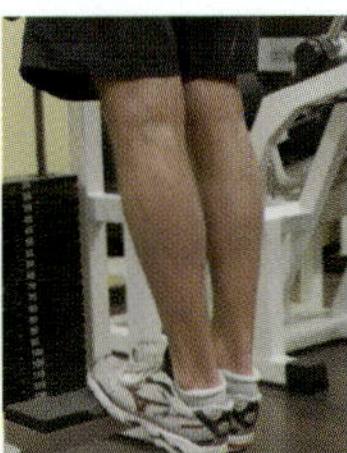
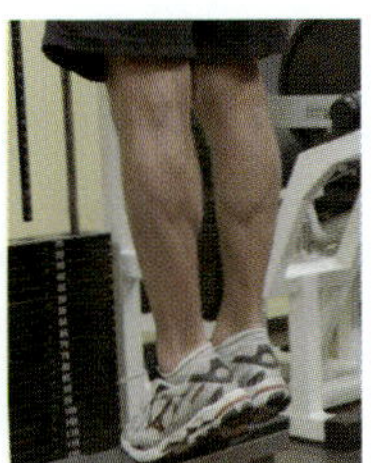

Reps	1st set: 15-20 2nd set: 15-20 3rd set: 15-20
Load	50% - 50% - 50%
Pace	steady

Sequence 45 p. 179

Table 7.20 Circuit training for high-level athletes to be performed during the periods of maximum workload

	Muscles and Joints	Exercises	Reps	Load	Pace
1	Abdomen + lower back muscles, synergy of anterior and Posterior kinetic chain Joints: knees, acetabulofemoral joint, vertebral column	Super combination: bending at the knees, leg raise in candle pose, return to plow pose, return to standing position, standing cable crunch alternated with stiff legged barbell deadlift	1st set: 12-15 2nd set: 12-15 3rd set: 12-15	70% 60% 50%	fast
2	Abdomen, synergy of anterior kinetic chain, acetabulofemoral joint	Hanging leg raise with knee bent	1st set: till exhaustion 2nd set: till exhaustion 3rd set: till exhaustion	bodyweight exercise	medium
3	Lower back muscles + synergy of posterior kinetic chain, acetabulofemoral joint	Good morning exercise with a light barbell	1st set: till exhaustion 2nd set: till exhaustion 3rd set: till exhaustion	barbell	medium
4	Abdominals, pelvis joints, acetabulofemoral joint	Hanging leg raises with legs straight	1st set: till exhaustion 2nd set: till exhaustion 3rd set: till exhaustion	bodyweight exercise	medium
5	Lower back muscles, pelvis joints	Lower back bench extension	1st set: till exhaustion 2nd set: till exhaustion 3rd set: till exhaustion	bodyweight exercise	medium
6	Quadriceps, acetabulofemoral joint, knee joints	Horizontal leg press exercises	1st set: 12-15 2nd set: 15-20 3rd set: till exhaustion	70% 60% 50%	medium
7	Quadriceps, knee joints	Alternate leg extension	20 each leg	50%	fast
8	Quadriceps, pelvis joints, knee and ankle joints	Jumping squat with a bar	1st set: till exhaustion 2nd set: till exhaustion 3rd set: till exhaustion	barbell	fast
9	Kinetic postural chain, acetabulofemoral joint, knee and ankle joints	Free walking on treadmill	10 minutes		

N.B. This circuit is suitable for freedivers with high-level athletic skills. There are no breaks, except the time it takes to change stations or exercises.
The circuit must be performed at least 3 times.

1 ABDOMEN + LOWER BACK MUSCLES, SYNERGY OF ANTERIOR AND POSTERIOR KINETIC CHAIN JOINTS: KNEES, ACETABULOFEMORAL JOINT, VERTEBRAL COLUMN

- Super combination: bending at the knees, leg raise in candle pose, return to plow pose, return to standing position, standing cable crunch alternated with stiff legged barbell deadlift

Reps	1st set: 12-15 2nd set: 12-15 3rd set: 12-15
Load	70% - 60% - 50%
Pace	fast

Sequence 89 p. 201

2 ABDOMEN, SYNERGY OF ANTERIOR KINETIC CHAIN, ACETABULOFEMORAL JOINT

- Hanging leg raise with knee bent

Reps	1st set: till exhaustion 2nd set: till exhaustion 3rd set: till exhaustion
Load	bodyweight exercise
Pace	medium

Sequence 90 p. 202

3 LOWER BACK MUSCLES + SYNERGY OF POSTERIOR KINETIC CHAIN, ACETABULOFEMORAL JOINT

- Good morning exercise with a light barbell

Reps	1st set: till exhaustion 2nd set: till exhaustion 3rd set: till exhaustion
Load	barbell
Pace	medium

Sequence 21 p. 169

4 ABDOMINALS, PELVIS JOINTS, ACETABULOFEMORAL JOINT

- Hanging leg raises with legs straight

Reps	1st set: till exhaustion 2nd set: till exhaustion 3rd set: till exhaustion
Load	bodyweight exercise
Pace	medium

Sequence 91 p. 202

5 LOWER BACK MUSCLES, PELVIS JOINTS

- Lower back bench extension

Reps	1st set: till exhaustion 2nd set: till exhaustion 3rd set: till exhaustion
Load	bodyweight exercise
Pace	medium

Sequence 22 p. 169

6 QUADRICEPS, ACETABULOFEMORAL JOINT, KNEE JOINTS

- Horizontal leg press exercise

Reps	1st set: 12-15 2nd set: 15-20 3rd set: till exhaustion
Load	70% - 60% - 50%
Pace	fast

Sequence 9 p. 164

7 QUADRICEPS, KNEE JOINTS

- Alternate leg extension

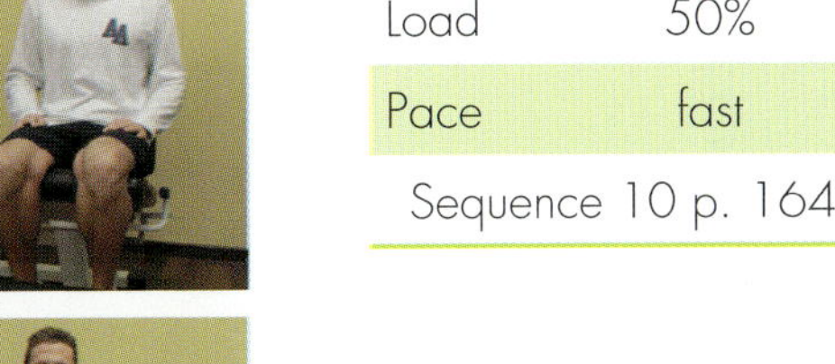

Reps	20 each leg
Load	50%
Pace	fast

Sequence 10 p. 164

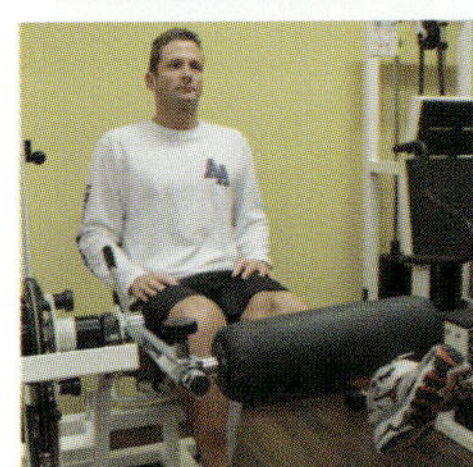

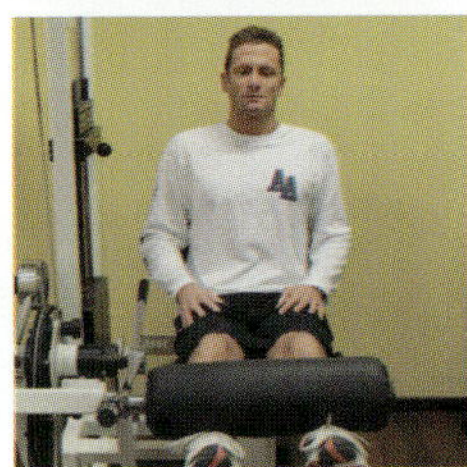

8 QUADRICEPS, PELVIS JOINTS, KNEE AND ANKLE JOINTS

- Jumping squat with a bar

Reps	1st set: till exhaustion 2nd set: till exhaustion 3rd set: till exhaustion
Load	barbell
Pace	fast

Sequence 49 p. 182

9 KINETIC POSTURAL CHAIN, ACETABULOFEMORAL JOINT, KNEE AND ANKLE JOINTS

- Free walking on treadmill

Reps	10 minutes

7.9 Sequences of the exercises given in the tables

1 DUMBBELL SHRUGS

2 PULL OVER

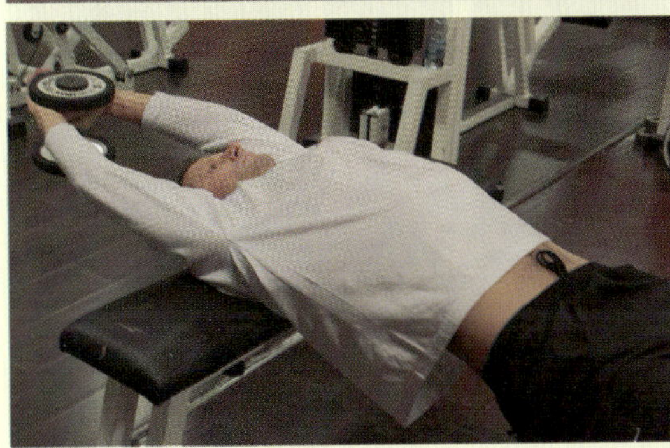
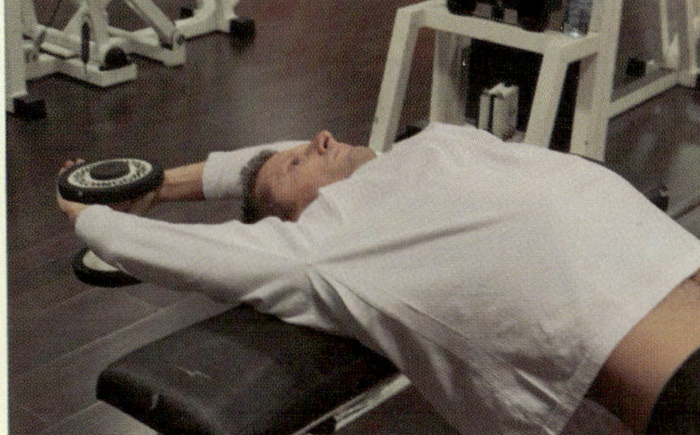

3 PECTORAL MACHINE

4 BEHIND NECK LAT PULL DOWN

5 BENT OVER BARBELL TRICEPS KICKBACK

6 DUMBBELL KICK BACK

7 DUMBBELL LATERAL RAISE

8 DUMBBELL FRONT RAISE

9 LEG EXTENSION

10 45 DEGREE LEG PRESS

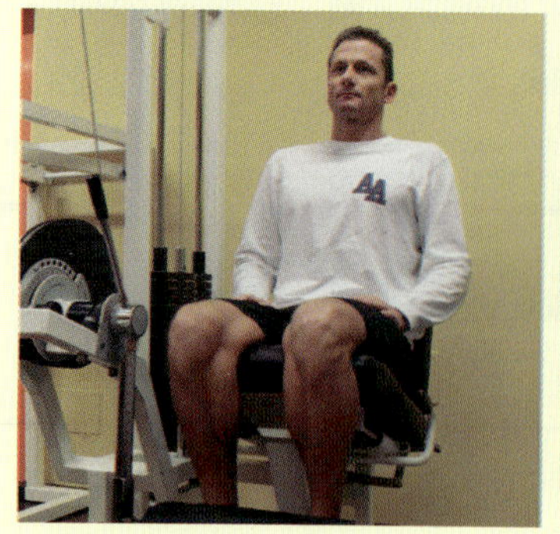

10 45 DEGREE LEG PRESS (*to be continued*)

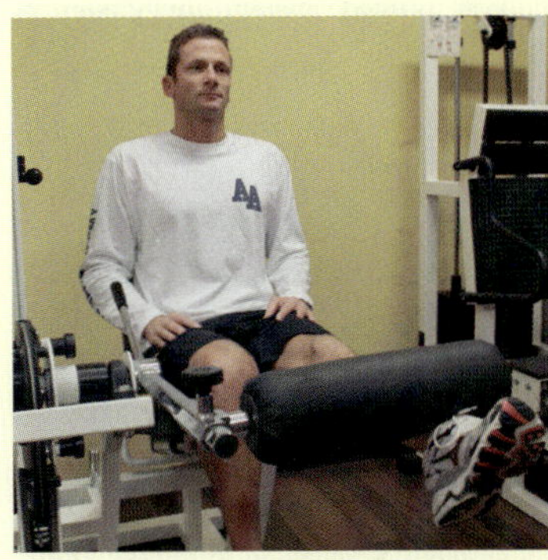

11 LEG CURL

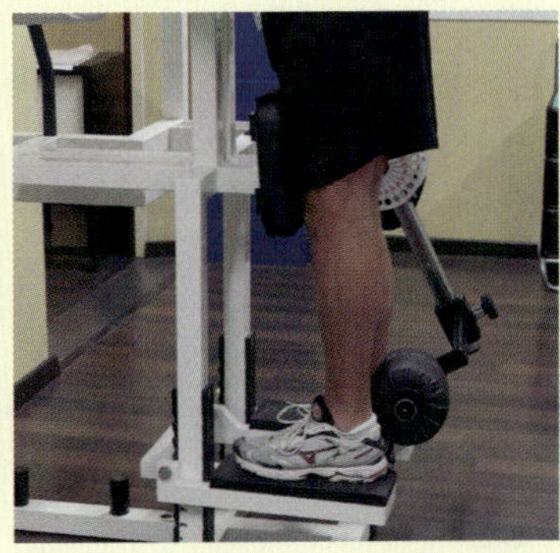

12 CRUNCH

13 BARBELL BENCH PRESS

14 CABLE CROSSOVER

15 INCLINED DUMBBELL FLY

16 PUSH-UPS

17 VERTICAL ROW

18 LOW PULLEY

19 DORSY BAR

20 BARBELL BENT OVER ROW

21 GOOD MORNING

22 LOWER BACK BENCH EXTENSION

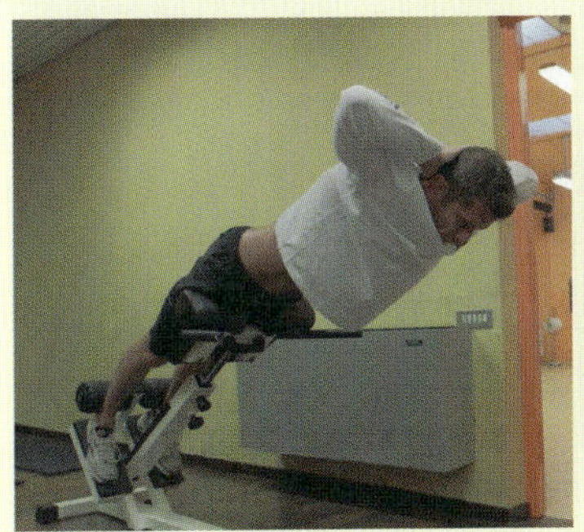

23 SQUAT

24 STIFF-LEGGED BARBELL DEADLIFT

25 ONE-LEGGED CABLE KICKBACK

26 STANDING BARBELL SHOULDER PRESS

27 INCLINE BENCH REVERSE FLY

28 DUMBBELL FRONT RAISE

29 DUMBBELL SHRUGS

30 BARBELL CURL

31 DUMBBELL ALTERNATE CURL

32 KNEELING CABLE TRICEPS EXTENSION

33 HANGING KNEE RAISE

34 COMBINED EXERCISES ON THE BENCH: BENCH PRESS + DUMBBELL FLY

35 DECLINE CRUNCH

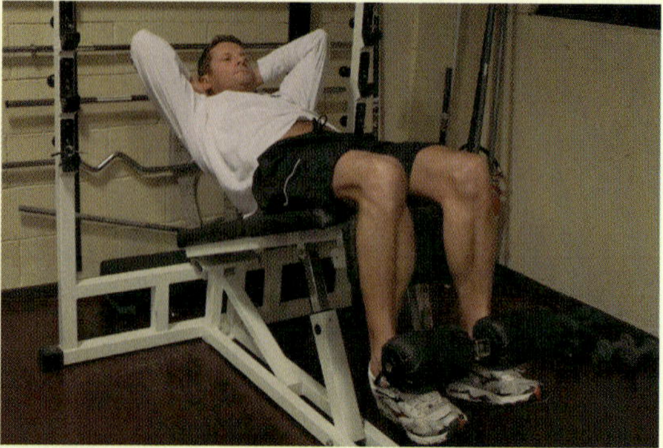

36 ABDOMINAL ROLLER

37 FITNESS PUMP

38 CURL + BENCH PRESS + OPEN + ARM SHOULDER PRESS + BARBELL UPRIGHT ROWING

38 CURL + BENCH PRESS + OPEN + ARM SHOULDER PRESS + BARBELL UPRIGHT ROWING (*to be continued*)

39 SHOULDER PRESS

39 SHOULDER PRESS (*to be continued*)

40 LOWER BACK BENCH EXTENSION

41 CHEST PRESS

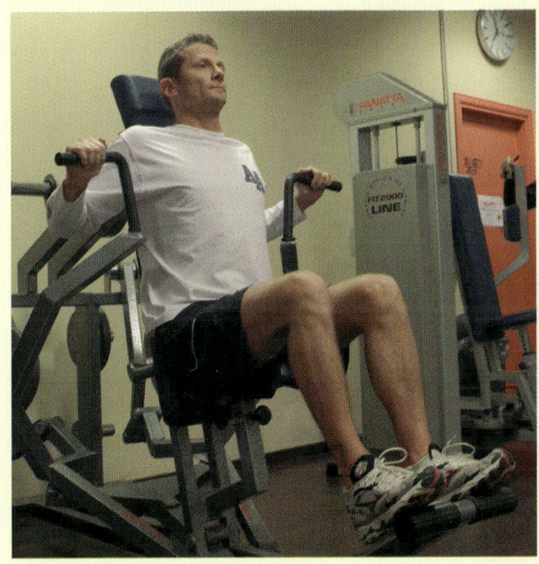

42 BICEPS MACHINE

43 TRICEPS WITH DUMBBELLS

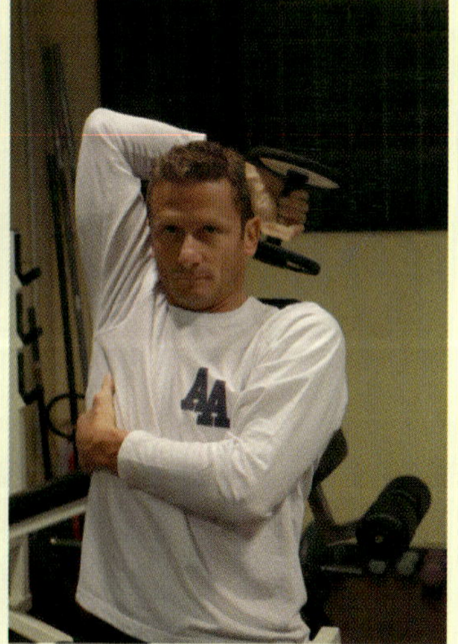

44 BARBELL UPRIGHT ROWING

45 CALF MACHINE

46 PULL DOWN CABLE CRUNCH WITH LAT MACHINE

47 FROM 90-DEGREE ANGLE LEG RAISE

48 LEG RAISE AS IN CANDLE POSE + LATERAL TWISTS

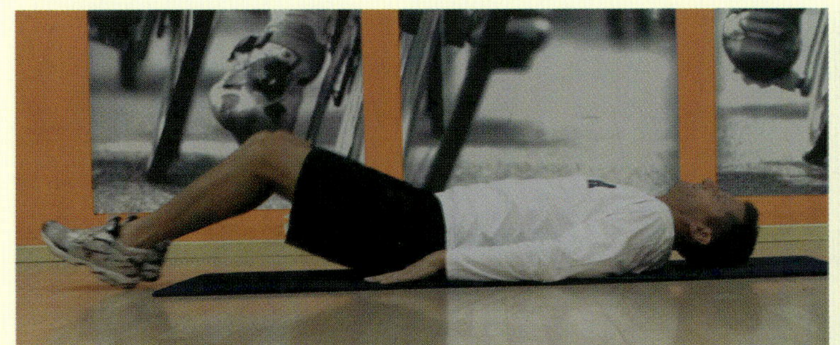

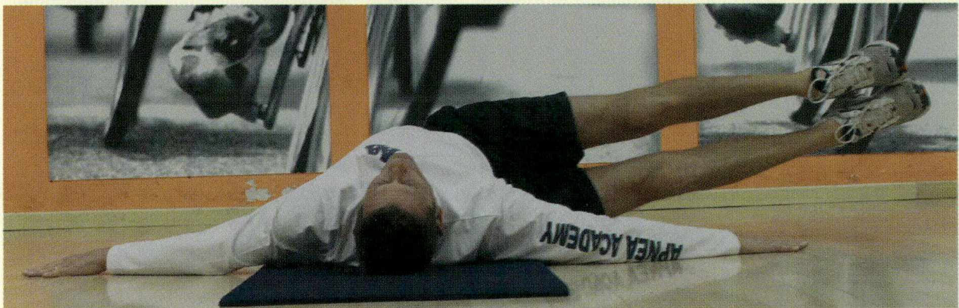

49 JUMPING SQUAT

50 FLEXION, EXTENSION, LATERAL BENDING, ROTATION, CIRCUMDUCTION OF THE HEAD

51 GRASP THE ELBOW UPWARDS WITH THE OTHER HAND AND PULL IT BEHIND THE HEAD

52 EXTEND THE ARMS ON THE FRONT AND UPWARD OVER THE HEAD WITH THE PALMS TURNED UPWARD (BALLISTIC STRETCHING)

53 KNEE CIRCUMDUCTION

54 FORWARD AND BACKWARD CIRCUMDUCTION OF ARMS OUTSTRETCHED

54 FORWARD AND BACKWARD CIRCUMDUCTION OF ARMS OUTSTRETCHED *(to be continued)*

55 SQUAT WITH LEGS WIDE APART

56 HIP CIRCUMDUCTION

56 HIP CIRCUMDUCTION (*to be continued*)

57 BEND KNEES ON THE FLOOR WIDE OPEN AND BEND ELBOWS TO THE FLOOR

58 FLEXION EXTENSION, CIRCUMDUCTION OF ANKLES STANDING OR SEATED

59 CHIN-UPS WITH ARMS WIDE OPEN AND PALMS FACING DOWN

60 TRICEPS DIPS WITH LEGS SUSPENDED

61 QUADRUPED ABDUCTION + EXTENSION WITH LEGS OUTSTRETCHED

62 SIDELYING LEG RAISES

63 LATERAL WIDE LUNGE AND THEN RETURN TO YOUR STANDING POSITION

64 TRICEPS DIPS BETWEEN TWO BENCHES

65 TRICEPS CABLE PUSHDOWNS

66 CABLE STRAIGHT ARM PULLDOWNS

67 STANDING CABLE CROSSOVER

68 HANGING KNEE RAISES

69 STANDING HALF FORWARD BEND KEEPING THE BACK FLAT

70 CURL + BENCH PRESS + OPEN ARM SHOULDER PRESS + BARBELL UPRIGHT ROWING

71 STRAIGHT LEGS CIRCUMDUCTIONS WITH ANKLE WEIGHTS

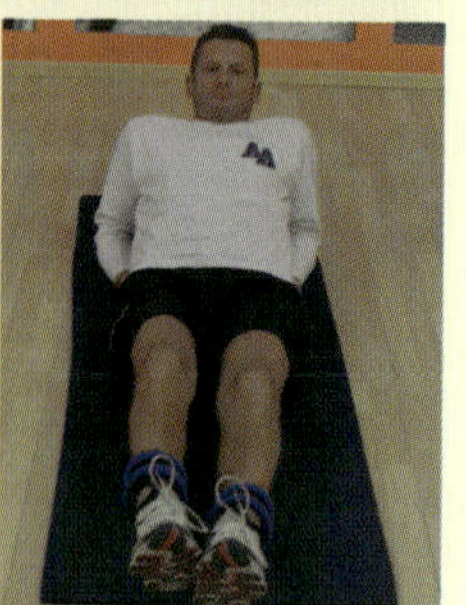

72 SIMULATION BREASTSTROKE ARM MOVEMENT AT CABLE MACHINE

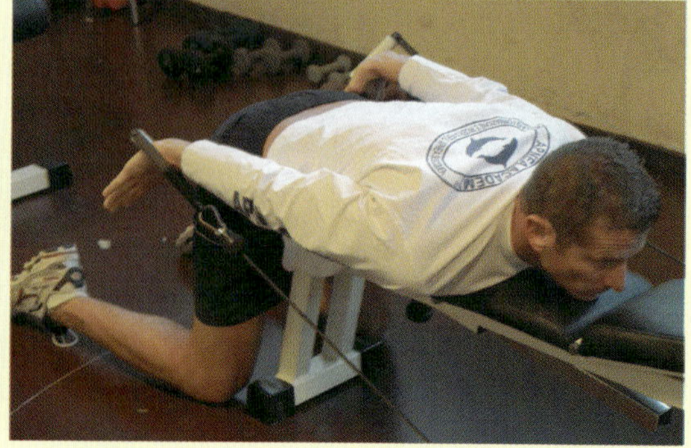

73 SIMULATION BREASTSTROKE LEG MOVEMENT AT CABLE MACHINE

74 BARBELL SISSY SQUAT

75 ADDUCTOR MACHINE

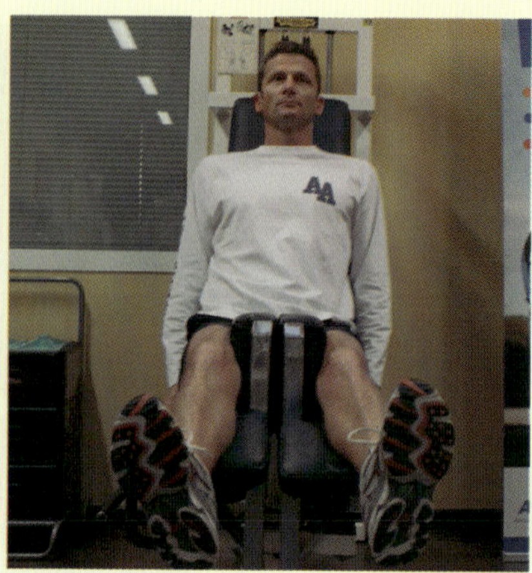

76 STANDING CABLE HIP ABDUCTION

77 BENT ARM PECTORAL STRETCH

78 BEHIND THE BACK STRETCH WITH HANDS AT THE GYMNASTIC LADDER

79 FORWARD AND BACKWARD CIRCUMDUCTION OF THE ARMS WITH THE STICK

80 COBRA POSE

81 HAMSTRING STRETCH, STANDING OR SEATED

82 PLOW POSE - LIFT YOUR LEGS OFF THE FLOOR BEHIND YOUR HEAD WITH TORSO PERPENDICULAR TO THE FLOOR

83 LIFT YOUR LEGS TO FORM A 180 ANGLE, LEG RAISE AS IN CANDLE POSE

84 EXTENSION AND RAISES OF THE TRUNK WHILE SEATED ON THE PARTNER'S KNEES

85 BACK EXTENSION WITH LEGS STRAIGHT HELD BY YOUR PARTNER-PRONE

86 LEG RAISES WITH THE PARTNER PUSHING THEM - SUPINE

87 FLEXION AND EXTENSION OF THIGHS ON THE LEGS WITH TRUNK STRAIGHT

88 FLEXION AND EXTENSION OF LEGS ON THIGHS IN PRONE POSITION, WITH PARTNER PUSHING IN THE OPPOSITE DIRECTION

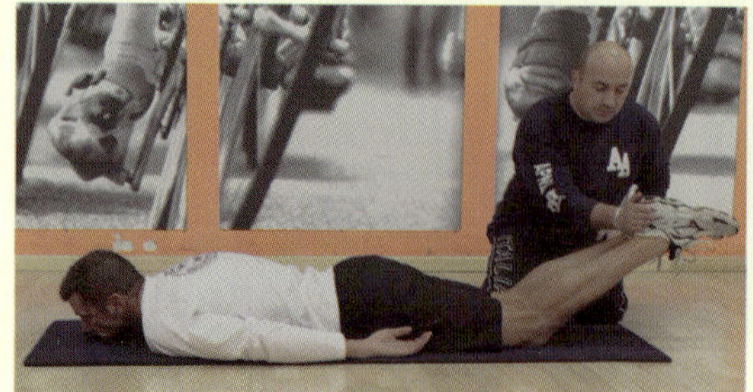

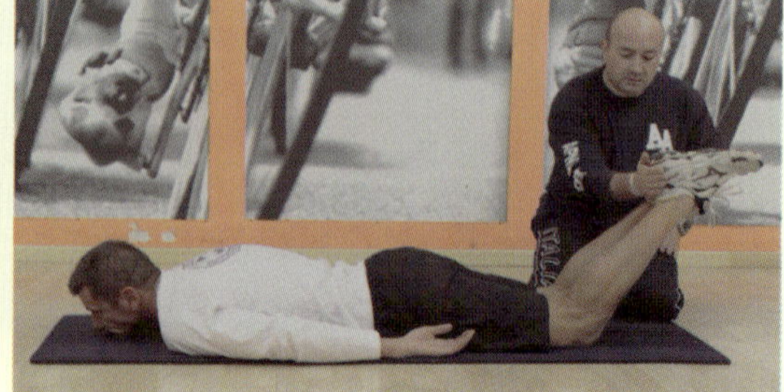

88 FLEXION AND EXTENSION OF LEGS ON THIGHS IN PRONE POSITION, WITH PARTNER PUSHING IN THE OPPOSITE DIRECTION
(*to be continued*)

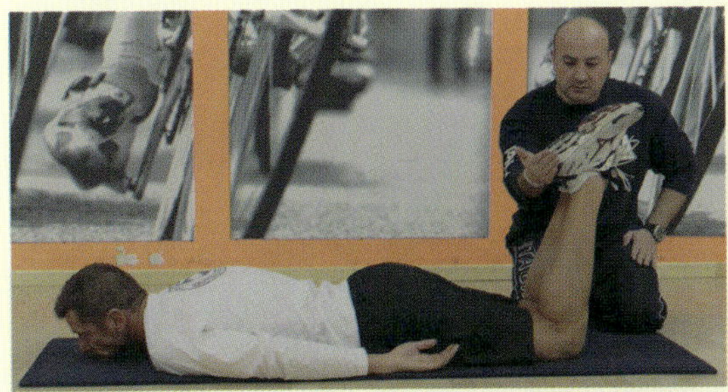
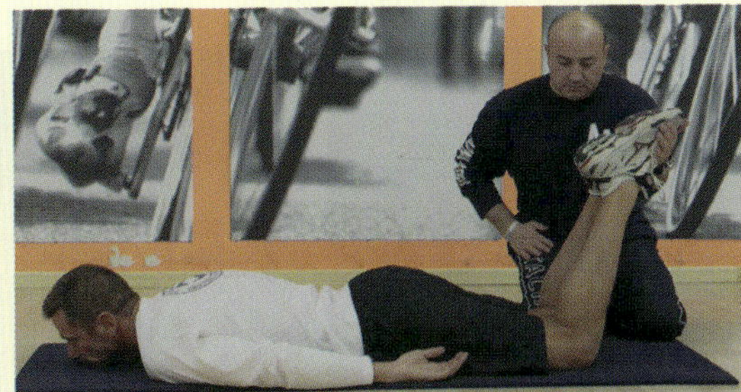
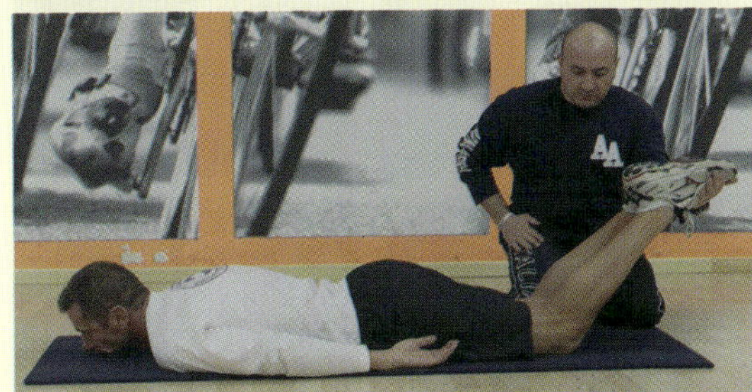
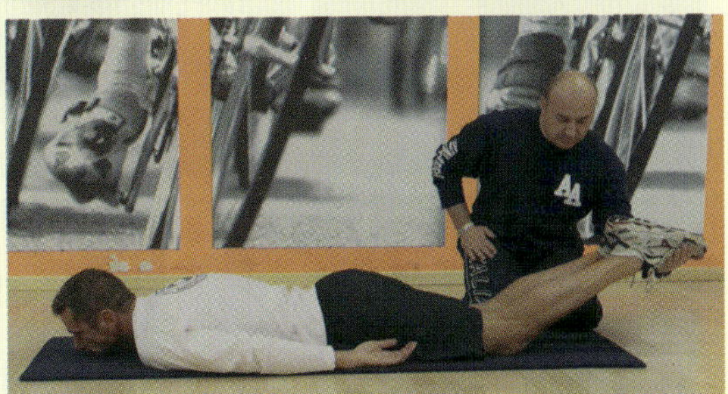

89 BENDING AT THE KNEES, LEG RAISE IN CANDLE POSE, RETURN TO PLOW POSE, RETURN TO STANDING POSITION, STANDING CABLE CRUNCH ALTERNATED WITH STIFF LEGGED BARBELL DEADLIFT

89 BENDING AT THE KNEES, LEG RAISE IN CANDLE POSE, RETURN TO PLOW POSE, RETURN TO STANDING POSITION, STANDING CABLE CRUNCH ALTERNATED WITH STIFF LEGGED BARBELL DEADLIFT

(to be continued)

90 HANGING LEG RAISE WITH KNEE BENT

91 HANGING LEG RAISES WITH LEGS STRAIGHT

Chapter 8

SWIMMING

8.1 Reasons for swimming

In this chapter, we talk about why freedivers need to swim as part of their training regimen. If we were presenting a comprehensive training program for competitive swimmers, we would go into a lot more detail, including many other variables, and analyse more technical issues. Some concepts are not thoroughly described from a technical point of view because we aim to make the training concept easy to understand, even by those who are not competitive swimmers. Bear in mind that our goal is to use swimming as a training method for freediving.

The freediver will benefit more from training designed for a middle-distance swimmer than from sprinter training. Therefore, if you have the opportunity to train with competitive swimmers, train with those who do 200 m or 400 m freestyle, rather than those who do 50 m or 100 m.

We will focus on how to implement a swimming training regimen for the freediver, focusing on volume, intensity, frequency and density. This will allow us to avoid the mere goal of swimming more laps than we did the day before There is nothing more monotonous than swimming without a targeted workout. In that situation, you would probably change sport after just a few weeks!

Before going into detail on the workout, we will define the main kinds of training (aerobic and anaerobic) with letters. We will use the first three letters of the alphabet (A, B, C) in combination with numbers (1, 2) to refer to specific paces and their related trainings. These letter-number combinations are nothing more than a communication shortcut; they create a simple way to refer to the levels of intensity and the performance procedures of a specific training.

In addition, the following paragraphs will refer to the Borg Scale, which is used to assess physical condition through perceived exertion.

Borg Scale	Scale Level	Perceived Exertion
Based on subjective perceived exertion, it is useful to assess the different levels of athletes' physical condition.	0	no exertion at all
	1	very light
	2	light
	3	moderate
	4	demanding
	5	pretty heavy
	6	heavy
	7	notably heavy
	8	very heavy
	9	hard
	10	extremely hard, up to the maximum

A

This letter designates a workout aimed at developing endurance and aerobic capacity. A high aerobic capacity enables the swimmer to maintain a certain level of speed as long as possible without decreased mechanic efficiency. In training, freedivers use two different types of aerobic swimming workouts:

A1

This includes active recovery workouts between one set and the next – that is, all exercises that improve technique, the warm-up at the beginning of the training session and the cool-down. During A1, the pace is very mild, and the heart rate is below 120 beats per minute.

A2
OR AEROBIC CAPACITY

This includes basic aerobic endurance (or capacity) workouts.

Physiological parameters of A2 training

- **Heart rate:** approximately 140 beats per minute or below. It can increase gradually during the workout, but by no more than 10% of the expected value. A higher increase indicates a need to further develop aerobic resistance.
- **Lactic acidemia**: usually lower than 2.5 mmol/L during the workout and steady over time. Distance swimmers usually have lower figures than other athletes.
- **Level of fatigue**: no higher than the 3rd level of the Borg Scale.
- **Ventilation:** mild change in respiratory rate.

B

This letter indicates a workout that not only triggers the aerobic energy system but is also near the anaerobic threshold. The numbers 1 and 2 are used with B to define the kind of workout performed. With regard to this labeling system, there are several schools of thought. One school considers B1 to be simply a level higher than A2, with similar features in terms of the energy systems, but including aerobic power training (threshold workout) that leads to employing the anaerobic energy system with a VO_2max workout. Meanwhile, other trainers and sports physicians believe that B1 includes an intensity workout of the anaerobic threshold (aerobic power) in a condition of maximal consumption of oxygen, while remaining within the aerobic system framework. For freedivers, these details are simply formalities. What we are interested in is how to train those energy systems through swimming because they are very important for us. In the following description, we adhere to the second school of thought.

B1
OR ANAEROBIC THRESHOLD

Anaerobic threshold intensity corresponds to the maximum aerobic power obtainable without the lactic acid mechanism contributing to overall energy production. It is expressed as the percentage of maximal oxygen consumption (VO_2max).

Physiological parameters of B1 workout

- **Heart rate:** usually between 160 and 180 BPM. Heart rate related to the intensity of the anaerobic threshold increases as seasonal training steps up. This parameter can be evaluated through specific tests.
- **Lactic acidemia:** ranges from 3 and 5 mmol/L and remains steady over time. In the same individual, it will generally be 1.5 to 2 mmol/L higher than the A2 standard values. Lower values are often seen in long-distance swimmers.
- **Level of fatigue:** third and fourth level of the Borg Scale.
- **Ventilation:** slight increase of respiratory rate.

B2
OR MAXIMAL OXYGEN CONSUMPTION (VO_2MAX)

VO_2max represents the maximal amount of oxygen that can be taken, carried and used in a specific unit of time. It can be achieved with help from the anaerobic systems. A proper definition of B2 may be: The maximum level of an aerobic workout using anaerobic mechanisms.

Physiological parameters of B2 workout

- **Heart rate:** includes values that are not as easily recognizable through manual methods compared to those of B1. They are commonly higher.
- **Lactic acidemia:** values ranging from 4 to 7 mmol/L (normally lower for long-distance swimmers). The quantity of lactic acid in the blood progressively rises as a constant-speed workout is performed.

- **Level of fatigue:** ranges from the fifth to the seventh level of the Borg Scale.
- **Ventilation:** significant increase in breathing.

C

This letter refers to a "lactate workout", where the anaerobic mechanism is in action. C is divided into C1, C2 and C3, but freedivers will work in C1 only. For the sake of completeness, we have to explain that a C2 workout aims for the peak of lactate, which is the maximum concentration of lactate the swimmer can store in the blood. C3 is a speed workout with the objective of increasing maximum speed through improved swimming performance and a rise in muscle power. We reiterate that in this book, we will analyse the lactate workout of C1 only, since it is the most useful for freedivers who uses swimming as physical preparation.

C1
OR LACTATE TOLERANCE

Building up this tolerance allows the swimmer to keep, for as long as possible, a certain level of speed while in a state of muscle acidosis without reducing mechanical performance. This tolerance is necessary in order to cope with a large amount of lactic acid being produced over a prolonged period of time (to put it plainly, when we have suffering arms that in the end do not work anymore).

Physiological parameters

- **Heart rate:** near maximal values.
- **Lactic acidemia:** near maximal values and higher than those corresponding to VO_2max. Beyond 8 mmol/L.
- **Fatigue degree:** beyond the seventh level of the Borg Scale.
- **Ventilation:** maximal respiratory rate.

8.2 Swimming starting test

We have described the main features of the various workouts used in training. Now we will analyse the pace of A2, B1, B2 and C1, which is very important to outline in a training schedule. First, we have to create a table of our pace. Methods are different, some clearer than others and some easier to apply.

The only scientific test that gives us clear evidence of the energy system we are using while training is the lactate measurement. For this test, the physician takes a blood sample from the athlete and analyzes the concentration of lactic acid in that sample. If it is up to 2,5 mmol/L, the athlete trains the aerobic capacity (A2). If it is about 4 mmol/L, he trains the threshold speed (B1). If it is between 5 and 7 (B2), he trains VO_2max. If it is higher than 7 mmol/L, he is using lactic acid power, so the anaerobic system is involved. However precise the test is, it is very difficult to apply. There are more empirical, precise and easy-to-apply methods through which it is possible to outline a comprehensive pace table. They can calculate times for different distances depending on the skill to be trained. It is important to bear in mind that timings obtained from this type of test are merely indicative. They are not precise, nor are they intended to be. In fact, while a long-distance swimmer may be able to meet the times outlined in the table for long distances, he may have trouble meeting the times for short distances. For a sprinter, the opposite may be true. Regardless, tests and relevant tables give us important information needed to start the training. As the table is updated, timings of individual paces will become increasingly precise until they will match the athlete's level.

8.2.1 1500-meter freestyle test

Using the 1500-Meter Freestyle Test, it is possible to identify the threshold speed of the 100-meter freestyle, defined as B1 (100). Starting with this figure we can determine all the paces.

Let's see how to do it:

Swim 1500 meters freestyle. You should be very tired and keep the average speed as uniform as possible for the entire distance.

Divide the total time of the 1500 freestyle by 15, and you will obtain the average time for a B1 100-meter freestyle.

Put this value in the slot of the table at the crossing point of the B1column and 100 meters row. Using this value, you can determine the others until you have completed the table of paces.

	A2	B1	B2	C1
50 meters	B1(100)/2	A2(50) – 5%[A2(50)]	A2(50) – 10%[A2(50)]	A2(50) – 15%[A2(50)]
100 meters	B1(100) + 5%[B1(100)]	B1(100)	2[B1(50)]	2[B2(50)]
200 meters	B1(200) + 5%[B1(200)]	2[A2(100)]	2[B1(100)]	4[B1(50)]
400 meters	B1(400) + 5%[B1(400)]	2[A2(200)]	4[A2(100)]	4[B1(100)]

Now, let's create an example and calculate all the other paces of 100 meters (in C1, B1 and A2) and those of the other distances that you will use during training (50, 200, 400).

Let's suppose that we cover 1500 meters in 25 minutes (which equals 1500 seconds). Take the total time of 1500 seconds, divide it by 15 and you will have the threshold speed time for the 100-meter free style. The threshold time should be 100 seconds.

25 minutes multiplied by 60 = 1500 seconds.

1500 seconds divided by 15 = 100 seconds (or 1 minute, 40 seconds).

B1 (100) is the x value of the table. Physiological qualities are shown in the rows, and distances are recorded in the columns. The crossing point between the B1 column and the 100 (x) row will have, in this example, a value of 1 minute, 40 seconds (written 1'40"). Having defined that, as you move diagonally across the table, you will double this value every time you go down and halve this value every time you go up.

Therefore:

A2(50) = x/2 = 50"

B2(200) = 2x = 200" = 3'20"

C1(400) = 4x = 400" = 6'40"

Let's fill in the table with the following values.

	A2	B1	B2	C1
50 meters	50"			
100 meters		1'40"		
200 meters			3'20"	
400 meters				6'40"

Let's focus on the row of 50 and try to assign times to the different physiological qualities in this distance (B1, B2, C1).

$$B1(50) = 50'' - 5\%[A2(50)] = 47{,}52''$$

$$B2(50) = 50'' - 10\%[A2(50)] = 45''$$

$$C1(50) = 50'' - 15\%[A2(50)] = 42{,}5''$$

The previous table will become:

	A2	B1	B2	C1
50 meters	50"	47,5"	45"	42,5"
100 meters		1'40"		
200 meters			3'20"	
400 meters				6'40"

Based on these new values, starting from the time of B1(50) and applying the rule previously described of moving diagonally across the table, you will have:

$$B2(100) = 2(B1(50)) = 2(47{,}5'') = 1'35''$$

$$C1(200) = 2(B2(100)) = 2(1'35'') = 3'10''$$

Starting from B2 timing (50) and applying the same rule, you will have:

$$C1(100) = 2(B2(50)) = 2(45'') = 1'30''$$

The table will be filled in as follows:

	A2	B1	B2	C1
50 meters	50"	47,5"	45"	42,5"
100 meters		1'40"	1'35"	1'30"
200 meters			3'20"	3'10"
400 meters				6'40"

Let's calculate the value of A2(100):

$$A2(100) = B1(100) + 5\%\ B1(100) = 1'45''$$

By applying the same rule of the diagonal to this value, you will get:

$$B1(200) = 2[A2(100)] = 2(1'45'') = 3'30''$$

$$B2(400) = 2[B1(200)] = 2(3'30'') = 7'$$

The table will be filled in as follows:

	A2	B1	B2	C1
50 meters	50"	47,5"	45"	42,5"
100 meters	1'45"	1'40"	1'35"	1'30"
200 meters		3'30"	3'20"	3'10"
400 meters			7'	6'40"

One step more, and your table will be completed. By applying the previous rules:

$$A2(200) = B1(200) + 5\%\ B1(200) = 3'30" + 5\%(3'30") = 3'40{,}5"$$

You apply the diagonal rule on this value and calculate a time of:

$$B1(400) = 2[A2(200)] = 2(3'40{,}5") = 7'21"$$

$$A2(400) = B1(400) + 5\%\ [B1(400)] = 7'43{,}05"$$

Your final table will be as follows:

	A2	B1	B2	C1
50 meters	50"	47,5"	45"	42,5"
100 meters	1'45"	1'40"	1'35"	1'30"
200 meters	3'40,5"	3'30"	3'20"	3'10"
400 meters	7'43,05"	7'21"	7'	6'40"

8.2.2 Differential test

In the 1500-meter test, we looked at the freestyle, which must be included in a training program. Breaststroke, backstroke or dolphin kick swimmers can improve their aerobic skills using freestyle. In fact, it is best not to swim too much in styles other than freestyle. It is not possible to swim 3x400 dolphin kick or breaststroke.

There is no one "right" swimming style for a freediver. We swim in the style we prefer, the one which provides the most satisfaction, or the one in which we have the best technique. The breaststroke can be used in training just as well as the backstroke or freestyle. The key factors are technique, effort intensity, workout volume, etc. If we want to improve and train for swimming styles other than freestyle, we have to use the differential test (since it is not possible to swim 1500 m dolphin kick, for example!). For the breaststroke, backstroke, dolphin kick, etc., in order to calculate paces, we have to measure maximal distances of 200, 100 and 50 m and apply differentials. This test shows the difference between the best time for 200 m and the best time for 100 m and gives the B2 time for 100 m. If we halve it, we obtain the B1 time for 50 m.

Let's suppose we have the following figures as peak performance values (calculated in the same period of the year, with the same level of physical condition):

3'10" in 200 backstroke

1'30" in 100 backstroke

42" in 50 backstroke

The differential test shows that:

B1(50) = (timing 200 backstroke – timing 100 backstroke)/2 = 50"

B2(50) = (timing 100 backstroke – timing 50 backstroke) = 48"

B2(100) = (timing 200 backstroke – timing 100 backstroke) = 1'40"

Insert these values in the table:

	A2	B1	B2	C1
50 meters		50"	48"	
100 meters			1'40"	
200 meters				

As we said about the 1500 test, given the value of a certain moment, if you move diagonally across the table, you will double that time every time you go down and halve it every time you go up.

Therefore:

C1(200) = 3'20"

C1(100) = 1'36"

Insert these values in the table:

	A2	B1	B2	C1
50 meters		50"	48"	
100 meters			1'40"	1'36"
200 meters				3'20"

As far as the 1500 test is concerned, if you move horizontally to the right, you take 5% off from every slot, therefore C1 (50) will be about 45".

Applying the other formulas, you will easily have the A2 values of the three distances: 100 and 200 in B1: 200 in B2.

8.3 Swimming training program

Here we propose two different approaches to training, depending on how much time you have available during the week. These two approaches are both designed on a 6-month micro-cycle. The first approach includes 2 training sessions per week; the second, 5 sessions. If you swim only once a week or less, it is best to perform an aerobic workout (A1 or A2) that includes long but light swimming sessions.

8.3.1 6-month training program with 2 sessions per week

Here is a hypothetical swimming training schedule consisting of 2 cycles of 3 months each.

Cycle 1 - Twice a week for 3 months (12 weeks) = 24 training sessions

Within our training period, we always have a start-up stage and a cool-down stage, which are included in the A1 workout. In each session we have two main parts, conventionally defined as blocks. For the 24 training sessions in the first cycle, we will have:

- *First block: the workout to be performed is A2.*
- *Second block: includes 13 sessions of A2, 7 sessions of B1 and 4 sessions of B2.*

The whole cycle is summarized in the following table:

1st cycle - 24 sessions	Warming-up	Block 1	Block 2	Cooling-down
A1	24	—	—	24
A2	—	24	13	—
B1	—	—	7	—
B2	—	—	4	—

* *Do not perform the B1 or B2 workout during the first 2 weeks of training.*

Cycle 2 - Twice a week for three months (12 weeks) = 24 training sessions

For the 24 training sessions in Cycle 2, we will have:

- *First block: performing only the A2 workout*
- *Second block: 9 sessions of the A2 workout, 9 sessions of B1 and 2 sessions of C1.*

The whole cycle is summarized in the following table:

2nd cycle - 24 sessions	Warming-up	Block 1	Block 2	Cooling-down
A1	24	—	—	24
A2	—	24	9	—
B1	—	—	9	—
B2	—	—	4	—
C1	—	—	2	—

1500 meter test, calculation of pace table.

1	2	3	4	5	6	7	8	9	10	11	12
A2	A2	A2	A2	A2	A2	A2	A2	A2	A2	A2	A2
A2	A2	A2	A2	A2	A2	B1	B1	A2	B1	B1	A2

Sessions 1-12 of the 1st cycle

13	14	15	16	17	18	19	20	21	22	23	24
A2	A2	A2	A2	A2	A2	A2	A2	A2	A2	A2	A2
B1	B2	A2	B1	B2	A2	B1	B2	A2	B2	A2	A2

Sessions 13-24 of the 1st cycle

Differential test and recalculation of pace table.

1	2	3	4	5	6	7	8	9	10	11	12
A2	A2	A2	A2	A2	A2	A2	A2	A2	A2	A2	A2
A2	B1	A2	B1	A2	B1	A2	B2	A2	B2	A2	C1

Sessions 1-12 of the 2nd cycle

13	14	15	16	17	18	19	20	21	22	23	24
A2	A2	A2	A2	A2	A2	A2	A2	A2	A2	A2	A2
B1	B2	B1	B2	B1	C1	B1	A2	B1	A2	B1	A2

Sessions 13-24 of the 2nd cycle

1500 meter test compared to the timing of the same test carried out at the beginning of the season.

8.3.2 6-month training program with 5 sessions per week

Let's suppose we schedule our swimming training program in 2 cycles of 3 months each.

Cycle 1: 5 times per week for 3 months (12 weeks) = 60 training sessions.

As we stated above, within our training period we always have a start-up stage and a cool-down stage, which are included in the A1 workout. Now, take a look at the following tables showing how workout sequences are performed within the two main blocks.

For 60 sessions of the first cycle, we will have:

- *First block: workout in A2 for 44 sessions and workout in B1 for 16 sessions.*
- *Second block: workout in A2 for 24 sessions, workout in B1 for 16 sessions (you do not have to repeat B1 workout in the second block if you have already performed it in the first block), B2 workout for 12 sessions and C1 workout for 8 sessions.*

What we stated so far is summarized as follows:

1st cycle - 60 sessions	Warming-up	Block 1	Block 2	Cooling-down
A1	60	—	—	60
A2	—	44	24	—
B1	—	16	16	—
B2	—	—	12	—
C1	—	—	8	—

* Do not perform B1 or B2 (least of all C1) workout in the first 2 weeks of training.

Cycle 2: 5 times per week for 3 months (12 weeks) = 60 training sessions.

For 60 training sessions in the second cycle, we will have:

- *First block: workout in A2 for 38 sessions, workout in B1 for 13 sessions and workout in B2 for 9 sessions.*
- *Second block: workout in A2 for 24 sessions, workout in B1 for 16 sessions, workout in B2 for 10 sessions and C1 for 10 sessions. (You do not have to repeat the B1 workout in the second block if you have already performed it in the first block; the same is true for B2).*

What we stated so far is summarized as follows:

2nd cycle - 60 sessions	Warming-up	Block 1	Block 2	Cooling-down
A1	60	—	—	60
A2	—	38	24	—
B1	—	13	16	—
B2	—	9	10	—
C1	—	—	10	—

Test 1500 and calculation of pace table.

1	2	3	4	5	6	7	8	9	10	11	12	13	14	15
A2	A2	A2	A2	B1	A2	A2	A2	B1	A2	A2	B1	A2	A2	A2
A2	A2	A2	B1	A2	A2	B1	B2	A2	B1	B2	A2	B1	C1	A2

Sessions 1-15 of the 1st cycle

16	17	18	19	20	21	22	23	24	25	26	27	28	29	30
B1	A2	A2	B1	A2	A2	A2	B1	A2	A2	B1	A2	A2	A2	B1
A2	B2	B1	B2	A2	B1	B2	A2	B1	C1	A2	A2	B1	B2	A2

Sessions 16-30 of the 1st cycle

Differential test and recalculation of pace table.

31	32	33	34	35	36	37	38	39	40	41	42	43	44	45
A2	A2	B1	A2	A2	A2	B1	A2	A2	B1	A2	A2	A2	B1	A2
C1	B1	B2	A2	B1	B2	C1	A2	A2	B2	C1	B1	A2	B2	B1

Sessions 31-45 of the 1st cycle

46	47	48	49	50	51	52	53	54	55	56	57	58	59	60
A2	B1	A2	A2	A2	B1	A2	A2	B1	A2	A2	A2	B1	A2	A2
A2	C1	B1	A2	A2	B2	B1	A2	B2	B1	A2	B1	C1	C1	A2

Sessions 46-60 of the 1st cycle

1500 meter test and calculation of pace table.

1	2	3	4	5	6	7	8	9	10	11	12	13	14	15
A2	A2	B1	A2	A2	B1	A2	A2	B1	A2	A2	B1	A2	A2	B2
B1	B2	A2	C1	B1	B2	A2	B1	A2	C1	B1	A2	A2	B2	A2

Sessions 1-15 of the 2nd cycle

16	17	18	19	20	21	22	23	24	25	26	27	28	29	30
A2	A2	B1	B2	A2	A2	B2	A2	A2	B1	A2	A2	B1	A2	A2
B1	C1	A2	A2	B1	B2	B1	B1	B2	A2	A2	B1	A2	C1	B1

Sessions 16-30 of the 2nd cycle

Differential test and calculation of pace table.

31	32	33	34	35	36	37	38	39	40	41	42	43	44	45
B1	A2	A2	B2	A2	A2	B1	B2	A2	A2	B2	A2	A2	B1	A2
A2	A2	B2	A2	C1	B1	A2	B1	B2	C1	A2	C1	B2	A2	A2

Sessions 31-45 of the 2nd cycle

46	47	48	49	50	51	52	53	54	55	56	57	58	59	60
A2	B1	A2	A2	B1	A2	A2	B2	A2	A2	B1	B2	A2	A2	A2
B1	A2	C1	B1	A2	A2	B2	A2	B1	C1	A2	A2	C1	B2	B1

Sessions 46-60 of the 2nd cycle

1500 meter test compared to the timing of the same test carried out at the beginning of the season.

8.4 Workout with different energy systems

A2 workout

To understand the A2 workout, bear in mind this phrase: "I give little, so I ask for little."

The typical workout for aerobic capacity includes swimming lengths at low intensity, but enjoying short recovery periods. (I give little in terms of effort, and I ask for little in terms of recovery time.) We arrive at the end of the length with a heart rate of 150 BPM (not so high), but we have very little time to rest, so we restart with 130 BPM. If you perform the A2 workout, you apparently train more during the recovery time than during the training session itself!

In the A2 workout, effort intensity is pretty low, but after a high number of repetitions (in the A2 workout, the total volume is always very large) we have trained our body, even though we do not realize it. Any distance can be chosen for this kind of training, ranging from 50 to 1500 meters. For a set in the A2 workout, recovery times range from 5 seconds to 40 seconds, depending on the distance. (The longer the distance, the longer the recovery time.)

***Some examples of A2 workout for an average swimmer may be*:**

- *20 × 50 fs, start every 45" (recovery time from 5" to 10")*
- *10 × 100 fs, start every 1'40" (recovery time from 10" to 15")*
- *5 × 200 fs, start every 3'40" (recovery time from 15" to 25")*
- *3 × 400 fs, start every 7'30" (recovery time from 30" and 45")*
- *10 × 50 legs with 10" rest*
- *3 × 200 arms with 30" rest.*

B1 workout

Any full or split distance can be used with intervals ranging from 10 to 30 seconds depending on distance. (The longer the distance, the longer the recovery time.)

Training is based on distances ranging from 50 to 400 meters. The average performed on 50 meters is obviously lower than that one performed on 400. Speed needs to be as steady as possible in each length. If we want to swim 200 m freestyle in 2'30" at threshold speed (B1), it is extremely important to swim each 100 m freestyle at about 1'15". If we swam the first one in 1'10" and the second one in 1'20", we did not carry out our expected task.

Compared to A1, the B1 workout entails a higher intensity (speed). Either we keep the total volume unchanged with slightly longer recovery periods, or we maintain the same recovery time as in A2, but with a slightly smaller volume.

***Some examples of B1 workout, starting from the previous example in A2, may be*:**

- *20 × 50 fs, start every 50", speed in B1*
- *16 × 50 fs, start every 45", speed in B1*
- *10 × 100 fs, start every 1'50", speed in B1*

- *8 × 100 fs, start every 1'40", speed in B1*
- *5 × 200 fs, start every 3'50", speed in B1*
- *4 × 200 fs, start every 3'40", speed in B1*
- *Leg workouts*
- *Arm workouts*

B2 workout

Workouts to improve VO_2max are organized by repetitions, each of them lasting from 3 to 6 minutes. Intervals range from 1 to 3 minutes, with the option of taking longer recovery time (6 to 8 minutes) to ensure higher intensity.

The total volume is generally smaller than the volume of the A2 or B1 workout, but it also can be equal. The B2 workout, on longer distances, may be split. A total volume of 1200 meters, for example, can be divided into two sets consisting in 600 meters or into 3 sets consisting of 400 meters. Such distances can, in turn, be split into sets of 50 to 100 meters with short intervals of rest (for example, 5 seconds), but you should swim as fast as in B1.

In split workout-based training, sets can be as long as 800 meters. If the distance is not split, you should not exceed 400 meters.

Let's take an example: A workout based on three repetitions of 400 meters split into 100 meters, 3 × (4 × 100). The time you spend recovering from one split before starting the next one is about 10 seconds, and speed ranges from 80% to 90% of the peak performance. After the 400-meter sets, there is a long cool-down, consisting of swimming very slowly for about 4 or 5 minutes. After that, you start another set.

In B2, it is necessary to ensure that speed is as steady as possible in each length by swimming the last length a little bit faster. For example, on a 400 m freestyle, split every 100 meters (4 × 100 fs), in the last 100 meters it is better to have a time slightly faster than the first 300 m. Taking the previous example into account, when you schedule the training cycle at the beginning of the season and you start to include the B2 workout, we suggest you start with a split track on 50 and increase gradually to 100, and then 200.

Example of B2 workout, starting from the previous examples in A2 and B1:

- *12 × 50 fs, start every 1'40", speed B2*
- *5 × 50 fs, start every 2'45", speed B2*
- *4 × 250 fs. The timing of each 250 meter needs to be equal to the time of the 50 fs in A2 multiplied by 5. Recovery = workout*
- *2 × 400 fs: 2 × [4 × 100 fs (B2)], interval between one 100-track and another is 15 seconds, interval between one 400m-track and another is 4 minutes of recovery.*
- *2 × (3 × 100 fs), with 10-second rest. Between a 300 m track and another 3 minutes of rest.*
- *3 × (4 × 50 fs), with 5 second rest. Between a 200 m track and another 2,30 minutes of recovery.*

C1 workout

This workout to improve tolerance to lactate includes training of relatively short duration with long recovery intervals. On distances of 100 meters or more, split workouts are commonly employed, with longer recovery intervals than those used in B2.

The speed for the total distance should be equivalent or faster than that of the competition. Paces in C1 tend to be the maximum attainable compared to the whole workout volume. In C, recovery is never active.

8.5 Workout proposals

A1	600 long-distance swimming + 8 × 50 mixed	1000
A2	16 × 50	800
A1	20 × 25 arms	500
B1	16 × 50	800
		3100

A1	12 × 50 at 1'	600
A2	5 × 200	1000
Legs	6 × (2 × 25 at 1"), rest 30"	300
B1	5 × 200	1000
		2900

A1	600 long-distance swimming	600
A2	10 × 100 (2 slow + 1 fast)	1000
Arms	3 × (4 × 25 at 45"), rest 30"	300
B1	10 × (2 × 50), rest 5"	1000
		2900

A2	200 + 200 (3 slow + 1 fast) + 200 progression	600
A2	3 × 400	1200
Arms	3 × (4 × 25 at 35"), rest 3'20"	300
B1	3 × 400	1200
		3300

A1	600 long-distance swimming	600
A2	16 × 50	800
Arms	20 × 25 fast at 1'	500
Legs	6 × 100 at 3'	600
B1	16 × 50	800
		3300

A1	400 long-distance swimming	400
A1	8 × 50 mixed	400
A2	16 × 50	800
B1	12 × 50	600
A1	100 long-distance swimming	100
A2	12 × 50 legs	600
A1	300 long-distance swimming	300
		3200

A1	300 long-distance swimming	300
A1	4 × 100 mixed	400
A2	2 × 400	800
B2	1 × 400	400
B2	2 × 200	400
A2	16 × 50, 1 fast relatively slow	800
		3100

A1	200 long-distance swimming	200
A1	8 × 50 style	400
A2	8 × 100	800
B1	8 × 100	800
B1	3 × (6 × 25) legs	450
A1	200 style	200
		2850

A1	300 long-distance swimming	300
A2	6 × 200	1200
B2	6 × (4 × 50) 1'-1'10" every 6'	1200
A2	4 × 100 arms	400
		3100

A1	400 long-distance swimming	400
A2	6 × 50	300
A2	6 × 200	1200
B2	2 × (8 × 50)	800
A1	200 long-distance swimming	200
		2900

A1	500 vary breathing	500
A2	6 × 100 mixed	600
A2	16 × 50	800
B2	16 × 50	800
A2	6 × 50	300
		3000

A1	300 long-distance swimming	300
A2	6 × 200	1200
B2	4 × (4 × 50)	800
A2	8 × 50 legs	400
A1	4 × 100 free style	400
		3100

A1	600 long-distance swimming	600
A2	3 × 400 free style	1200
B2	6 × 100	600
A2	6 × 50 legs	300
A1	200 long-distance swimming	200
		2900

A1	400 long-distance swimming	400
Legs	8 × 25	200
A1	6 × 100	600
	Test 1500	1500
		2700

A1	12 × 50 mixed	500
B1	12 × 50	600
A2	8 × 50 arms	800
C1	4 × 50	800
A1	8 × 50	300
		2200

A1	600 long-distance swimming	600
A2	8 × 50 legs	400
A2	10 × 100	1000
B1	8 × (2 × 50)	800
A1	200 long-distance swimming	200
		3000

A1	4 × 50 mixed + 4 × 50 workout	400
A1	12 × 50 (25 fly+ 25 fs)	600
B1	6 × 200 (1 complete + 1 split 4 × 50)	1200
C1	20 × 25	500
A1	6 × 50 free style	300
		3000

A1	400 long-distance swimming	400
Legs	8 × 50	400
B1	20 × 50	1000
C1	8 × 50	400
A1	300 long-distance swimming	300
		2500

A1	200 + 200 (1 fast + 1 slow) + 200 legs	600
Arms	10 × 50 (25 fly fast + 25 fs)	500
B1	3 × (5 × 100), rest 30"	1500
A1	300 long-distance swimming	300
		2900

A1	300 long-distance swimming	300
A2	2 × 600 (3 lengths slow + 1 fast)	1200
B1	12 × 100 (3 at 1'40" + 3 at 1'45" + 3 at 1'50"+ 3 at 1'40")	1200
	200 long-distance swimming	200
		2900

A1	600 long-distance swimming	600
Legs	6 × 50	300
C1	6 × 50	300
B1	2 × (10 × 50), rest 1'	1000
A1	200 long-distance swimming	200
		2400

A1	200 long-distance swimming	200
A1	10 × 50 mixed	500
	Technique 200 meter	200
B1	8 × 300	2400
	100 long-distance swimming	100
		3400

A1	100 long-distance swimming	100
A1	200 + 200 (1 slow + 1 fast) + 200 legs	600
C1	2 × (2 × 50 + 4 × 25)	400
Arms	10 × 50 (25 fly fast + 25 fs)	500
B1	2 × (6 × 100)	1200
	200 long-distance swimming	200
		3000

A1	200 long-distance swimming	200
A1	12 × 50 mixed	600
C1	200 meter technique	200
Arms	3 × 300	900
B1	3 × (3 × 100)	900
	200 long-distance swimming	200
		3000

A1	6 × 50 mixed	300
A2	3 × 400	1200
B1	2 × (6 × 100)	1200
A1	6 × 50	300
B2	2 × (6 × 50)	600
		3600

A1	400 long-distance swimming	400
A2	12 × 100	1200
B2	6 × (6 × 50)	1800
A1	200 long-distance swimming	200
		3600

A1	200 long-distance swimming	200
A1	600 meter technique	600
A2	6 × 50 at 1'10"	300
B1	16 × 50	800
B1	16 × 50	800
A1	100 swimming	100
		2800

A1	400 long-distance swimming	400
A2	12 × 100	1200
B2	6 × (6 × 50)	1800
	200 long-distance swimming	200
		3600

A1	8 × 75	600
C1	12 × 25 legs	300
A2	4 × 200	800
A1	4 × 50	200
B2	4 × 250, 1 complete, 1 split, 5 × 50	1000
		2900

A1	8 × 50 mixed	400
A2	6 × 200	1200
B1	4 × 100, rest 1'	400
B2	4 × 100, rest 1'	400
C1	2 × 100	200
		2600

A1	600 long-distance swimming	600
A2	4 × 400 (odd complete, even fractioned 4 × 100)	1600
C1	12 × 50 (25 fast + 25 normal)	600
A1	200 long-distance swimming	200
		3000

A1	400 long-distance swimming	400
A2	12 × 100	1200
B2	6 × (6 × 50)	1800
A1	200 long-distance swimming	200
		3600

A1	10 × 100 mixed	1000
B1	6 × (3 × 50)	900
	200 long-distance swimming	200
C1	4 × (4 × 25)	400
A1	6 × 50	300
		2800

Chapter 9
YOGA

In the past few decades, the ancient discipline of yoga has become very popular in Western countries. As a result, it is becoming increasingly easy to find knowledgeable yoga teachers. This book does not aim to replace trainers or teachers. Its aim is simply to present various activities that can complement training for freediving. The experiences of athletes training for freediving and other sports are useful tools, not only for trainees but also for trainers.

9.1 Reasons for practicing yoga

Yoga is a discipline that looks at the human being as a whole and takes into account all aspects of being human. Every workout includes aspects that the person is fully aware of and aspects that lie in the subconscious realm as well.

Each yoga workout, if properly performed, affects body, mind and soul. Even if we are performing what appears to be merely a physical exercise, we are also thinking, breathing and feeling. Exercise that includes all these elements enables athletes to improve faster and in a more comprehensive way.

One of the main aspects of yoga is that measurable results are put in the background. The main focus is, instead, to feel and listen to one's body and try to bring it gradually to its limits.

A good performance is not the goal, but it becomes the consequence of a path traveled by listening to one's body. In this book, we will focus on yoga's physical workout, since the aspect we want to emphasize is physical elasticity. Each posture described here helps train the freediver's joint mobility and muscular mobility. Skills acquired from practicing yoga will ensure greater agility to help perform the exercises required in other types of training. Those who would like to deepen their knowledge of yoga as it relates to freediving, including working on breathing and mental concentration techniques, can learn from books such as "Breathing Techniques for Freediving", by Federico Mana, and "Il Respiro nell'Apnea", by Umberto Pelizzari (coauthors L. Landoni and A. Seddone).

Breathing is important to any workout focusing on physical elasticity. When one stretches muscles or works on joint mobility, physical tension is perceived, as well as pain, causing him to shorten – or even stop – breathing and start holding his breath. In order to facilitate muscular stretching and joint flexibility, it is important to focus on long, deep inhalations, which help keep the muscles relaxed so they can stretch more easily.

9.2 Yoga starting test

This chapter presents a yoga workout that can help freedivers improve joint mobility and muscle stretching. In the analysis of the different disciplines, we emphasized how important mobility is, both to support advanced techniques and to allow the body to stay relaxed when diving. Stiffness wastes energy during a performance and hampers freediving skills. Each freediver has his own problem areas that are not as flexible as they could be. Using the tests presented in this chapter, you can identify which areas need to be trained more. You will need to complete 11 tests, each testing 4 areas of the body. The following illustration shows how you can record the results of the tests. When the tests are completed, add up each column, and by comparing one with another, you can identify which joints and muscles need the most training.

Evaluation of musculoskeletal mobility

	Shoulders/ shoulder blades	Back	Hips/pelvis	Joint of knee and ankle
Test 1				
Test 2				
Test 3				
Test 4				
Total score				

Each exercise is scored from 1 to 4, depending how difficult it was for the athlete to perform. The lower the score, the greater the difficulty. At the end of the test, the columns with the lowest total scores will indicate which areas need the most work.

TEST 1 • SHOULDERS AND SHOULDER BLADES

How to perform it

- *Lie on your back with both legs outstretched (picture 1).*
- *Stretch both arms outward and up toward the ceiling until your hands touch.*
- *Lift your hands above your head, and let them drop toward the floor.*
- *Evaluate the position gained.*

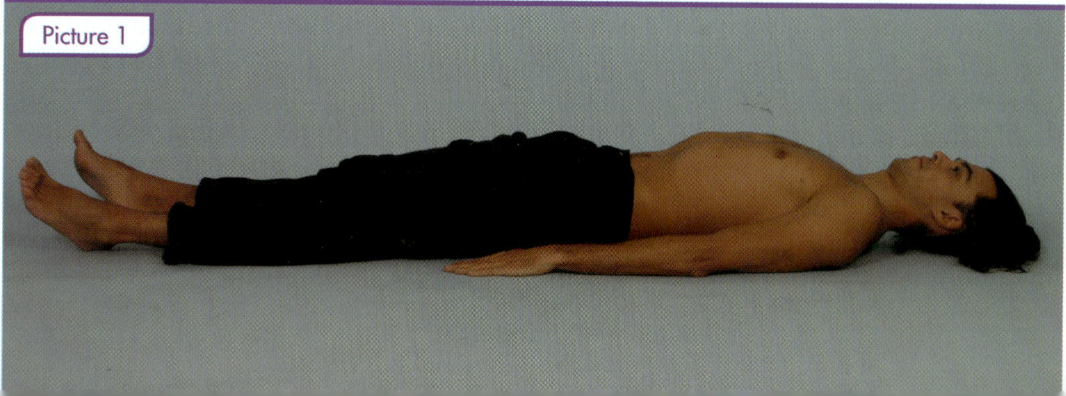
Picture 1

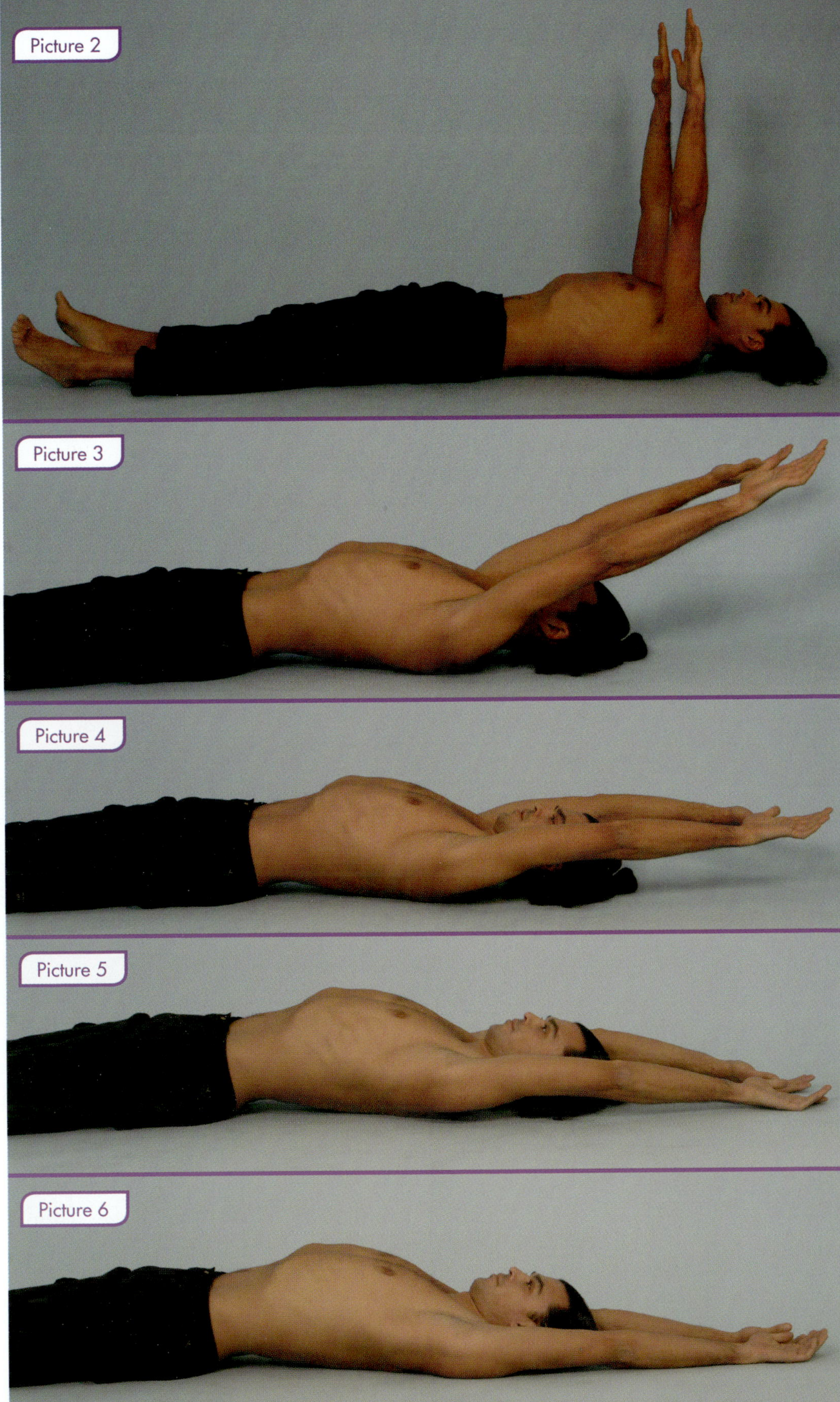
Picture 2
Picture 3
Picture 4
Picture 5
Picture 6

Score

1. *Arms, hands and shoulders are raised off the ground, and there is a feeling of tension (picture 3).*
2. *Hands are approaching the ground and they are slightly raised, but the position is uncomfortable (picture 4).*
3. *Hands and/or forearms touch the ground, and the position is comfortable (picture 5).*
4. *Shoulders, arms and hands are on the ground, and I feel comfortable in this position (picture 6).*

TEST 2 • SHOULDERS AND SHOULDER BLADES

How to perform it

- *Stand up with both legs straight but spread slightly.*
- *Weave both hands behind your back (picture 1).*
- *Rotate your palms toward your gluteus muscles (picture 2).*
- *Raise your outstretched arms.*

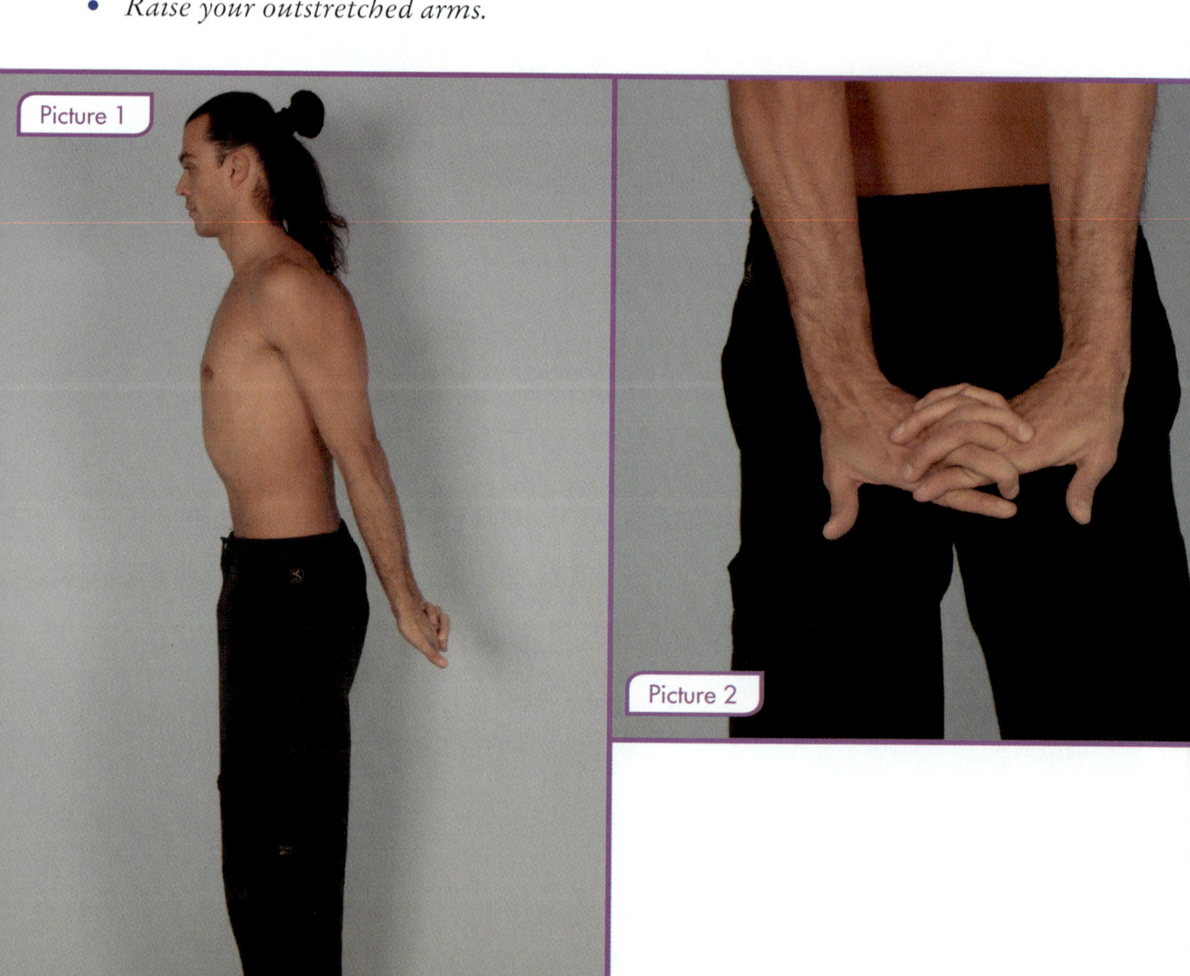
Picture 1
Picture 2

Score

1. *I feel pain in my arms and shoulders just by weaving my fingers (picture 3).*
2. *I cannot rotate my palms toward my gluteus muscles and raise my arms (picture 4).*
3. *I can rotate my palms toward my gluteus muscles and outstretch my arms, but I feel muscular tension (picture 5).*
4. *I can rotate my palms toward my gluteus muscles and outstretch my arms, and my muscles are relaxed (picture 6).*

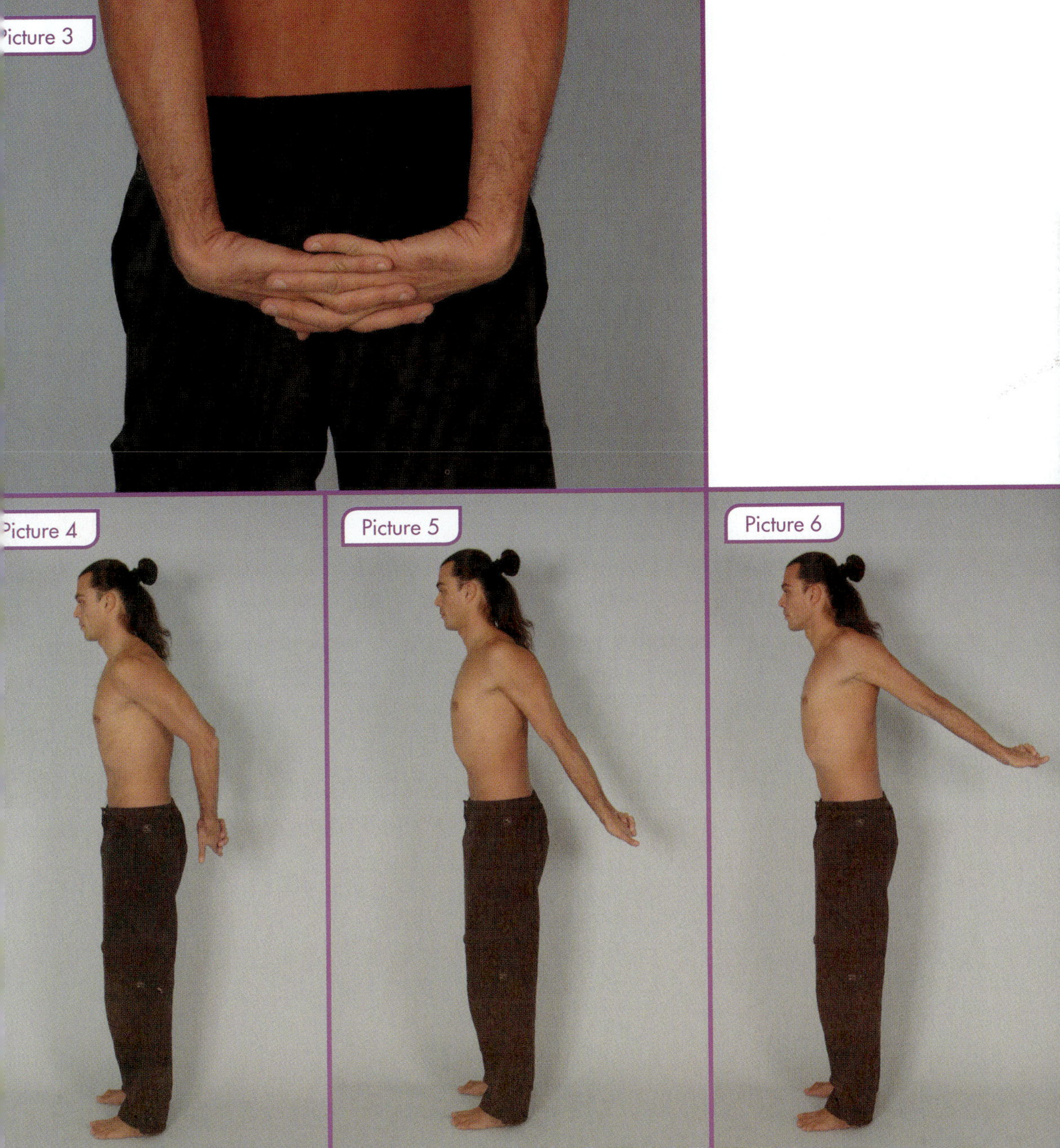
Picture 3
Picture 4
Picture 5
Picture 6

TEST 3 • SHOULDERS AND SHOULDER BLADES

How to perform it

- *Stand up with both legs straight but spread slightly.*
- *Stretch both arms outward.*
- *Flex your forearms 90° (picture 1).*
- *Let one arm pass below the other, and weave hands together (picture 2).*

Picture 1
Picture 2

Score

1. *I cannot to weave my arms.*
2. *I can weave my arms but not my hands (picture 3).*
3. *I can weave both arms and hands, but I feel my muscles contracting.*
4. *I can weave arms and hands and my muscles are relaxed (picture 4).*

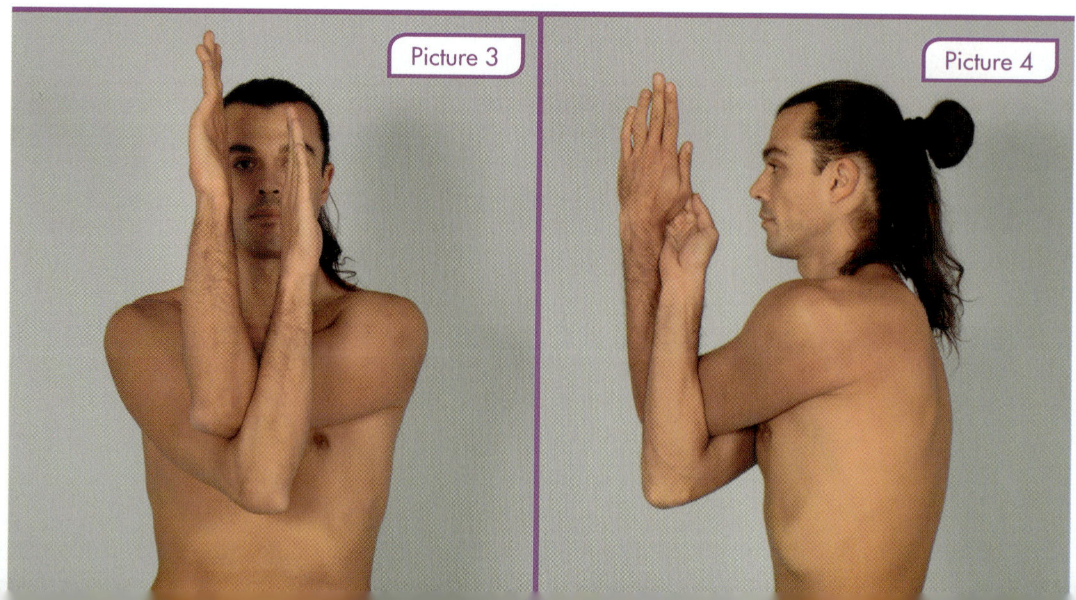
Picture 3
Picture 4

TEST 4 • BACK

How to perform it

- *Stand up with both legs straight but spread slightly (picture 1).*
- *Bend your trunk forward trying to touch your toes while holding your legs straight.*

Score

1. *I can touch my tibias slightly below the knees (picture 2).*
2. *I can easily touch my ankles (picture 3).*
3. *I can easily touch my toes (picture 4).*
4. *I can touch the floor with my palms (picture 5).*

TEST 5 • BACK

How to perform it

- *Lie down on your back with your legs out straight on the floor.*
- *Flex both legs, bringing your knees toward your chest and keeping your heels next to your gluteus (picture 1).*
- *Bring your knees toward your forehead, and let your legs stretch in a natural way (picture 2).*

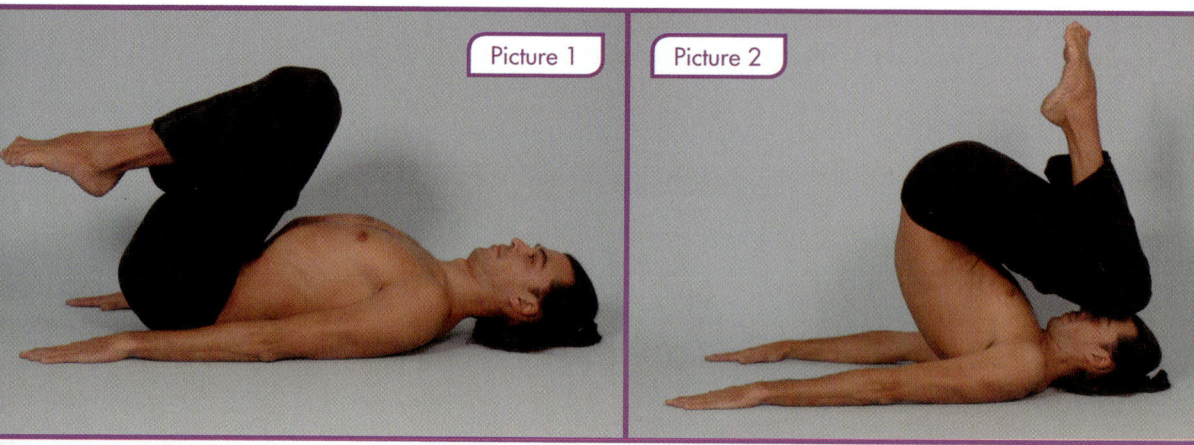
Picture 1
Picture 2

Score

1. *I cannot bring my knees toward my forehead.*
2. *I can bring my knees toward my forehead, but I feel stretching in my legs and I feel squeezed.*
3. *I can bring my knees toward my forehead and stretch both legs so that my feet lightly touch the ground.*
4. *I can bring my knees toward my forehead, and my feet easily touch the ground (picture 3).*

Picture 3

TEST 6 • BACK

How to perform it

- *Lie down with your knees bent behind you so you are sitting on your heels.*
- *Keep your back straight, and bring both hands to your heels (picture 1).*
- *Without removing your hands from your heels, lift your pelvis and push it forward until you arch your back properly (picture 2).*

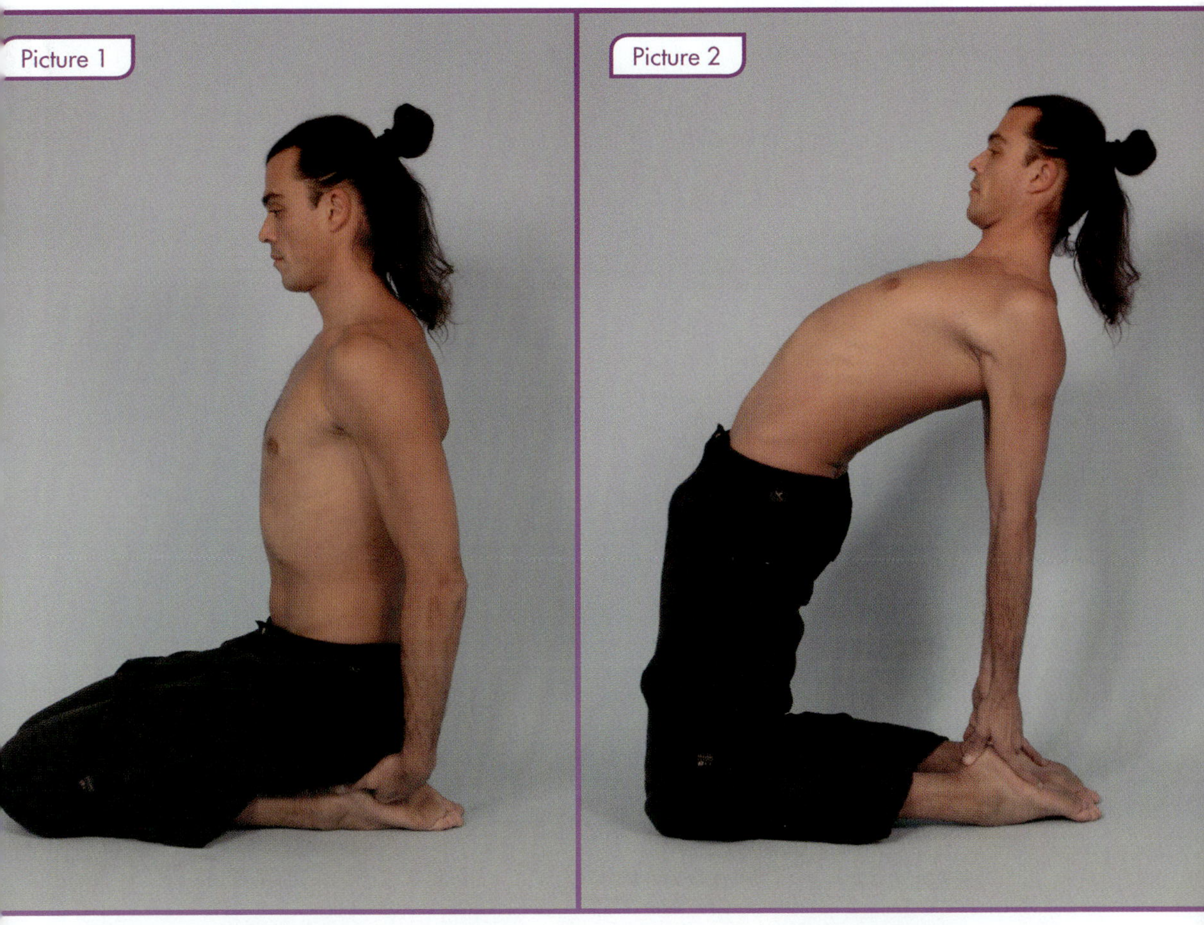
Picture 1
Picture 2

Score

1. *I cannot lift my pelvis without removing both hands from the heels.*
2. *I can manage to lift my pelvis, but I need to remove one hand from the heels temporarily.*
3. *I can lift my pelvis without removing my hands from the heels, but when I arch my back I feel uncomfortable.*
4. *I can lift my pelvis without removing my hands from the heels, and when I arch my back I feel comfortable.*

TEST 7 • HIPS AND PELVIS

How to perform it

- *Sit down with your legs crossed.*
- *Try to keep your back straight and your pelvis firm on the ground.*
- *Try to put your knees as close to the ground as possible (picture 1).*

Picture 1

Score

1. *I cannot keep my back straight, and my knees are far from the ground (pictures 2 and 3).*
2. *I cannot keep my back straight, and my knees are pretty far from the ground (pictures 4 and 5).*

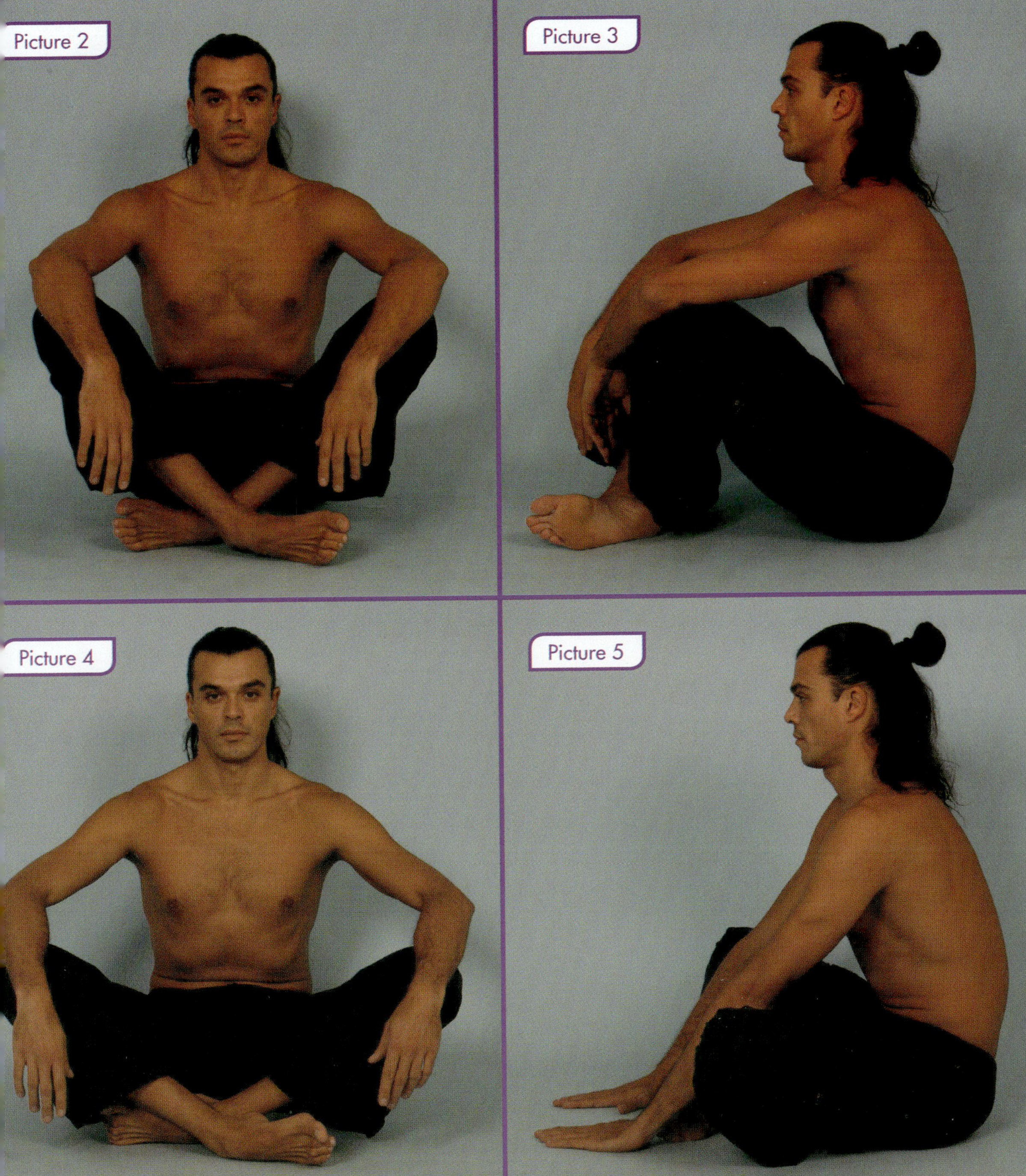

3. *My back is almost straight, and my knees are pretty close to the ground (pictures 6 and 7).*
4. *My back is straight, and my knees are on the ground (pictures 8 and 9).*

TEST 8 • HIPS AND PELVIS

How to perform it

- *Lie down on your back with both legs flexed and your feet touching the ground.*
- *Bring your right foot to your left knee.*
- *Let your right hand pass through the space between your legs, and grab your shin bone.*
- *Let your left hand grab your shin bone, and weave your hands together (pictures 1 and 2).*
- *Lie down on your back with your shoulders and head on the ground.*
- *Repeat the whole cycle on the other side.*

Score

1. *I cannot easily grab my shinbone with both hands.*
2. *I can grab my shinbone, but I cannot put my shoulders and head on the ground.*
3. *I can grab my shinbone and put my shoulders and head on the ground, but my hip hurts.*
4. *I can grab my shinbone and put my shoulders and head on the ground comfortably.*

Picture 1
Picture 2

TEST 9 • HIPS AND PELVIS

How to perform it

- *Stand up with both legs spread and feet rotated outward (picture 1).*
- *Flex your knees, bring your pelvis toward the ground and push your knees out with both hands (picture 2).*

Score

1. *I cannot let my pelvis go down easily (picture 3).*
2. *I can let my pelvis go down, but my knees tend to pivot forward (picture 4).*
3. *I can let my pelvis go down, my knees are spread open, but I feel my muscles straining.*
4. *I can let my pelvis go down, my knees are spread open, and I feel comfortable.*

Picture 1

Picture 2

TEST 10 • TIBIOTARSAL JOINT

How to perform it

- *Lie down on your back and sit on your heels (pictures 1 and 2).*
- *Keep this position for a few minutes.*

Score

1. *I cannot sit on my heels without pain because my insteps do not align with the ground.*
2. *I cannot sit on my heels because of knee-joint problems.*
3. *I can sit on my heels, but my insteps or knee joints hurt.*
4. *I can sit on my heels comfortably.*

Picture 1

Picture 2

TEST 11 • TIBIOTARSAL JOINT

How to perform it

- *Lie down on your back and spread your legs slightly (picture 1).*
- *Point your toes, pushing them down toward the floor as far as you can.*

Picture 1

Score

1. *My toes are 90° from the ground.*
2. *My toes are 45° to 80° from the ground (picture 2).*
3. *My toes are 30° to 45° from the ground (picture 3).*
4. *My toes are 15° to 30° from the ground (picture 4).*

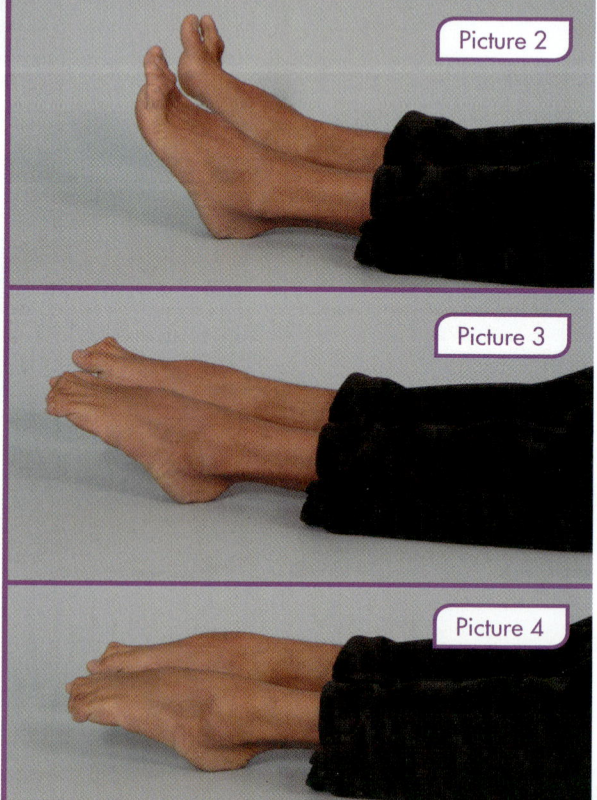

Picture 2

Picture 3

Picture 4

9.3 Improving shoulder and shoulder blade elasticity

Exercises that give tone and elasticity to shoulders and shoulder blades have two main objectives. The first is to help attain the position needed for constant weight descent or for breaststroke swimming or for using one fin.

Secondly, flexible shoulders and shoulder blades give more elasticity to chest, so freedivers can manage large air volumes more easily.

Physical elasticity also makes it easier to master technical skills, especially when freediving-related postures are required.

Here are some exercises specifically for shoulder and shoulder blade mobility:

EXERCISE 1 • SHOULDER AND SHOULDER BLADES MOBILITY

How to perform it

- *Stand up with feet spread to shoulder width. Gluteus and leg muscles should be tensed to support the lumbar band correctly. Arms are stretched straight up over your head in line with your ears (pictures 1 and 2).*
- *Every time you inhale, push your arms backward gradually, avoiding pain or excessive contraction. Feel the stimulation of the joints (picture 3).*
- *Repeat for 10 breathing cycles.*
- *Change the orientation of both hands, and repeat for 10 more breathing cycles.*
- *Rest for 2 minutes.*
- *Repeat the whole sequence 3 times.*

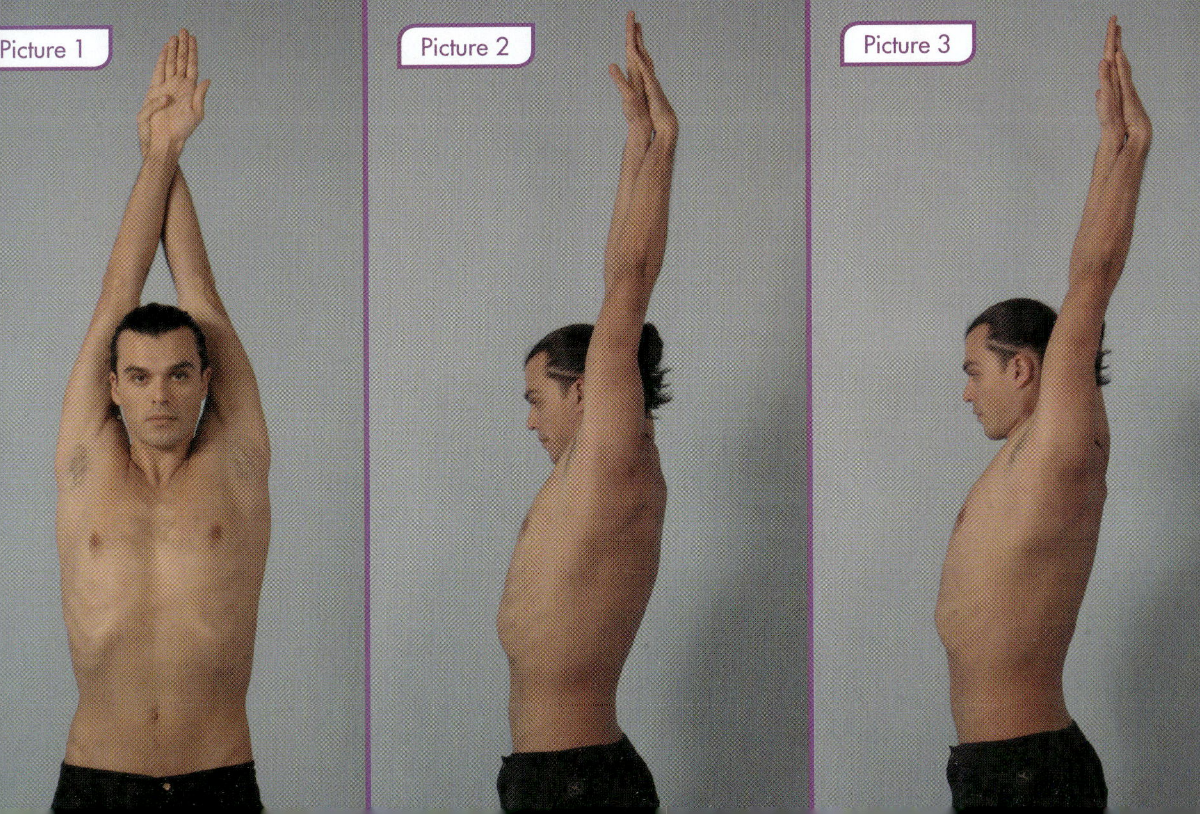

EXERCISE 1B • SHOULDER AND SHOULDER BLADES MOBILITY

Not every freediver has good joint mobility in the shoulders and shoulder blades, so it is possible that someone could have difficulty getting into the starting position required for the previous exercise. In fact, it might be difficult for many athletes. If you are one of them, there is an intermediate workout that allows you to get closer to exercise Number 1.

How to perform it

- *Stand up with both legs straight and your feet spread to shoulder width. Gluteus and leg muscles are tense to ensure proper support for the lumbar band. Arms are flexed so that the backs of your hands can be in contact with one another, and your arms are in line with your ears (picture 1).*
- *Every time you inhale, push your elbows back gradually to avoid feeling pain or excessive contraction. Feel the stimulation of the joints (picture 2).*
- *Every time you exhale, return elbows and arms to the starting position in line with your ears.*
- *Repeat for 10 breathing cycles.*
- *Rest for 2 minutes.*
- *Repeat the whole sequence 3 times.*

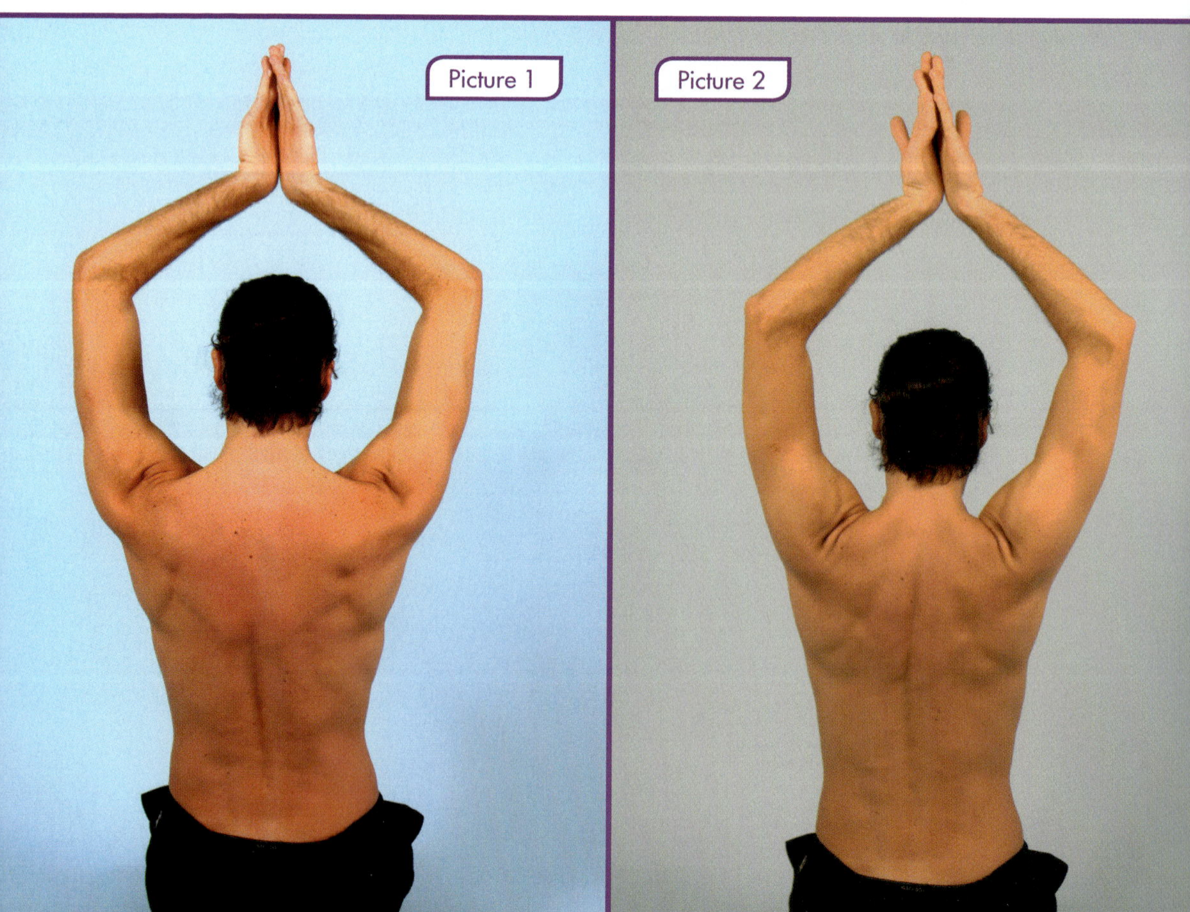
Picture 1
Picture 2

EXERCISE 2 • SHOULDER AND SHOULDER BLADES MOBILITY

How to perform it

- *Start in a prone position on all fours. Stretch out both arms and slightly rotate your hands under your shoulder blades (approximately 45°). Knees are on the floor in line with your hips. Your head is slightly raised so that you can look straight ahead (picture 1).*
- *While you are inhaling, flex both arms by pushing your elbows forward, and bring your chin to the floor. Your chin it is not between your hands, but slightly behind them. Such a position makes the shoulders and shoulder blades more elastic. A more forward position has less effect on your shoulders and can strain the pectoral muscles (pictures 2 and 3).*
- *Exhale, hold your breath for few seconds, and feel the joints and muscles stretching.*
- *Inhale slowly and arch your back. push both hands against the floor, bring your chin to your breast bone. By pushing your pelvis in retroversion you tend to arch your spine; in this position shoulders gradually move away from your shoulder blades (picture 4).*
- *Inhale by holding your breath for a few seconds.*
- *Repeat the sequence 10 times.*
- *Rest for 2 minutes.*
- *Repeat the whole cycle 3 times.*

Picture 1

Picture 2
Picture 3
Picture 4

EXERCISE 3 • SHOULDER AND SHOULDER BLADES MOBILITY

How to perform it

- *Lie face down, and bring your forehead and nose to the floor.*
- *Bring both hands behind the back of your neck, and keep your elbows raised off the floor (picture 1). Every time you exhale, stretch both arms out to the sides, but don't allow your arms and hands to touch the floor (picture 2).*
- *Every time you inhale, bring both hands behind the back of your neck.*
- *Repeat for 15 to 20 breathing cycles.*
- *Repeat the whole sequence 3 to 5 times.*

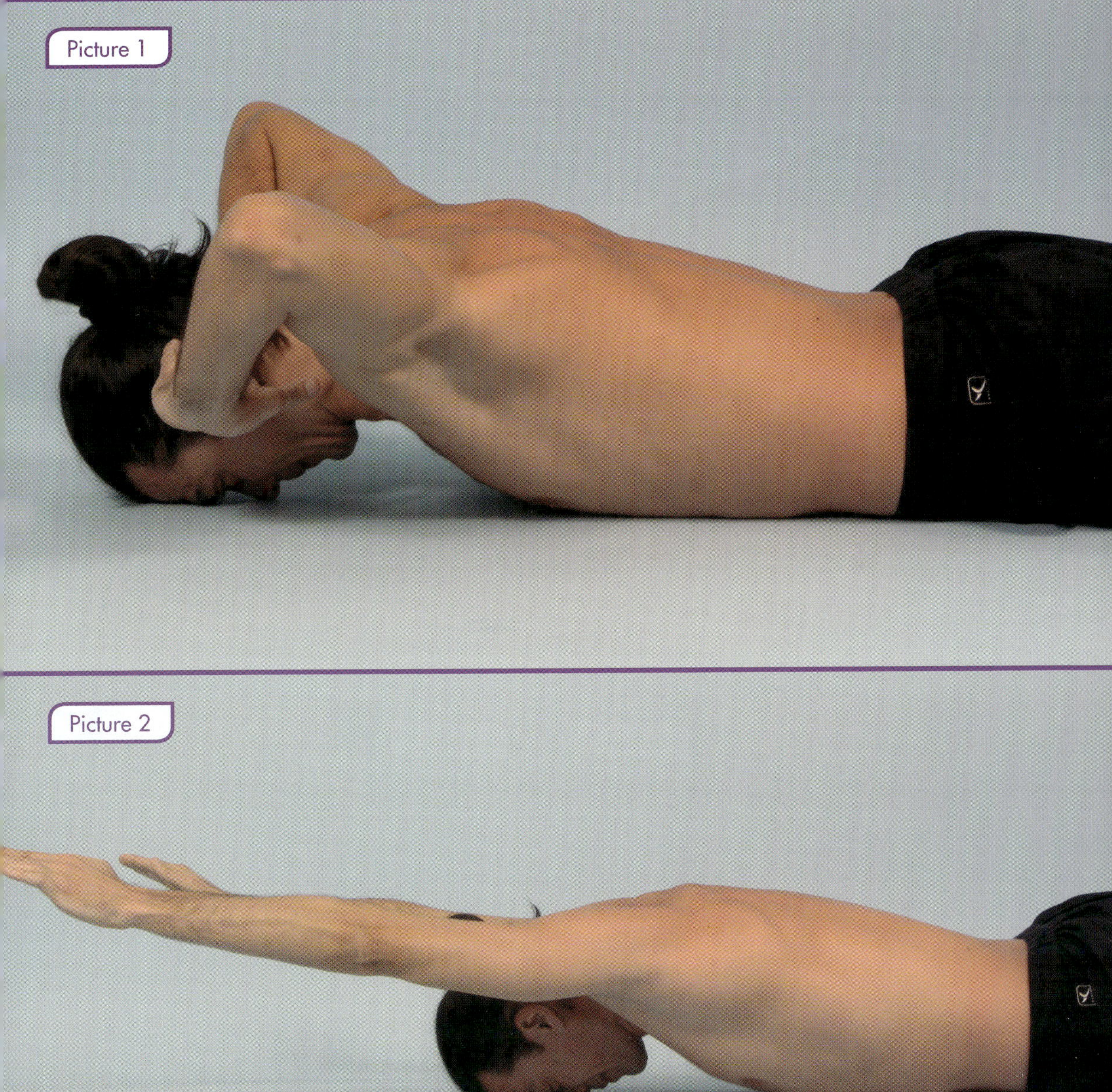

EXERCISE 4 • SHOULDER AND SHOULDER BLADE MOBILITY

How to perform it

- *Start out on all fours, with your arms vertically aligned with your shoulders. Bring your head down until your forehead and nose (or chin) touch the ground. Elbows do not touch the ground. Your back is slightly arched and your hips are vertically aligned with your knees (picture 1).*
- *Breath slowly. Every time you exhale, bring your shoulders close to your shoulder blades and feel the muscles and joints working (picture 2).*
- *Every time you inhale, move your shoulders away from you shoulder blades and feel the muscles and joints relax (picture 3).*
- *Repeat for 15 to 20 breathing cycles.*
- *Repeat the whole sequence 3 to 5 times.*

Picture 1

Picture 2

Picture 3

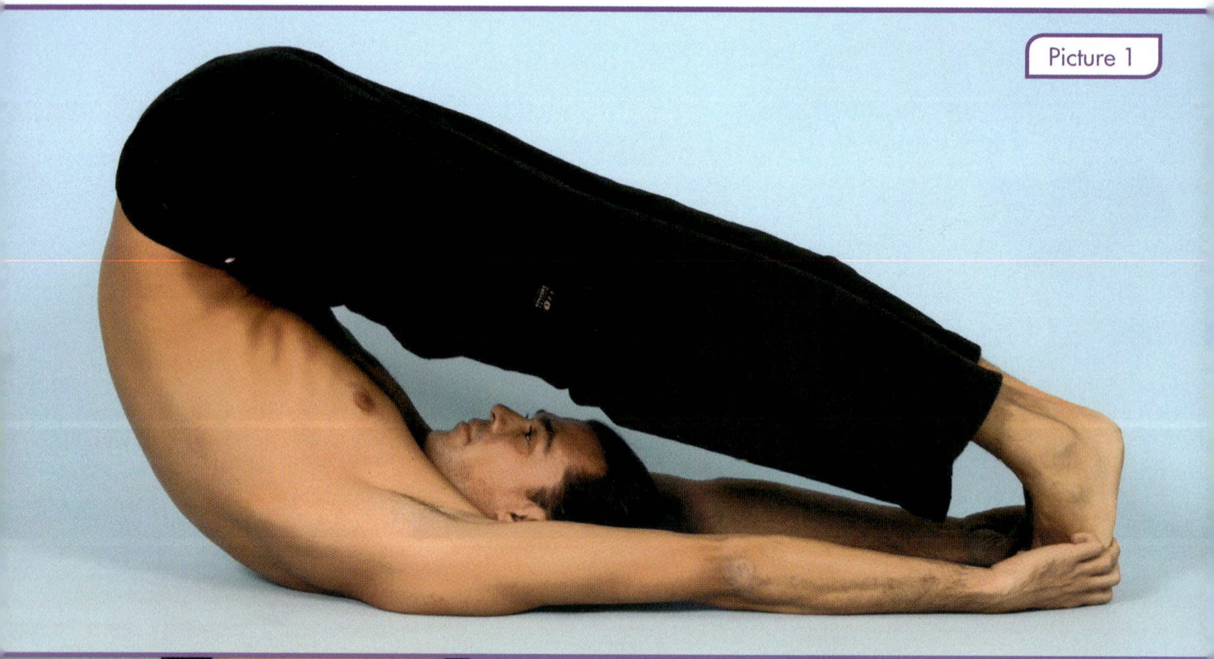

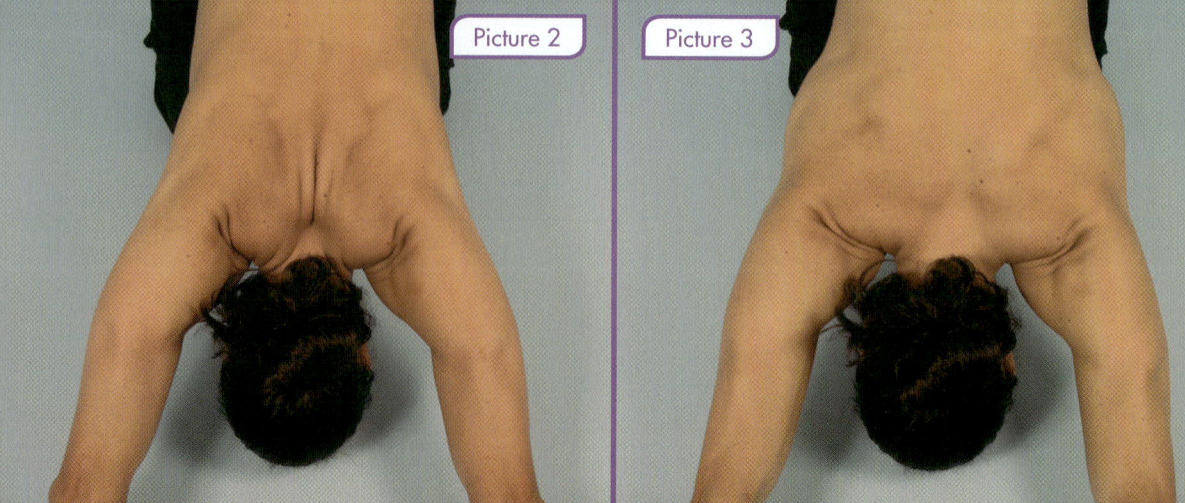

EXERCISE 5 • SHOULDER AND SHOULDER BLADE MOBILITY

How to perform it

- *Stand up straight with your feet shoulder width apart. Gluteus and leg muscles are tense to ensure proper support of the lumbar band. Intertwine your hands behind your back, and stretch your arms out to keep your shoulders open and your shoulder blades close (picture 1).*
- *When you exhale, keep your back and legs straight. When you reach the maximum flex forward, continue to exhale and bring both hands upward (picture 2).*
- *Every time you exhale, try to lift your arms a bit higher. Repeat for 15 breathing cycles.*
- *Repeat the whole sequence 3 to5 times.*

9.4 Improving the flexibility of spine and lumbar regions

The spine is affected by all motion and posture defects. While mobility of the spine isn't considered essential to the propulsion movement when using fins, it becomes very important to the propulsion movement when using the monofin, which is a tool increasingly used by freedivers.

And, as all would surely agree, having a strong and elastic back is a benefit for any athlete.

The back, especially the lumbar region, is subjected to repeated flexation, contractions and rotations during training and workouts. Having a back that moves harmoniously is of great help to a freediver.

The exercises below are aimed at toning and strengthening the back.

EXERCISE 6 • SPINE MOBILITY

How to perform it

- *Lie on your back with the spine and lumbar region flat on the floor. Put your arms at your sides with the palms facing down. Bend your knees until your fingers are able to touch your heels (picture 1).*
- *As you exhale, start raising the hips to lift first the sacral region and then the lumbar region from the floor (picture 2).*
- *Keep breathing and progressively raise your hips so that your body forms a straight line from your shoulders to your knees. Your shoulders and cervical region are completely on the floor. (picture 3 and picture 4).*
- *When you have raised your hips to the highest level, hold that position for 3 to 5 breathing cycles.*
- *Exhale and return to the starting position, slowly lowering the back, starting with the cervical vertebrae and continuing down the spine to the sacral vertebrae.*
- *Repeat the whole sequence 3 to 5 times.*

Picture 1

Picture 2

Picture 3

Picture 4

EXERCISE 6B • VARIATION OF EXERCISE 6

When you have achieved a good level of performance in the exercise above, you are ready to move on to the following similar exercise, which enable you to perform higher hip raises.

How to perform it

- *Lie flat on your back with the spine and lumbar region completely on the floor. Put your arms at your sides, and bend your knees until you are able to grab your heels with your hands. (picture 1).*
- *Exhale as you start to raise your hips, lifting from the floor first the sacral region and then the lumbar region (picture 2).*
- *Keep breathing and progressively raising your hips until your body forms a straight line from your shoulders to your knees and the shoulders and cervical region are completely on the floor. (picture 3).*
- *Once you raise your hips to the highest level, hold the position for 3 to 5 breathing cycles.*
- *Exhale and return to the starting position, slowly lowering the back, starting with the cervical vertebrae and progressing down the spine to the sacral vertebrae.*
- *Repeat the whole sequence 3 to 5 times.*

Picture 1

Picture 2

Picture 3

EXERCISE 7 • SPINE MOBILITY

How to perform it

- *Lying on your stomach with nose and brow touching the floor, grab your left wrist with your right hand and hold your arms behind your back. Keep your elbows close to each other, allowing the shoulder blades to get close to each other (picture 1).*
- *Every time you exhale, raise your legs from the floor, trying to keep them fairly straight (picture 2).*
- *Every time you inhale, slowly return legs to the floor.*
- *Repeat the exercise for 10 breathing cycles.*
- *Rest for a few seconds.*
- *Return to the starting position (picture 1).*
- *This time, every time you exhale, raise your chest and shoulders from the floor, holding your legs straight and tightening your gluteus muscles (picture 3).*
- *Every time you inhale, return your face close to the floor without touching it.*

Picture 1

Picture 2

- *Repeat the exercise for 10 breathing cycles.*
- *Rest for a few seconds.*
- *Return to the starting position (picture 1).*
- *Now, every time you exhale, raise both your chest and your legs from the floor, trying to hold your legs straight, and tighten your gluteus muscles (picture 4).*
- *Every time you inhale, slowly lay your whole body straight with the floor.*
- *Repeat the exercise for 10 breathing cycles.*
- *Rest for 2 minutes.*
- *Repeat the whole sequence 3 times.*

EXERCISE 7B • VARIATION OF EXERCISE 7

Once you have achieved a good level of performance with Exercise 7A, try doing the whole sequence while keeping the heels together. This enables you to further strengthen the relevant muscles.

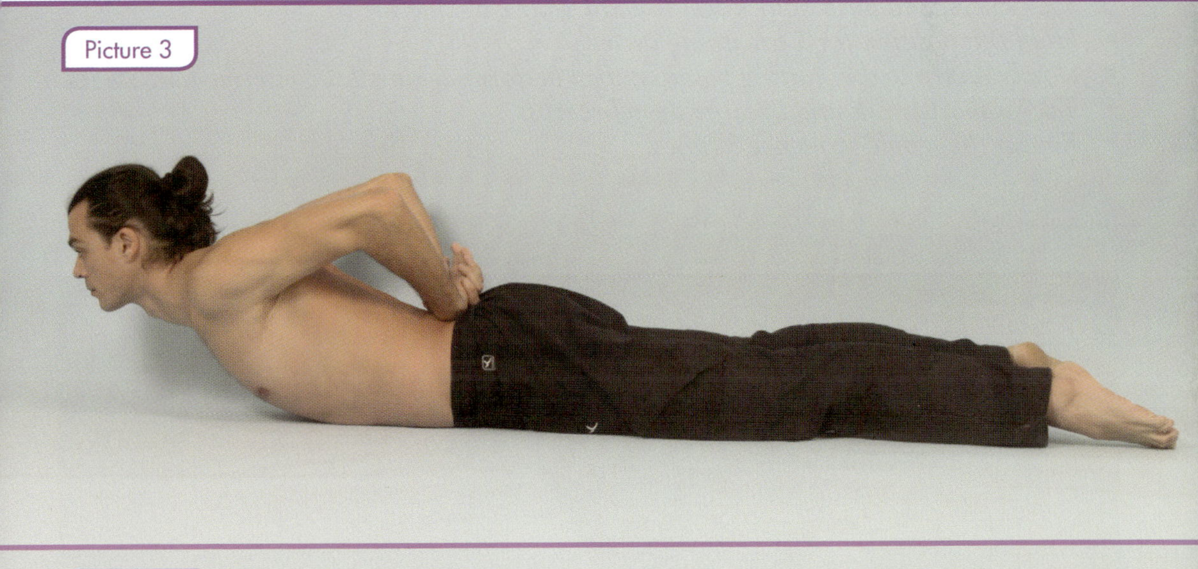
Picture 3

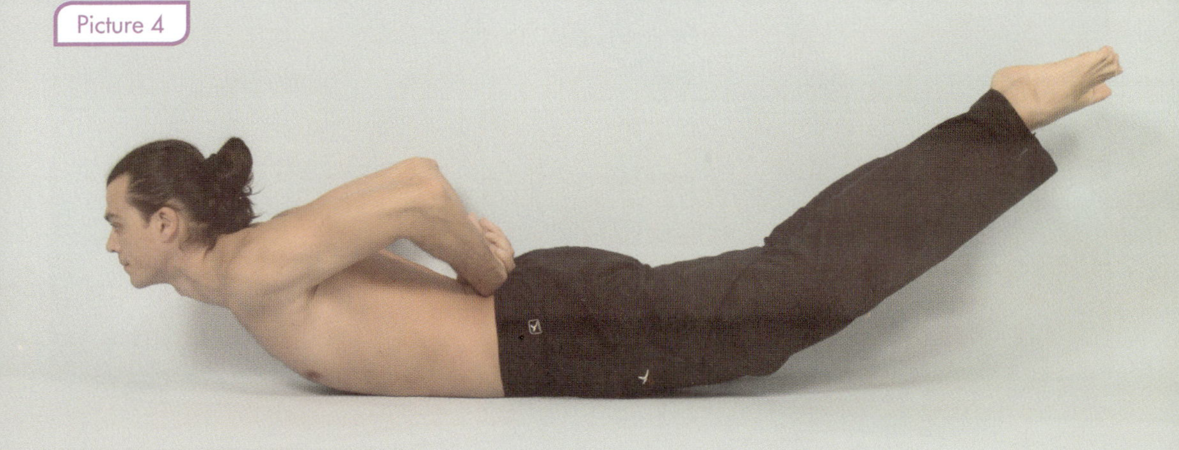
Picture 4

EXERCISE 8 • SPINE MOBILITY

How to perform it

- *Lying on your back with your spine and lumbar regions flat on the floor, bend your knees (picture 1).*
- *Exhale and raise your hips from the ground, bringing your knees to your brow while trying to keep your heels close to the gluteus muscles and pointing your toes toward the ceiling (picture 2).*
- *Hold this position for 5 breathing cycles.*
- *Exhale and allow the weight of your legs to bring your feet down until your toes touch the floor (picture 3).*
- *Hold this position for 5 breathing cycles.*
- *Bring your hands to your feet (or to your ankles if you cannot reach your feet) and while exhaling completely stretch out your legs (picture 4).*
- *Hold this position for 5 breathing cycles.*
- *The following steps are optional, designed for those who perform the previous steps with ease. Exhale and bring your knees next to your ears, wrapping your arms over your knees, and push your knees toward your ears (picture 5).*
- *Hold this position for 5 breathing cycles.*
- *Slowly return to the starting position, then perform again all the intermediate stages.*
- *Take a short break and breathe deep breaths.*
- *Repeat the whole sequence 3 times.*

Picture 1

Picture 2
Picture 3
Picture 4
Picture 5

EXERCISE 9 • SPINE MOBILITY

How to perform it

- *Kneel on the floor seated on your heels.*
- *Hold your back straight and bring your hands to your heels (picture 1).*
- *While exhaling, push your hips forward, trying to arch your back without letting go of your heels (picture 2).*
- *Hold this position for 5 breathing cycles.*
- *Exhale as you return to the starting position.*
- *Rest for 2 minutes.*
- *Repeat the whole sequence 3 to 5 times.*

Picture 1 Picture 2

EXERCISE 9B • EASIER VERSION

How to perform it

- *Kneel on the floor seated on your heels.*
- *Hold your back straight and bring your hands to the floor (picture 1).*
- *While exhaling, push your hips forward, trying to arch your back, tighten the gluteus muscles and hold both hands on the floor (picture 2).*
- *Hold this position for 5 breathing cycles.*
- *Exhale as you return to the starting position.*
- *Rest for 2 minutes.*
- *Repeat the whole sequence 3 to 5 times.*

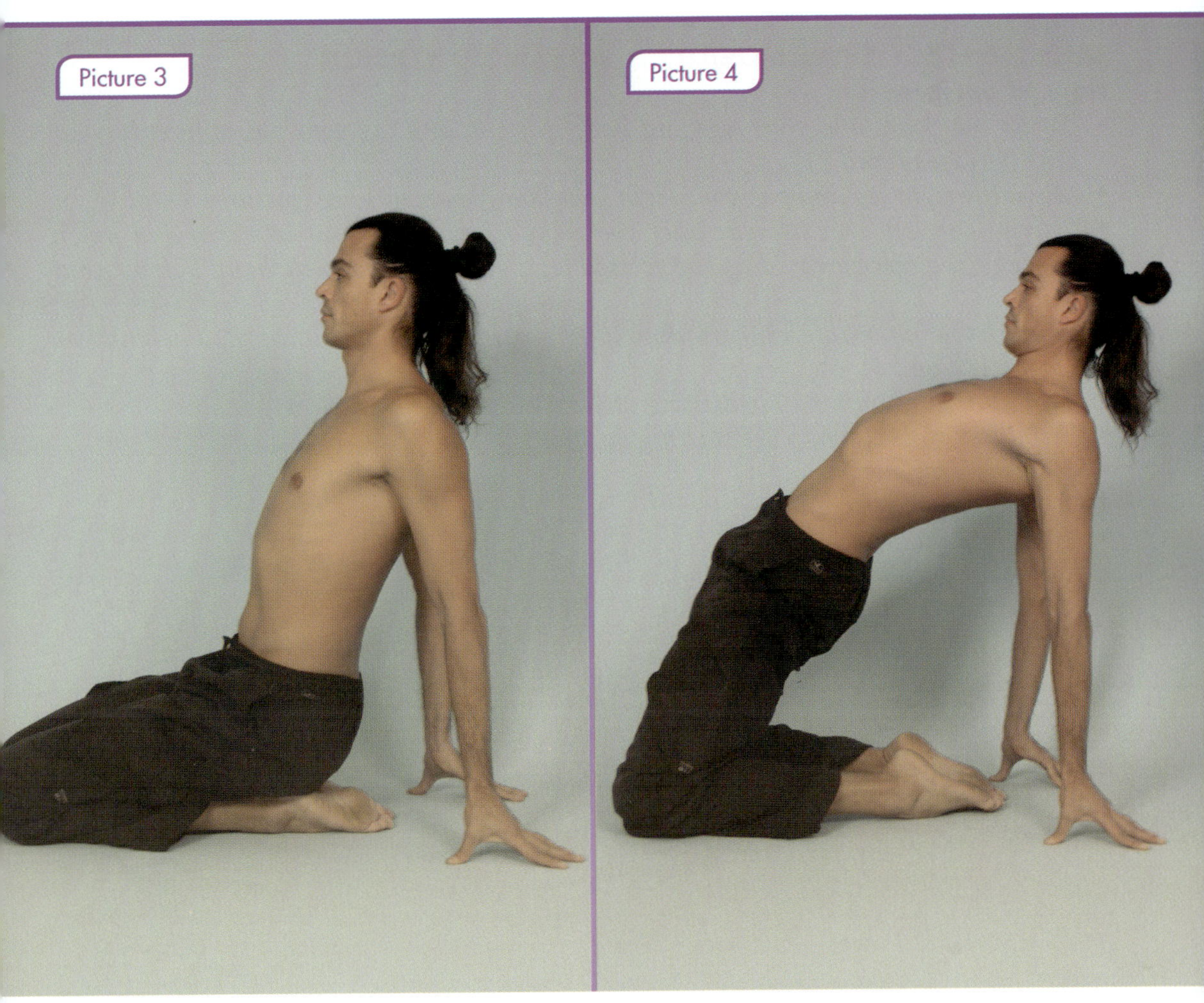
Picture 3
Picture 4

EXERCISE 10 • SPINE MOBILITY

How to perform it

- *Sit on the floor, hold your legs and back straight and lay your palms next to your legs (pictures 1 and 2).*
- *Bend the right leg and put the right foot over your left knee (picture 3 and 4).*
- *Bring the left arm straight over the right knee and grab your left tibia with your left hand (picture 5).*
- *While exhaling, rotate your trunk to the right, trying to look at the wall behind you (picture 6).*
- *Hold this position for 10 breathing cycles.*
- *Exhale as you return to the starting position.*
- *Rest for 2 minutes.*
- *Repeat on the other side.*
- *Rest for 2 minutes.*
- *Repeat the whole sequence 3 times.*

EXERCISE 10B • SPINE MOBILITY • ADVANCED VERSION

How to perform it

- *Sit on the floor, hold your legs and back straight, and lay your palms next to your legs (pictures 1 and 2).*
- *Bend the right leg and put your right foot over your left knee (pictures 3 and 4).*
- *Bring your left arm straight over the right knee; bend your left arm and put it through the space created by the crossed legs; grab your opposite hand behind your back.*
- *While exhaling, rotate your trunk to the right, trying to look at the wall behind you (pictures 5 and 6).*
- *Hold this position for 10 breathing cycles.*
- *Exhale as you return to the starting position.*
- *Rest for 2 minutes.*
- *Repeat on the other side.*
- *Rest for 2 minutes.*
- *Repeat the whole sequence 3 times.*

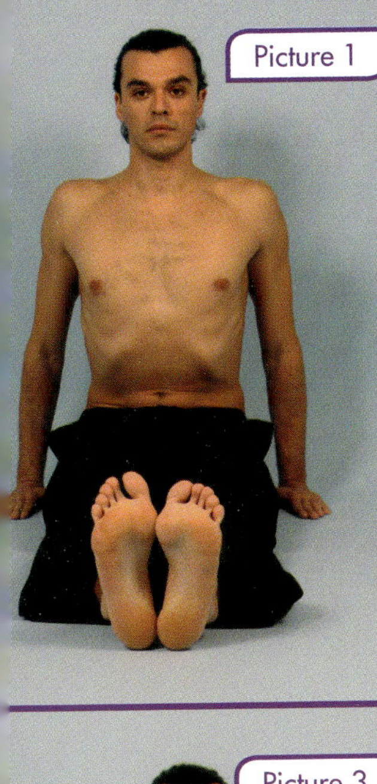
Picture 1

Picture 2

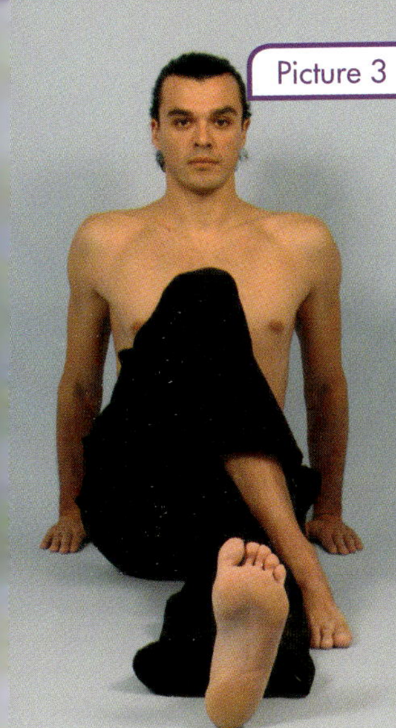
Picture 3

Picture 4

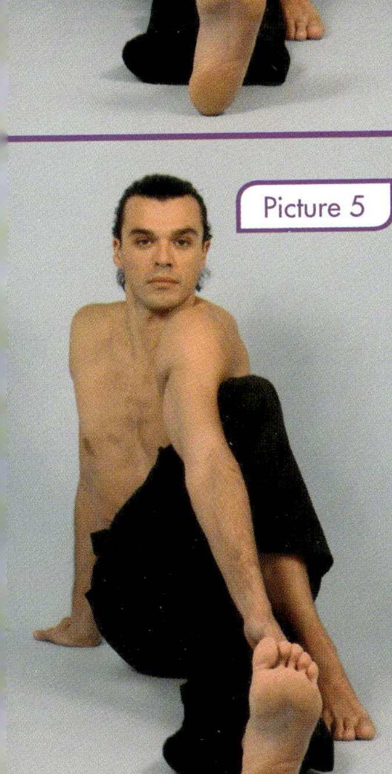
Picture 5

Picture 6

9.5 Improving the flexibility of hips and pelvis

The legs are an important means of propulsion for a freediver. Therefore, they are constantly and carefully trained during all stages of training.

There are many exercises for leg muscles, but it is equally important to exercise the leg joints.

The joint that suffers the most from awkward motions or bad habits is the hip joint. Although it is designed to move in a wide radius approaching 180°, it often suffers from significant motion limitations.

The hip joint and the pelvis are closely linked. That is why, in this section, we will deal with the mobility of both these structures.

EXERCISE 11 • MOBILITY OF HIPS AND PELVIS

How to perform it

- *Stand up straight with legs slightly wider than shoulder width apart and feet turned out (picture 1).*
- *Bend your legs until you can place your hands on your knees. Push your knees away from each other with your hands (picture 2).*
- *Every time you exhale, hold your hips down and push your pelvis in retroversion. feeling the strong stretching of muscles and the involvement of the joints (picture 3).*
- *Every time you inhale, hold the hips down and push your pelvis in anteversion, feeling the relaxation of muscles and joints (picture 4).*
- *Repeat for 15 breathing cycles.*
- *Rest for 2 minutes.*
- *Repeat the whole sequence 3 to 5 times.*

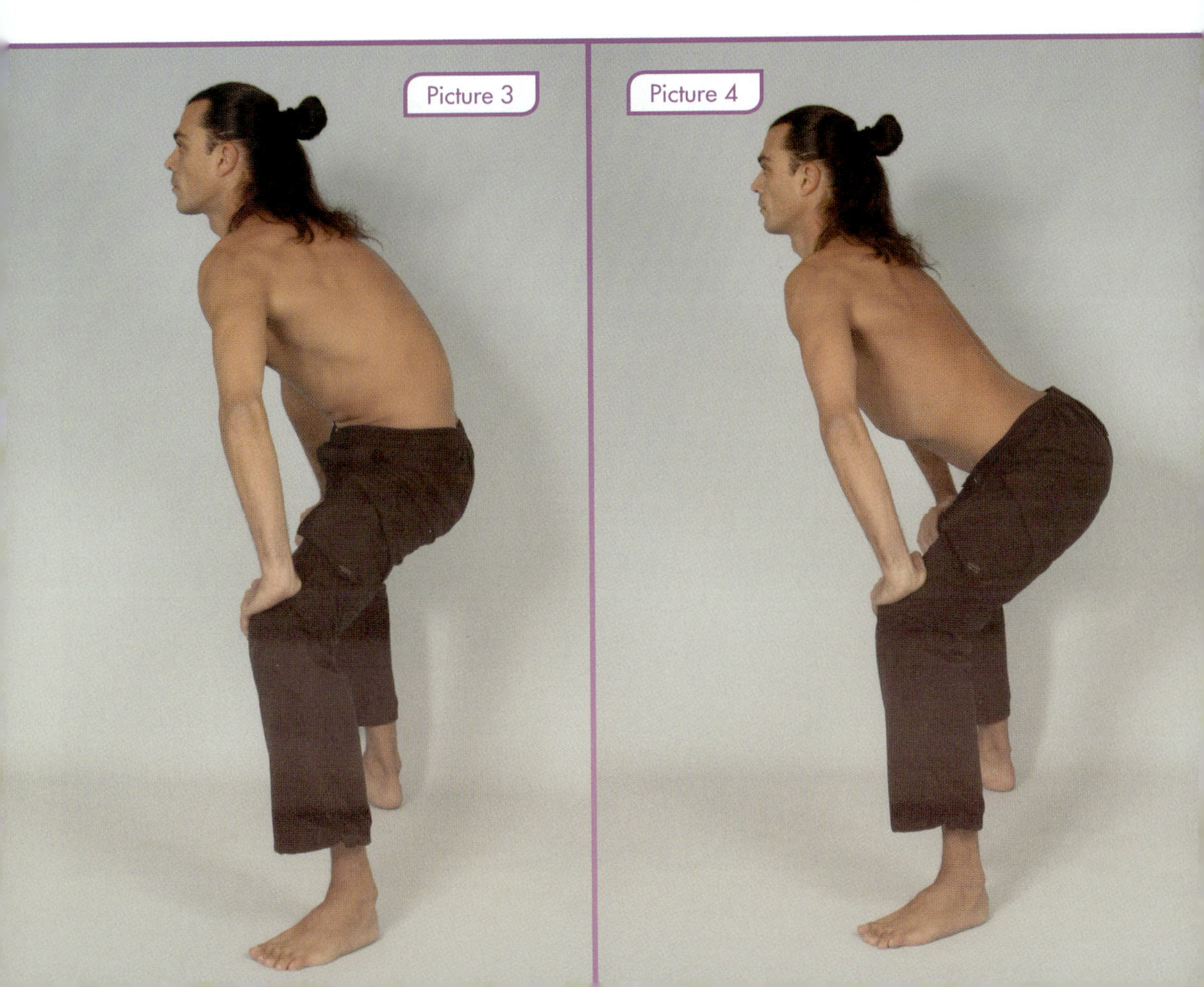
Picture 3

Picture 4

EXERCISE 12 • MOBILITY OF HIPS AND PELVIS

How to perform it

- *Sit with legs bent and the soles of the feet touching each other. Grab your feet with your hands, and try to hold your back straight. (pictures 1 and 2).*
- *Every time you exhale, push your knees to the floor, keeping your back straight (picture 3).*
- *Repeat for 5 breathing cycles.*
- *Put your hands on the floor next to the gluteus muscles. Raise the gluteus muscles from the floor and horizontally align them with the heels (picture 4).*
- *Every time you exhale, push your knees to the floor, trying to hold your back straight (picture 5).*
- *Repeat for 5 breathing cycles.*
- *Return to the starting seated position.*
- *Rest for 2 minutes.*
- *Repeat the whole sequence 3 times.*

Picture 1

Picture 2
Picture 3
Picture 4
Picture 5

EXERCISE 13 • MOBILITY OF HIPS AND PELVIS

How to perform it

- *Stand up with legs straight and open. Feet must be turned outward and wider than shoulder width apart. Put your hands in a prayer position. holding the forearms parallel to the floor (picture 1).*
- *Bend your legs until the gluteus muscles are lower than your knees. Heels must be flat on the ground (picture 2).*
- *Bring your elbows to the insides of your knees, and every time you exhale, push the knees outward with the arms to gradually increase the hip opening (picture 3).*
- *Hold this position for 5 breathing cycles.*
- *Bring your hands to the floor and return to the starting position.*
- *Rest for 2 minutes.*
- *Repeat the whole sequence 3 times.*

Picture 1

Picture 2

Picture 3

EXERCISE 14 • MOBILITY OF HIPS AND PELVIS

How to perform it

- *Stand with legs straight and open. Feet must be turned outward and wider than shoulder width apart.*
- *Bend your legs and trunk forward until the palms of your hands touch the floor. Keep bending the legs until your heels are flat on the floor. Try to hold your back straight (picture 1).*
- *Every time you exhale, using your hands for support, move your body weight to one side without raising the heels (picture 2).*
- *Inhale and return to the center position.*
- *Exhale and move your body weight to the opposite side without raising your heels (picture 3).*
- *Repeat for 20 breathing cycles.*
- *Rest for 2 minutes.*
- *Repeat the whole sequence 3 times.*

EXERCISE 15 • MOBILITY OF HIPS AND PELVIS

How to perform it

- *Start on all fours, holding your arms straight with your hands at shoulder width (picture 1 and 2).*
- *Put your right foot just inside your right hand, and put your left knee a few centimeters back (picture 3 and 4).*
- *Let your right foot slide toward your left hand. While exhaling, push your right knee forward and try to bring it to the floor, holding your right shinbone parallel to the shoulder line (picture 5 and 6).*
- *If the knee does not touch the floor, hold this position for at least 10 breathing cycles, pushing the knee toward the ground every time you exhale.*
- *If the knee touches the floor, push your pelvis to the ground and hold this position for at least 10 breathing cycles, pushing the knee toward the ground every time you exhale (picture 7 and 8).*
- *Return in the starting position.*
- *Rest for 2 minutes.*
- *Repeat on the opposite side.*
- *Return in the starting position.*
- *Rest for 2 minutes.*
- *Repeat the whole sequence 3 times.*

Picture 1

Picture 2

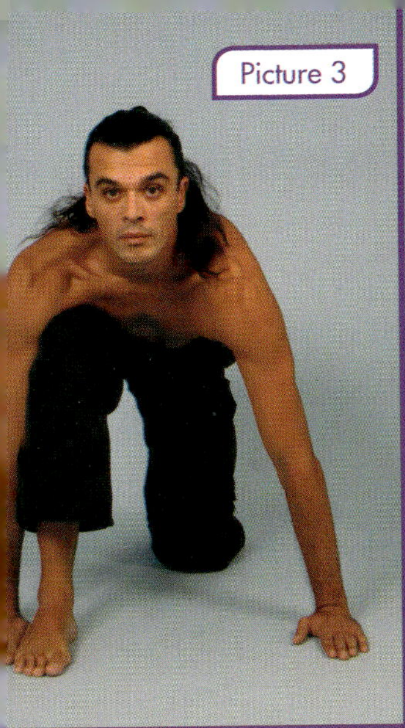
Picture 3

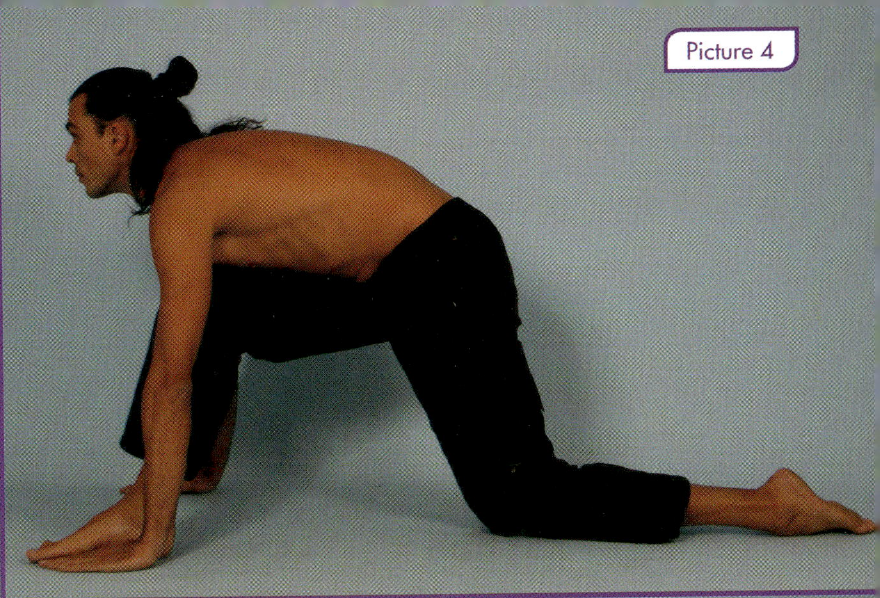
Picture 4

Picture 5

Picture 6

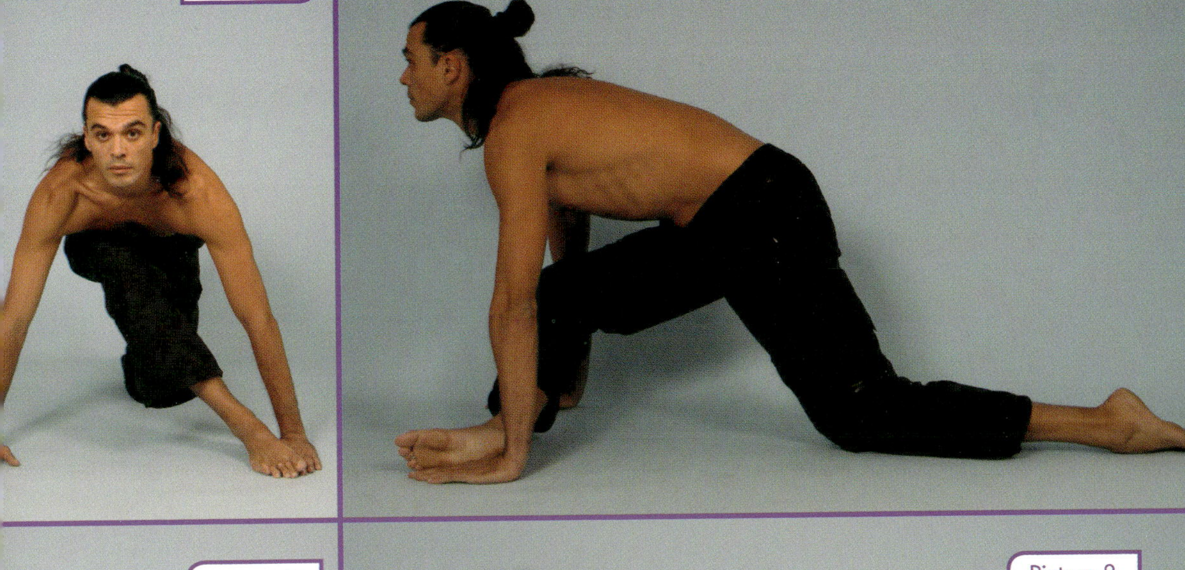

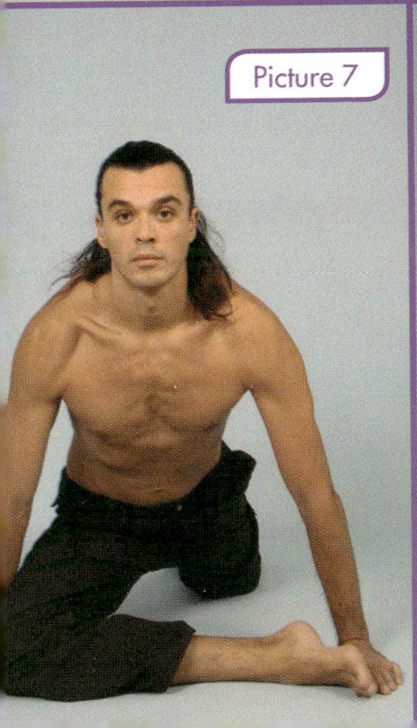
Picture 7

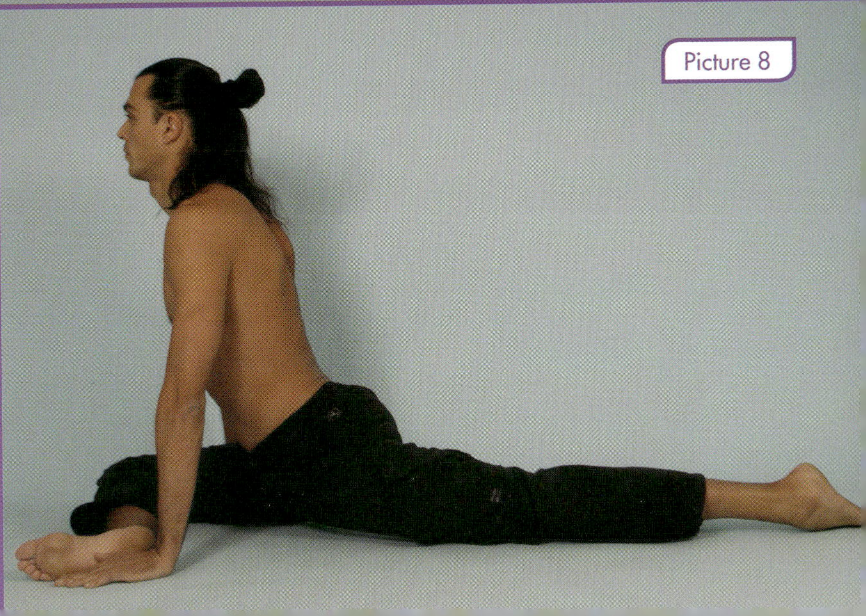
Picture 8

9.6 Improving the flexibility of tibiotarsal joint

The freediver who trains in other non-freediving disciplines often does exercises that put a load on the ankles that is significantly different from the load experienced in freediving-specific training. Exercising to increase joint mobility and reaction in this region enables the freediver to be wear fins or the monofin with less pain.

Since fins and monofins move a huge quantity of water, they subject the tibiotarsal joint to great loads and sprains. The following exercises are designed to improve the strength and mobility of this area.

EXERCISE 16 • MOBILITY OF TIBIOTARSAL JOINT

How to perform it

- *Kneel on the floor, sitting on your heels (picture 1 and 2).*
- *Bring your hands to the floor, and while exhaling raise your knees from the floor, distributing your body weight between your arms and the insteps of your feet (picture 3).*
- *Hold this position for at least for 5 breathing cycles.*
- *Rest for 2 minutes.*
- *Repeat the whole sequence 3 times.*

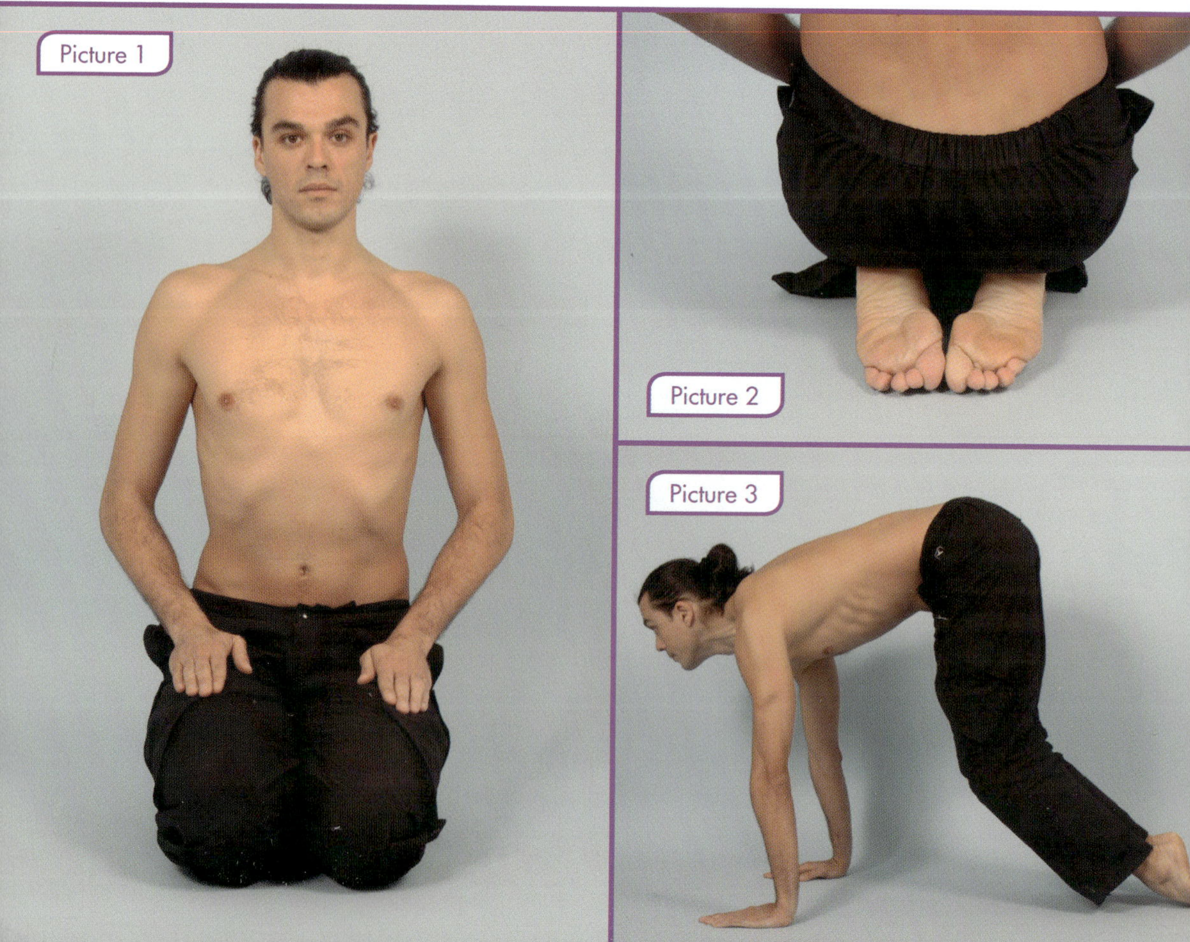
Picture 1
Picture 2
Picture 3

EXERCISE 17 • MOBILITY OF TIBIOTARSAL JOINT

How to perform it

- *Kneel on the floor, sitting on your heels (picture 1).*
- *Bring your hands to the floor next to your feet or behind them. While exhaling, raise your knees from the floor, shifting your body weight onto the tibiotarsals (picture 2).*
- *Hold this position for at least 5 breathing cycles.*
- *Rest for 2 minutes.*
- *Repeat the whole sequence 3 times.*

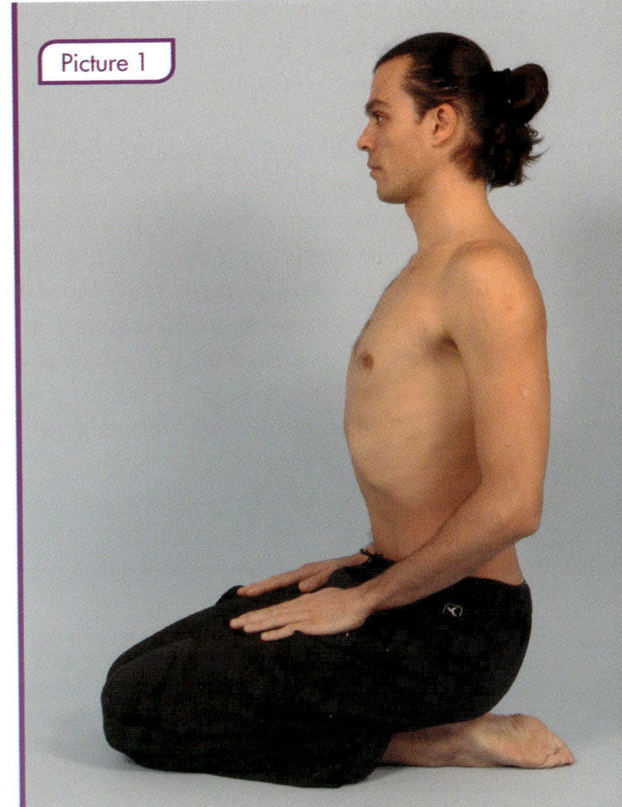

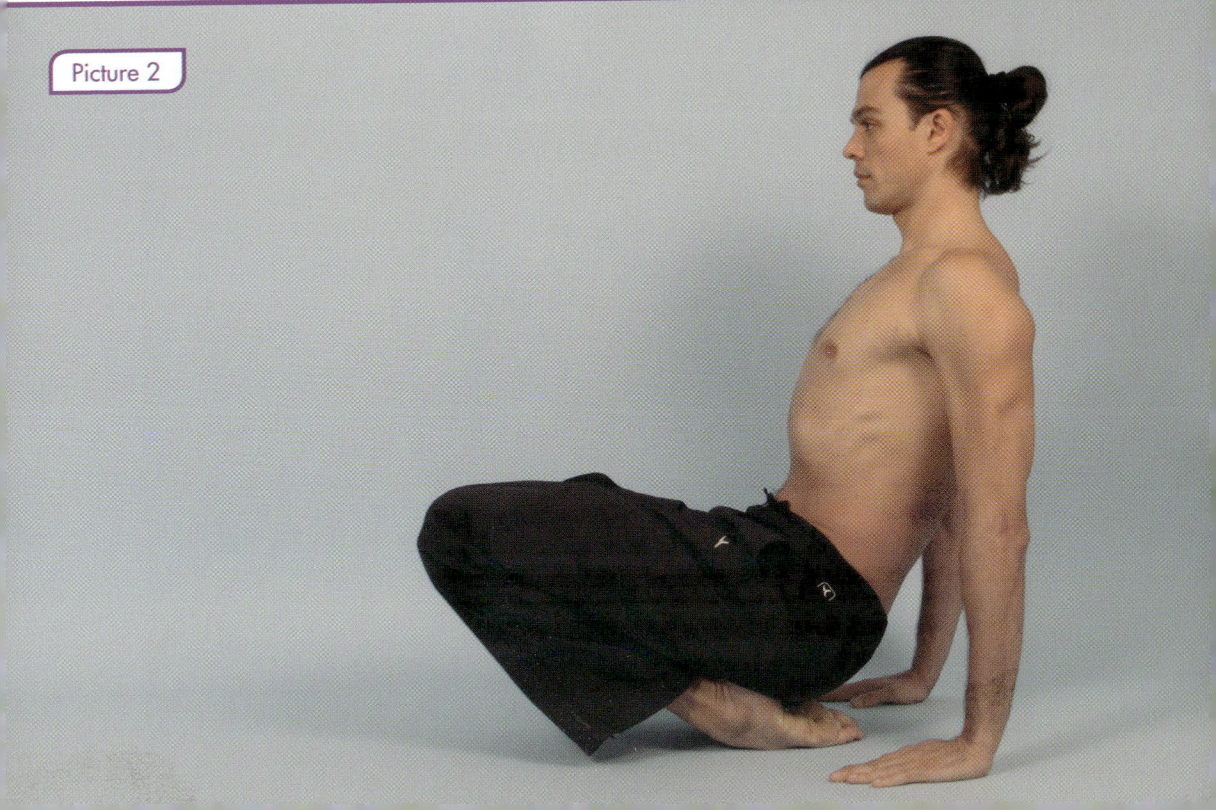

Picture 2

EXERCISE 18 • MOBILITY OF TIBIOTARSAL JOINT

How to perform it

- *Crouch down on tiptoe with your hands next to your feet to hold your balance (picture 1).*
- *Move your ankles in a lateral direction from right to left, trying to reach the joint limit (picture 2 and 3).*
- *Perform this movement for about 1 minute.*
- *Move your ankles in a vertical direction pushing the heels up and then down, trying to reach the joint limit (picture 4 and 5).*
- *Perform this movement for about 1 minute.*
- *Rotate your ankles, trying to reach the joint limit.*
- *Perform this movement for about 1 minute, then change the direction of the rotation and continue for another minute.*
- *Rest for 2 minutes.*
- *Repeat the whole sequence twice.*

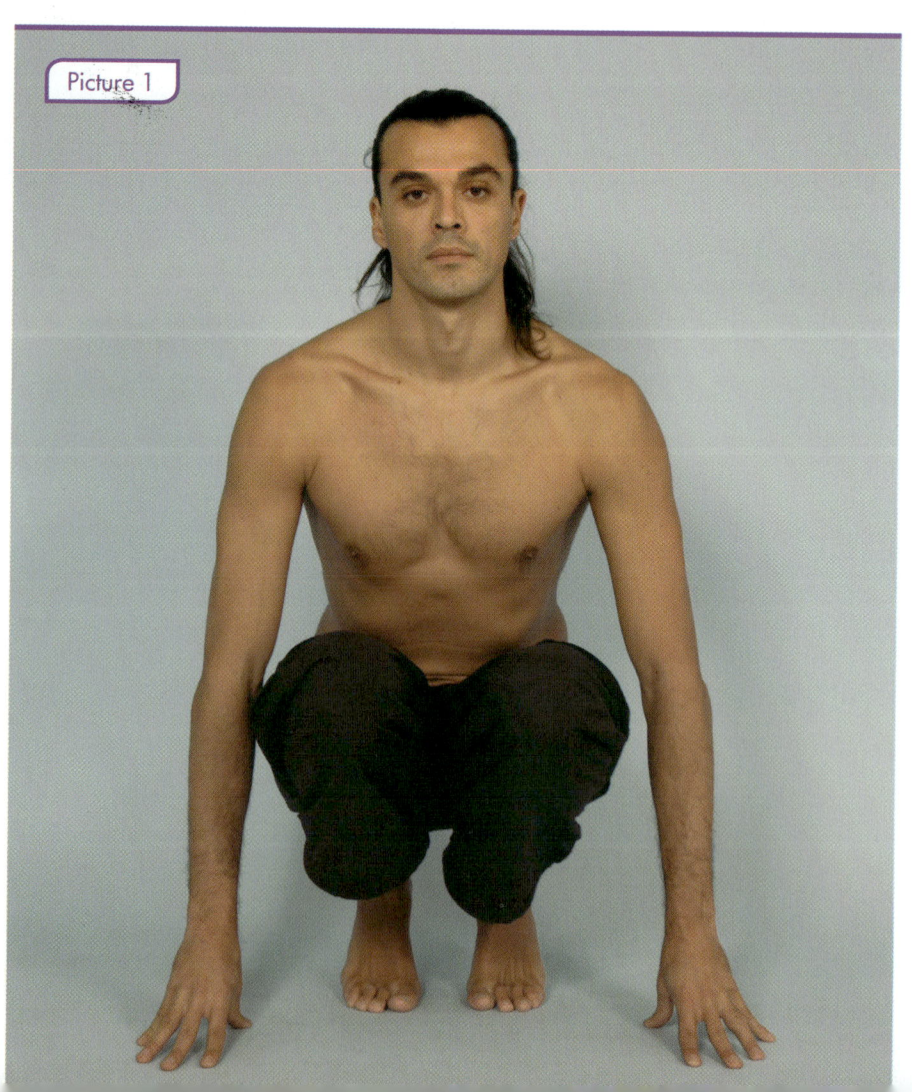

Picture 1

Picture 2

Picture 3

Picture 4

Picture 5

9.7 Training proposals

Yoga training can be performed independently, or it can be paired with another type of training.

Performing yoga exercises before or after running, weight lifting or swimming is something many athletes are coming to appreciate.

Yoga is an intense muscle stretching and joint mobility workout For this reason, it is both a good warm-up and a good cool-down.

If you include yoga as part of your training routine, it will be up to the you to choose how to benefit the most. A yoga session before or after training is very useful, but it is important to assess how much time will be needed to properly perform both disciplines. Performing yoga independently from your other training sessions may allow you to focus more on your yoga performance.

We also remind you that it is better to train for 30 minutes every day than for two hours straight once a week.

Basic Yoga Program

Region	Reference Exercise	Reps
Example 1		
Shoulders/Shoulder blades	Exercise 1	3
Spine/Lumbar region	Exercise 2	3
Hip/Pelvis	Exercise 1	3
Tibiotarsal joint	Exercise 2	3
Example 2		
Shoulders/Shoulder blades	Exercise 2	3
Spine/Lumbar region	Exercise 3	3
Hip/Pelvis	Exercise 3	3
Tibiotarsal joint	Exercise 3	5
Example 3		
Shoulders/Shoulder blades	Exercise 4	3
Spine/Lumbar region	Exercise 5	3
Hip/Pelvis	Exercise 3	5
Tibiotarsal joint	Exercise 4	3

Example 4		
Shoulders/Shoulder blades	Exercise 3	3
Spine/Lumbar region	Exercise 3	3
Hip/Pelvis	Exercise 3	5
Tibiotarsal joint	Exercise 3	5
Example 5		
Shoulders/Shoulder blades	Exercise 2	3
Spine/Lumbar region	Exercise 3	5
Hip/Pelvis	Exercise 5	3
Tibiotarsal joint	Exercise 1	3
Example 6		
Shoulders/Shoulder blades	Exercise 5	3
Spine/Lumbar region	Exercise 4	5
Hip/Pelvis	Exercise 3	3
Tibiotarsal joint	Exercise 3	5
Example 7		
Shoulders/Shoulder blades	Exercise 5	3
Spine/Lumbar region	Exercise 5	5
Hip/Pelvis	Exercise 5	5
Tibiotarsal joint	Exercise 2	5
Example 8		
Shoulders/Shoulder blades	Exercise 3	5
Spine/Lumbar region	Exercise 1	3
Hip/Pelvis	Exercise 5	3
Tibiotarsal joint	Exercise 1	5

Advanced Yoga Program

Region	Reference Exercise	Reps
Example 1		
Shoulders/Shoulder blades	Exercise 1 Exercise 3	3 5
Spine/Lumbar region	Exercise 2 Exercise 1	3 5
Hip/Pelvis	Exercise 1 Exercise 4	3 5
Tibiotarsal joint	Exercise 2 Exercise 1	3 5
Example 2		
Shoulders/Shoulder blades	Exercise 5 Exercise 3	3 5
Spine/Lumbar region	Exercise 5 Exercise 3	3 5
Hip/Pelvis	Exercise 3 Exercise 4	3 5
Tibiotarsal joint	Exercise 1 Exercise 3	3 5
Example 3		
Shoulders/Shoulder blades	Exercise 1 Exercise 2	3 5
Spine/Lumbar region	Exercise 3 Exercise 4	3 5
Hip/Pelvis	Exercise 5 Exercise 1	3 5
Tibiotarsal joint	Exercise 2 Exercise 5	3 5

Region	Reference Exercise	Reps
Example 4		
Shoulders/Shoulder blades	Exercise 5 Exercise 4	3 5
Spine/Lumbar region	Exercise 3 Exercise 2	3 5
Hip/Pelvis	Exercise 1 Exercise 5	3 5
Tibiotarsal joint	Exercise 2 Exercise 1	3 5
Example 5		
Shoulders/Shoulder blades	Exercise 1 Exercise 3 Exercise 5	3 3 5
Spine/Lumbar region	Exercise 2 Exercise 3 Exercise 4	3 3 5
Hip/Pelvis	Exercise 1 Exercise 2 Exercise 4	3 3 5
Tibiotarsal joint	Exercise 1 Exercise 2 Exercise 3	3 5 5

The possible combinations of exercises are many. The workouts may range from 10 minutes to more than an hour. When choosing a combination of exercises, be sure to include at least one exercise for each joint region into each session, focusing more on areas that showed the worst results during the starting tests.

9.8 Practical tips to practice yoga

The exercises above come from classical yoga poses, but some have been adjusted to meet freedivers' needs. The variation of some poses may be great.

As mentioned before, this book is not intended to replace a trainer or a yoga teacher. There are many yoga schools with great teachers, who can work with you and make this discipline increasingly exciting for you.

Those who want to study yoga in detail can work with a yoga teacher to find interesting points to integrate into their freediving training.

Chapter 10

A SUPPORT TO TRAINING

Athletes are increasingly turning to professionals in the medical and paramedical fields to help make their bodies and minds work their best, even when they are subjected to high workloads and physical and psychological stress during training and competition.

Incorrect posture resulting from an abnormal jaw closure may prove, in the long run, detrimental or even traumatic if combined with frequent and intense workouts.

Or, high-level athletes, as the result of an injury or a period of overtraining, may lose their enthusiasm, which is a key aspect of success.

The following chapter presents two techniques that can help the freediver. These methods are usually used near the end of training: After having made so much important progress, the athlete can best understand and appreciate the benefits of these supporting techniques.

10.1 Hypnosis and NLP: the mind potential among myths and beliefs

Dr. Marco Alessandria[1]

The intuitive mind is a sacred gift
and the rational mind is a faithful servant.
We have created a society that honors the servant
and has forgotten the gift.

This was how Albert Einstein (an eminent scientist whose intuition was a key part of his brilliance) honored the deepest and most unconscious part of our mind, raising it to the rank of a sacred entity as a meeting tool between the human being and the great mastermind of the universe.

With wise management of the mind, a human being is sometimes able to activate powers deemed to be superhuman. Take, for example, the astonishing achievements

---

[1] Graduate in Motor and Sport Sciences and in Physiotherapy. Osteopath registered at R.O.I. (Registry of Italian Osteopaths) holding a postgraduate diploma in Osteopathy and a Master in Clinical Posturology. Healthcare professional specialized in hypnotic communication, NLP practitioner and NLP Master practitioner.

He is a professor at S.U.I.S.M. in Turin, as external expert for the course of Physical Medicine and Rehabilitation.

of martial arts masters of the East. Those masters, many with not-so-young bodies, are able to do things that would leave 20-year-olds with their mouths agape. Or, think about shamans who are able to pierce their skin with sharp objects without a groan and without losing a drop of blood. For examples more in line with our experiences, we can recall single-handed ocean passages in small vessels with only a cell phone and a few cans of food; ultramarathon races in the desert at temperatures near 50 ° C, where the athlete covers distances of 200 km in less than 40 hours; or the climbing of tall mountain peaks without supplemental oxygen and in adverse weather conditions.

We could go on with thousands of examples, but what is crucial to understand is that we all have this important mind structure, this "gift," and our task is to learn how to control it and direct it to help us overcome challenges and achieve goals.

Ancient books and religious texts are full of references to the use of mind potentials. From meditation to prayer, all of them have the goal of making tangible the visual imagery potential of the mind.

Hypnosis is an effective method for developing such potential. All of us have heard that we use only a small part of our brain. Hypnosis is the access key that helps us communicate with other parts of our brain. Tapping into this latent potential, which is there at our disposal and eager to express itself, allows us to improve, at a rapid pace, any aspect of our lives: work, school, sports, etc.

Hypnosis is based on an immutable principle: **Any idea that occupies the mind for an adequate time has the potential to transform its content into action**. This is done with the help of the will, intention and motivation to give the unconscious a chance. It can be done through self-talk or with the guidance of a trained expert in hypnotic communication.

The uncritical acceptance by the unconscious of a new idea leads to the development and manifestation of the idea, much to the astonishment of the individual who had never before been aware of having such capabilities.

This principle can be summed up in a single concept widely supported by hypnotists: ideoplasy, or plastic monoideism. It means that an idea can take shape and become a tangible reality, observable in all its potential. The mental representation becomes a powerful tool through which you can meet your needs.

"**Hypnosis doesn't exist; everything is hypnosis**", said Milton H. Erickson, one of the greatest hypnotists in the world. Unfortunately our idea of hypnosis has always been linked to the image drawn around distorted information from TV and movies. Such misinformation, which relegates hypnosis to a subtle, coercive and submissive practice, collapses with this statement, since Erickson makes us understand that hypnosis is already within us; it is part of a genetic ancestral power that resides in one of the most ancient areas of our brain structure. We cannot be afraid of something that is ours and works for us.

We all experience hypnosis several times during the day, but we often don't stop to realize it. We spend moments without conscious control that allow us to rest and to perform automatic gestures. Such moments enable us to do something else and think about something else; they isolate us from the world, allow us to increase our level of attention and memory, allow us to adopt quick and effective solutions to our problems, and much more.

From this we can deduce that hypnosis is not sleeping and it is not wakefulness; it is a modified psychophysical state that is able to produce mental and physical phenomena that cannot be experienced through simple voluntary control.

A hypnosis session allows us to recognize these skills, control them and direct them. It is necessary to be supported by a hypnotist, who uses special techniques to bring the individual to this particular state of consciousness and leads him to discover his inner world, evoking appropriate suggestions to achieve the goals set at the beginning of the session. This establishes a relationship between the hypnotist and the subject characterized by a feeling of empathy, mutual willingness and motivation. Hypnosis is a path, and the relevant feedback becomes an essential element for the effectiveness and accuracy of the hypnotic induction.

The person in hypnosis is not totally disconnected from reality nor is he at the total mercy of the hypnotist, because during the session the mind keeps a watchful eye on the rational part of his brain, relegating it to the role of observer and not disturbing the process, and giving the subject the ability to come out of the hypnotic state at any time in the event that situations morally or ethically contrary to his system of values occur, or if the subject is faced with an unconscious reality that he does not want to investigate.

In some sports, the tool of hypnosis is used as a method to increase performance, and nobody can deny the importance of managing the mental dynamics, particularly in sports where concentration for long periods of time is necessary or where voluntary breath-holding forces the athlete to increase inner talk, which works with imagination, evokes memories and initiates the dreaming activity.

Dreaming is one of the voices of the unconscious, one of its ways of expressing itself. In the dream state, mental activity can create a fantasy world that is able to make us live situations built around a series of sensory experiences, which are tangible and unambiguous, although they seem real to us at that time. During a dream, we truly see, feel, perceive and experience real emotional states, although there are no real environmental stimuli that cause these situations.

Many believe that dreaming is totally spontaneous and cannot be controlled on the basis of our desires, but it is equally true that the mental processes that bring about the evocation of such experiences can be directed according to our goals, making use of their potential.

Contrary to what we have always been taught, we are not slaves to our mind, but potential drivers of it. We just have to decide whether to play the role of driver or of passive passenger.

Hypnosis allows you to communicate with the unconscious part of your mind, giving you the opportunity to develop phenomena believed to be impossible by the conscious mind.

The unconscious does not need to choose, decide or discriminate in order to implement its program. It has an uncritical acceptance of the ideas developed by our minds. Thanks to this ability, the phenomenology of hypnosis covers a very broad scope.

Hypnosis has been used in all areas of medicine and surgery, in psychotherapy and sports, and even in business to improve the performance of managers and executives.

One of the most spectacular abilities of hypnosis is the control of pain. Many studies have documented how it is possible, thanks to this technique, to achieve analgesia and anesthesia in such a way as to be able to face surgery or other painful medical procedures, as well as experience postoperative pain relief.

The effects of hypnosis during surgery are amazing. It can cause a peripheral vasoconstriction that lessens or prevents bleeding caused by a surgical incision. Hypnosis has been used in the field of dentistry for dental extractions, in dermatology for removal of lymphomas, in gastroenterology for the removal of the appendix and in otolaryngology for tonsillectomies.

Currently, hypnosis is gaining ground in the rehabilitation field to speed recovery after surgery, and periods of immobilization to decrease muscle wasting.

Other phenomena that may occur in a state of hypnosis are:

- **hyperesthesia**, that is, the strengthened ability of receptors to capture stimuli, both endogenous and exogenous ones. Such ability is essential in sports for fine control that makes movements effective and efficient, and for control of cardiorespiratory information to optimize resources and improve performance;
- **time distortion**, which allows you to make time subjective (determined by your own internal clock) rather than objective (which is the same for everyone). Subjective time can be manipulated by contracting or expanding it, giving the perception that a long time has elapsed in a few minutes, or vice versa. Time distortion can be used to achieve the feeling that time has flown by during a difficult or unpleasant situation;
- **influence on motility**, that is, the ability to obtain surprising muscle phenomena, such as increasing muscular strength to perform actions that require a greater strength than you thought you had, or improving endurance by optimizing the use of energy resources;
- **hypermnesia**, that is, an enhancement of the memory that is used for learning in school, work and sports;
- **amnesia**, which is the loss of selective memory. This can be useful for the deconstruction of an incorrect sporting gesture that leads to a decrease in performance.

Many other phenomena can be induced during a hypnotic trance, including age regression, which serves to recall information from our past that we didn't think we remembered.

Hypnosis can instill in athletes specific suggestions, which can be accessed without the help of the hypnotist during a competition to help improve performance. During hypnosis, the hypnotist can provide a post-hypnotic command that will act as a reminder of the suggestions evoked during the sessions. A post-hypnotic command can be triggered by a simple gesture chosen by the athlete (such as adjusting the cap or pinching the thumb and forefinger together), so he can quickly use it at any time during the competition.

But are all people hypnotizable and able to develop these phenomena?

There are no rigorously scientific statistics to answer this question, because techniques are too varied and the people studied are too diverse. Experience has shown that all people are hypnotizable, but at different levels of hypnotic trance and with different abilities to experience hypnotic phenomena. Not all people respond the same way to the same suggestion, nor does the same person respond in the same way to the same suggestion in a different session. In addition, each of us experiences some phenomena better than others. Though not consistent, hypnotic induction can hardly be called ineffective.

However, there are some factors that negatively interfere with hypnosis and some factors that can aid it.

Negative factors that sometimes cause a person to resist going into a trance include: the fear of not waking up, fear of revealing secrets, and fear of not being respected. This last feeling often results from the distorted image of hypnosis that is frequently presented in the media, combined with an extremely rational mindset with a high degree of critical judgment.

Factors that can affect hypnosis positively are a high level of education (to be able to better focus on a task), gender (it is believed that women are more easily hypnotized than men), age (a high level of hypnotizability from ages 7 to 20, becoming gradually lower as we age), sports (athletes are generally more easily hypnotized, likely because of their natural ability to perceive body signals, to listen to themselves, and to be introspective).

It is understandable, therefore, that there may be a personal aptitude for the hypnotic practice with a resulting difference in sensitivity, psychophysical phenomenology and level of hypnotic trance. This variation in the ability to use mental potential may explain why two athletes with the same physiological values can have vastly different competition results.

What is the difference between an athlete and a champion? What is the difference between a professional and a world-beater? What is the difference between a pursuer and a leader? In sports, you do not win only because of your muscles but also because of your mind. The level you reach does not matter. What's important is the goal you set in order to be satisfied with yourself.

In sports, the management of mind processes becomes a key factor in achieving the goals you set. "It's the difference that makes a difference," said Richard Bandler, co-creator of Neuro-linguistic Programming (NLP).

Bandler argues that the mind does not learn according to goals, but according to directions. It is therefore necessary to build "mental roads" that lead to those goals.

The goal is the finish line, and we can decide to reach it either along a difficult, unpaved path, with stops and weeds, or along a highway with three lanes, no speed limits and no traffic. It is about forming an alliance with your own potential so that you will have a faithful travel companion who can alleviate the tedious and tiring moments that divert your attention from the goal.

Our rigid mindset, brought about by of our convictions and beliefs, prevents the physiological flow of hidden potential and imposes limits on what we see as possible. Our doubts, our fears and our limits are all by-products of our way of thinking, which inevitably affects our behavior.

Sometimes, though, a word, an image or an experience is enough to make us change our mind, and we are often not aware of what gave rise to such change. Indeed, mental blocking is not innate, but learned. Therefore, if you have learned to have mental blocks, you can just as easily learn to eliminate them.

During the deep relaxation of hypnosis, it is possible to acquire some simple mental techniques to help create and build mental images and experiences that determine what path the mind can take to achieve your goals and to overcome constraining beliefs and convictions.

All this, together with the post-hypnotic command, makes the athlete independent from the hypnotist and free to use what he has learned whenever he needs it. He can also create new and more effective mental images to use in relation to new issues that emerge during competition or training.

Many sports include numerous different events, which subsequently involve numerous techniques and many forms of physical training. Thanks to the "tools" provided by hypnosis, you can:

- structure or restructure the best techniques to optimize performance;
- minimize the interference of your weaknesses in competitions involving compulsory exercises;
- overcome critical moments: air hunger, muscle fatigue, negative thoughts, etc.;
- identify in advance the onset of critical moments in order to better manage and direct them, thanks to a greater perception of body stimuli;
- reduce loss of concentration caused by external factors that cannot be controlled, such as weather conditions and noisy spectators.

Many other disturbing factors can be blocked out using of the mental approach experienced during an altered psychological and physical state. Each of us has our own specific weaknesses that can be improved in order to increase performance.

Through a careful analysis of the competition and the individual athlete's technique, it is possible to identify what will make it difficult to achieve the best performance. This can be done by the athlete himself, who is able to provide his mind with the most accurate information.

For each negative situation, the athlete can identify the mental image that causes the development of negative elements. The image can then be reshaped during the relaxation stage of hypnotic communication or NLP.

In this way, the athlete can link the new image to a post-hypnotic command so that he can call up this mental support tool whenever necessary during a performance. It is also possible to link a specific strengthening image to a specific disturbing element. For instance, if the athlete is able to accurately recognize the moment in which he is about to face an obstacle, he can block its onset.

The most effective mental images are created by change in submodalities (color, brightness, position, size, distance, sound, volume, tone, etc.), by associating sensations and feelings, or by modeling an outstanding performance of your own or of another athlete and then associating it with the visual image.

The modeling process is a key moment in NLP and can be equally essential for hypnotic induction. You can use an outstanding performance of your own, or that of another athlete, as a model in order to grasp the characteristics of excellence that enhance a performance. Then, you can create a mental recording of it, reproducing in your mind all that has been observed. Playing it back with your eyes closed, you live, you see, you sense, you feel the movement of muscles and joints, and you even anticipate the mental and physical feelings that are going to occur. Then you bring them forward into your reality. This is a very powerful weapon, which can give you unexpected and often unconscious results. Modeling is not the mere act of copying; it is an extrapolation of physical and mental strategies using a collection of verbal and nonverbal communication methods. All this helps to understand how the athlete perceives himself and how he positions himself in his overall representation of the world.

This requires becoming allied with your own mind and defining unified intentions in order to meet your expectations.

This mental training can produce immediate effects, and the athlete can often feel a change as soon as the first performance after such training. As you keep working with this method, the effects will be more striking and more exciting. It is not uncommon for an athlete to be surprised by the speed at which he achieves his goals, especially when he aims to make such behavior unconscious and automatic. For such phenomenology to occur, the person must have the adequate will, motivation and ability to have a dialogue with himself.

The path we have described so far has led us to understand the potential the mind can develop in different situations: how it can do it, in which contexts, and to what extent.

But deeds must follow words! All this talk may have fascinated you and made you curious, but our rational mind is always in desperate search of verification. It needs something to hang onto in order to bring back experiences within its old frame of reference. Otherwise, our mind ends up considering any phenomenon a trick, a drama. In Erickson's words: "You know how human behavior is: What is unusual is unacceptable, unless you consider it to be something mystical."

I must confess that I have been a victim and a prisoner of this mental prison too, before administering Conconi Tests to triathletes in connection with hypnosis.

Here I will show you tests taken before and after hypnosis sessions, omitting the names of the athletes who participated in the tests for privacy reasons. I believe the results were satisfactory and surprisingly homogeneous. Therefore, I invite anyone to express any doubt, question, inquiry or suggestion.

The study was aimed at investigating the possibility of increasing endurance through the use of hypnosis. In this study we set as a criterion for inclusion the anaerobic threshold of 175 bpm. Athletes with a lower anaerobic threshold were not included in the test. The athletes selected participated in a working protocol which included:

1. carrying out the Conconi Test on the treadmill before the hypnosis sessions;
2. identification of a post-hypnotic command decided by the athlete;
3. from 3 to 5 sessions of hypnosis, depending on the individual's ability to achieve plastic monoideisms;

4. carrying out the Conconi Test again after the hypnosis sessions;
5. analysis of data, drafting and comparison of graphs (heart rate pattern during the test, anaerobic threshold, maximum heart rate, maximum speed achieved during the test, maximum duration of the tests, slope of the treadmill).

The tests were performed during the season when performances were at the highest level possible. The athletes were ordered not to change their training methodology during the testing.

A few parameters were set to perform the Conconi Test:

1. a steady inclination at 4%. This was chosen because of the speeds achieved by the athletes during previous Conconi Tests. Such speeds exceeded 20 km/h. Since the maximum speed of the treadmill was 20 km/h, we had to increase the inclination in order to increase the difficulty;
2. initial speed: 10 km/h;
3. increasing speed: 0.5 km/h every 100 m. Such frequent increases were chosen in order to get a more accurate reading of the anaerobic threshold from the graph.

After taking the first Conconi Test, the athlete was subjected to a preliminary interview to identify a post-hypnotic command. The chose commands were simple, easy-to-perform gestures: adjusting the cap, touching the thumb and forefinger together, etc.

Then, the hypnosis sessions took place, presenting the athletes' hypnotic suggestions according to various techniques for the development of plastic monoideism.

The second Conconi Test was performed right after the last session of hypnosis. Athletes were requested to carry out their warm-up activities and then begin the test. During the test, the athletes chose when to use their post-hypnotic commands.

We will name the athletes we tested **Person A** and **Person B.**

Person A *First test (blue) and second test (red)*
Recorded figures at 5%-6%-7% inclination levels

The second graph shows how difficult is to recognize the deflection point, therefore the threshold too, compared to the first graph. In addition, the athlete reached a speed well over the speed allowed by the treadmill (20 km/h), forcing the operators to increase the inclination to 7%.

Person B *First test (blue) and second test (red)*

This shows how difficult it is to identify the deflection point. The comparison graph (which follows) shows the heart rate trend in the second test to be much lower than in the first test. The conducted experiment revealed data worthy of further investigation.

Unfortunately, the low number of people tested does not allow us to draw any conclusions. However, it is possible to develop new and exciting hypotheses for further studies, such as:

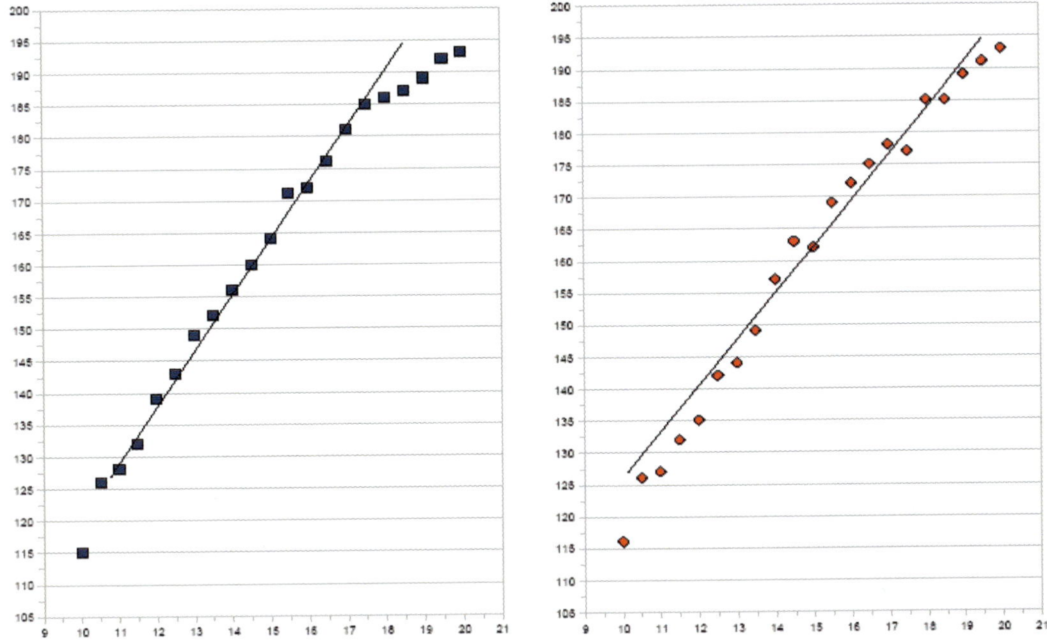

Person A First test (blue) and second test (red)
Recorded figures at 5%-6%-7% inclination levels

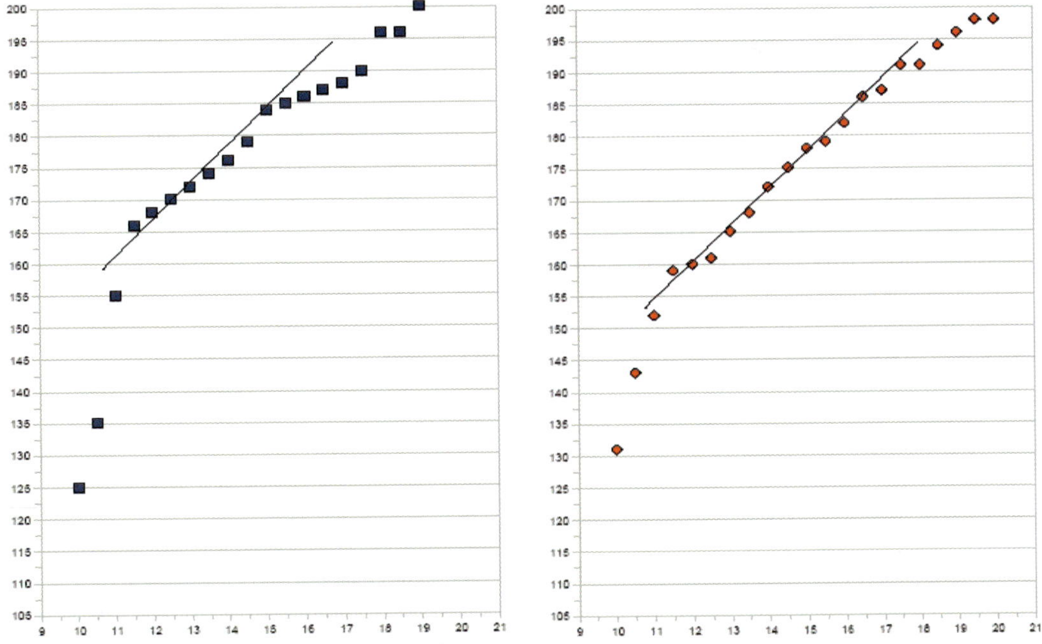

Person B First test (blue) and second test (red)

- the possibility of measuring blood lactate, since above the threshold it significantly increases in concentration and the graphs of the second test show that the deflection point is very indefinite and fading;
- the change in VO_2max, a parameter dependent on the anaerobic threshold and on the heart rate trend.

I hope my invitation to clarify the effects of the dynamics of our brain in sports performances in a more pragmatic and accurate way could be positively regarded among athletes. Furthermore, I hope that the world of sports at all levels (from managers to athletes) can become more aware that more research is needed to help provide further tools to improve performances. Indifference and close-mindedness contribute to keeping the number of samples low and prevent experts from providing these useful tools.

To the athletes who participated enthusiastically in this experiment, I hope they could take advantage of what they learned to improve their performances at national, European and worldwide levels. And, I invite them to keep cultivating their potentials through mental imagery. There is no easy or difficult, simple or demanding competition. It's all about you and how you frame the competition in your mind. This makes a big difference.

When I began to test triathletes, one of them told me: "Sometimes it seems to me that the shortest race of a triathlon is endless, and other times the longest race proves to be easier."

I asked him: "According to you, what color is that difference?"

After a moment of surprise at the question, which appeared to be nonsense at first glance, he took a deep breath, smiled and said: "In the first case, my race has an annoying and depressing color. In the second case, the color is lively, intense and pleasant."

Our brains work through frameworks, models and images. We do not act directly. Instead, we create maps that we use to guide our behaviors. This largely determines the way we live, the way we feel and the choices we have at our disposal. Hans Vaihinger, in his book "The Philosophy of 'As If,' " states: "The whole world of representations … is not at all designed to be an image of reality …; it is instead a tool that helps us find a way through reality itself."

The holder of the Nobel Prize for neuroscience in 2000, E.R. Kandel, proved it scientifically. He said: "Colors, sounds, scents … are mental patterns developed by our brain, and they do not exist outside of it."

Our mind is a production line of continuously changing images, feelings and thoughts, made up to satisfy our way of being and the way we feel. We are culturally linked to the idea that learning is a long, hard and boring process. In fact, our mind is able to learn very quickly. When we create a mental image that is perfect in all its components, we can improve our performance very quickly. We do not need to wait for the learning process to take place; it is immediate. It can delete what we do not like and replace it with something we like.

Some athletes object to the idea that we don't need a long time to learn an athletic technique, but we only need a long time if we do not have a clear image of what we have to do. Let's try to create a clear mental image of what we have to do. Let's try to create a mental image of an athletic technique that you want to learn. Make sure that the movement is perfect in all its details. Take an image of someone who performs that particular technique very well, replace his body and his face with yours, imagine the movements of the arms, elbows, wrists and fingers, then the legs and so forth. Visualize every single area of your body. Imagine how you breathe and the sensations you feel. Maybe you can slow down the image so that you can focus on it more carefully and soak in every detail. It lasts just a few minutes, but it will result in a specific image created by all those feelings generated from the process. Learning this way is easy, quick and fun.

According to you, what is simple and what is difficult? What is easy and what is demanding? Where is the limit between possible and impossible? Was there a moment in your life when what you believed was impossible turned into possible?

I know these questions are not easy to answer. I'm sure you are recalling past experiences that can be labeled with those adjectives, and those experiences are probably being recalled as images. Maybe reality was different from what you recall. Maybe images create your reality.

Therefore, the quality of your results is determined by the questions you ask yourself and the mental representation you create depending on the goals you set. I want to stress the concept of quality of results, because it is not the result itself that dictates the success. It is, instead, whether the projection of your expectations of the success are gratifying to you.

If you do nothing to change your mental representations, you cannot take advantage of all the resources you have. Only then will find out how best to manage your potential. As the old saying goes: "Insanity is doing the same thing over and over again and expecting a different result."

Some time ago, when I first became interested in freediving, I met wonderful people, such as Roberto Chiozzotto and Mike Marić, who helped me understand freediving and freedivers' requirements. The first concept they taught me was that in freediving, the ability to achieve the best performance is 90% mental.

It is clear, then, how important the management of the mental process is in static and dynamic apnea, or in constant weight, or in a 9-hour race such as a triathlon. The mind finds it difficult to stay focused. It wanders through memories and feelings. It starts recall conversations on different topics, even those that are not relevant to the race goal. All this is simply physiological. The mind is starting a process to distract if from the continuous physical stress.

Imagine trying to stay focused on one thought for a whole working day. I am sure you already know the answer: It is not possible to stay focused on one thought because other thoughts overlap it. However, because our mind has trouble sticking to one thought for a long period, it gives us the opportunity to create new channels of thought and lead our mind in directions that are beneficial rather than distracting.

Mental preparation starts with our ability to set well-structured goals that direct our mind to follow the right paths during training and competition. This allows us to stay focused and not be affected by internal or external distractions that can divert our mental "intentions." A well-structured goal, which is supposed to satisfy our mental requirements, should answer the following questions:

- Does it look positive?
- Does it describe a result or a process?
- Is it in harmony with you?
- How do you know you reached it?
- Is it under your control?

The hypnotic state enables you to extract deep, subconscious answers to these questions.

The next step is to identify internal and external interferences that can distract you from trying to achieve the best performance. Using the following equation can help you produce a well-structured plan:

$$p = \mathbf{P} - \mathbf{I}_{i,e}$$

Where *p* is performance, ***P*** is the physical and mental potentials (these aspects are closely linked; thanks to hypnotic states it is possible to increase physical potential, which is the value of this variable); $\mathbf{I}_{i,e}$ means internal and external interferences.

Internal interferences include all those mental and physical factors that can distract you during competition and get in the way of achieving your best possible performance. They can be controlled if you know how. For example, by eliminating constraining and negative thoughts, and by developing post-hypnotic commands, your thoughts can be channeled into potentiating states. **External interferences** include all those environmental factors you cannot control, but you can limit their influence on your performance by using well-constructed mental images to change the feelings that are perceived.

All this aims at giving back to one's faculties the management of potentiating mental and physical states. This is closely linked to physiological elements and internal representations that generate behaviors that are fitting to the goal. The change can be easy and immediate, provided you work to regain your innate skills. You will be free to decide to face important events without stress, fear or anxiety.

As mentioned above, the athlete can trigger the state of hypnosis using a post-hypnotic command. This process is called **autohypnosis**. It is a self-induced process that allows the athlete to develop the same goals as those experienced during hypnosis sessions that were directed by a hypnotist. This is possible because in hypnosis it is not the hypnotist or his powers that control the patient. Instead, what brings about most of the changes are the personal potentials and skills of the patient. One of the most effective techniques for gaining an altered mental state is breathing. The ancient yogic practice of pranayama is often effective in helping to reach that goal. The manual intervention of the nasal cycle that occurs during meditation (*dhyana*) is the best documented technique of self-induced alteration of conscience.

The credit for studying and assigning the name to the nasal cycle is ascribed to the German rhinologist R. Kaiser (1895). He described in detail the dynamic process through which nasal passages periodically change in size and shape, resulting in a variation of air inlet and outlet. When the right mucous membrane increases in volume and reduces the lumen of nasal choanae, the left one is pervious, and vice versa.

Other scientists have also studied this topic. Rao and Podtar in 1970 showed how predominance shifts from one nostril to the other when a person changes position, for example, from being seated to lying down.

One of the most interesting aspects of the nasal cycle is that it is possible to control it. Iyengar in 1981 showed the manual methods commonly used in yoga to alter the quantity and quality of the nasal cycle.

In 1981 Werntz analyzed the air flow of the nostrils on 43 people. According to his results, there is a "direct relationship between the activity of brain hemispheres and nasal cycle rhythm." Higher values recorded in one hemisphere by an electroencephalograph were found to be linked to predominant air flow through the opposite nostril.

Werntz and other scientists found it was possible to change the dominant nostril by forcing air to pass through the non-dominant nostril. In addition, such induced experimental alteration was linked to a switch of in brain hemisphere dominance. Therefore, it appears that the nasal cycle is closely linked to brain hemisphere activity and that changes voluntarily induced in nasal air flow might be used to alter the activity of the brain as it relates to the autonomic nervous system controlling the main functions of our body. This is similar to hypnosis, in that you can voluntarily control involuntary functions and communicate with the unconscious areas that are able to synthetize hidden potentials.

Sivananda in 1992 stated that: "*Prana* is the overcoat of the mind. If you are able to control *prana*, you are able to control mind and *virya* (seed) as well; because *prana*, *virya* and mind are under the same single link."

The above-described aspects of the nasal cycle help simplify the connection between mental states induced through hypnotic techniques and breathing and meditative methods. Their many common elements are the binding agents that link them in a way that makes separating the boundary almost invisible. That is why we invite readers to study the meditation-breathing topic and read more about it in publications written by others.

The mind is like a toy with just a few instructions but with a huge potential for satisfaction. You can play with it with the enthusiasm of a child and be unexpectedly surprised. This will become a path to regaining your potentials and teaching them how to satisfy your needs.

10.2 Odontostomatology: the use of the bite plane in sports

M. Marić, G. Pieraccini, M. Bosco[2], P. Gandini
School of Specialization in Orthodontics - University of Pavia[3]

It is well-known that dentistry and specifically occlusal rebalancing are used in various sports disciplines to improve athletes' performances. Joint repositioning and/or muscular relaxation through the use of occlusal devices has become popular in sports

[2] Professor of Oral Rehabilitation – University of Pavia.

[3] Director: Prof. Paola Gandini.

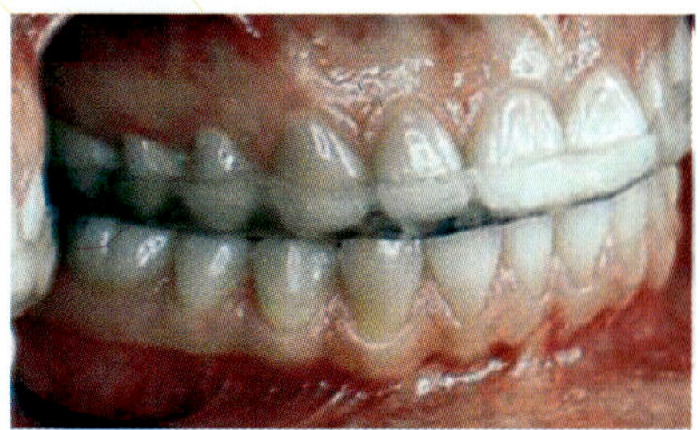

Picture 1

dentistry. Its aim is to reduce stress, improve body posture and improve physical performance by optimizing jaw alignment.

Occlusal devices (picture 1), including bite planes, repositioning devices and stabilization devices, are removable dental appliances commonly made of hard resin. They are inserted in occlusal and biting surfaces of one dental arch in order to create a correct interaction with the elements of the opposite dental arch. Other functions are to give the jaw a more stable orthopaedic position, to improve muscle activity and to protect teeth and their supporting structures from dangerous factors.

In sports, as in all activities requiring extraordinary performances, deficits in motor unit recruitment may occur. They can cause chronic and severe pain or underperforming. In fact, the postural system can have some flaws that are evident in the maximum requests of integration during a sports performance: An extraordinary effort can make it fall outside the adaptation range.

A repositioning device is an appliance used to correct oral problems. It also integrates a general plan of postural reprogramming in patients with painful or dysfunctional symptoms at various levels of the musculoskeletal system. According to some authors, dysfunctions of the stomatognathic system are closely related to problems in other areas of the body. For example, a pathological dental occlusion can cause a postural deficit resulting in a variety of symptoms, such as cervicalgia, pubalgia or backache.

The relation between the oral and the postural systems in high-level athletes is important because the athletes' posture needs to perfectly fit the specific gesture movements. In order to obtain maximum muscular strength, correctness in motion and neuromuscular activation, the patient finds the most comfortable position for his lower jaw during that specific movement, so that he ensures the best postural balance. Hence, there is not only one valid posture for the lower jaw. The Italian Society of Odontostomatology in Sports (*SIOS – Società Italiana di Odontostomatologia dello Sport*) is working on this. It is carrying out a considerable amount of research to create the most suitable bite-positioner for various sports. The goal is to design a bite plane that ensures the maximum freedom of lower jaw movement, maximum comfort, the best stabilization of the head in the position of reference and maximum postural balance to optimize both athletic performance and precision in the specific motor gesture.

The SIOS Panel of Physiology of Stomatognathic Systems conducted an investigation to determine the activity of the stomatognathic system while a person is playing sports. The panel was supported by professionals such as dentists, sports doctors, physiatrists, neurophysiologists and osteopaths in order to study most effectively this complex topic: mechanisms of occlusion and posture during sports. After one year of investigation, based on a sample of 47 athletes, the panel drew the conclusion that the need for a bite plane varies from person to person and the occlusal device can best perform its function by giving athletes maximum balance during the training stage, rather than during the performance itself.

Another study, carried out by the University of Sassari, focused on how occlusion affects sports performances. Results showed that patients do not always benefit from the use of a bite plane during sports. Furthermore, the same pathology can determine different physical performances in different patients since not all pathologies affect postural attitude in the same way. Italian scientists reported clinical cases where occlusal devices proved to be a useful tool in correcting algic disorders that limited ordinary life as well as sports performance.

A 1996 article reported six cases where postural deficits were treated with a bite plane. According to the authors of the study, the occlusal treatment not only solved the problem but, in some cases, also improved athletic performance.

Sports in which occlusal devices have been tried during the past few years include football, dance and skiing. The Italian Federation, through the Department of Research and Experimentation of the Italian National Olympic Committee (CONI) and the Scientific Research and Medical Commission of the Italian Winter Sports Federation (FISI), is following athletes from different teams to evaluate the need to act in this regard.

Apnea also has been listed among the disciplines using the bite plane. The first research was carried out in 2004 by the University of Pavia on the deep freediving world record holder, Umberto Pelizzari. In 2005, the Department of Odontostomatology of the University of Pisa, together with the School of Specialization in Orthodontics of Pavia, carried out an experimental study on four freedivers. It showed major improvements in athletes' performances after using occlusal devices at night, during training sessions and during free time.

In September 2009, the possibility of treating Roberto Chiozzotto with a bite plane was taken into consideration. One month later, he went to the Orthodontics ward of the Dentistry Clinic of the University of Pavia, where he met with a specialist.

A medical history was taken, including orthodontic and gnathologic data. Possible systemic and local diseases that could have caused alterations in the development of the stomatognathic system were examined. Great importance was attached to questions that allowed us to identify anything that would affect the temporomandibular joint: the absence of parafunctional activities, bad habits, or any other situation that can play a role in developing temporomandibular joint disorders (TMJ) from a dental, orthopaedic or psychological point of view. In the orthodontic history, an evaluation of the somatic aspect was reported (facial symmetry, facial and lips profile) and situations of malocclusion. Phonation, swallowing and breathing disorder analyses were carried out as well. The last part included a visit with a gnathologic specialist, taking into account the anamnestic and clinical fields.

Roberto had to answer some questions about current or prior pain linked to the temporomandibular joint and to masticatory and neck muscles, headaches, functional limitation, clicks or noises while chewing. Subsequently, an objective exam was carried out, which includes a series of evaluations allowing us to test the effectiveness of the stomatognathic system. The patient was asked to perform horizontal mandibular excursions in

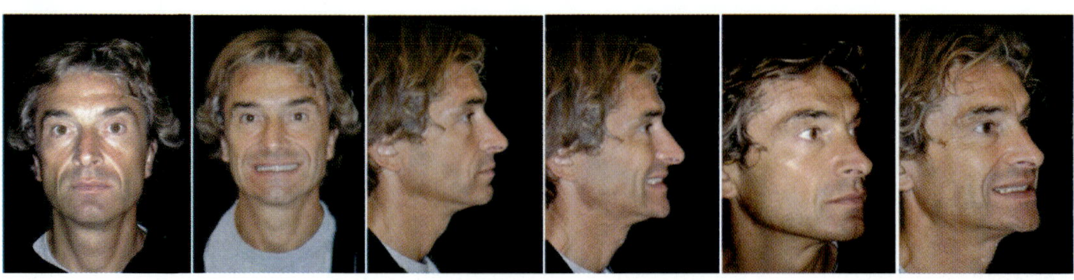
Picture 2

such a way that we could evaluate the shift and quantify laterality and protrusive direction, taking into account deviation from the middle line and overjet. Then he was asked to perform vertical mandibular movements to test the shift and the opening range, taking into account the overbite in absence of painful symptoms. The absence of joint noise was tested as well, through auscultation and palpation while opening and closing. To conclude, tests of inter-oral and extra-oral musculature were carried out through palpation, looking for pain or tenderness, hypertrophy, hypertonia/hypotonia, trigger or tender point presence. All the data collected gave us a comprehensive framework on the health of the joint, allowing us to rule out the presence of temporomandibular joint disorders.

Extraoral (picture 2) and intraoral (picture 3) pictures were taken. In extraoral pictures, the patient is standing in an upright position: two pictures have been taken from the front, two from the side and two from a ¾ perspective, respectively one in dental occlusion with touching lips and one smiling. One of the six intraoral pictures gives a complete front view, one of them focuses on the relationship between the upper and lower dental elements (overjet), two of them give a complete bitewings view, and two of them focus on the occlusal view of the upper and lower arches.

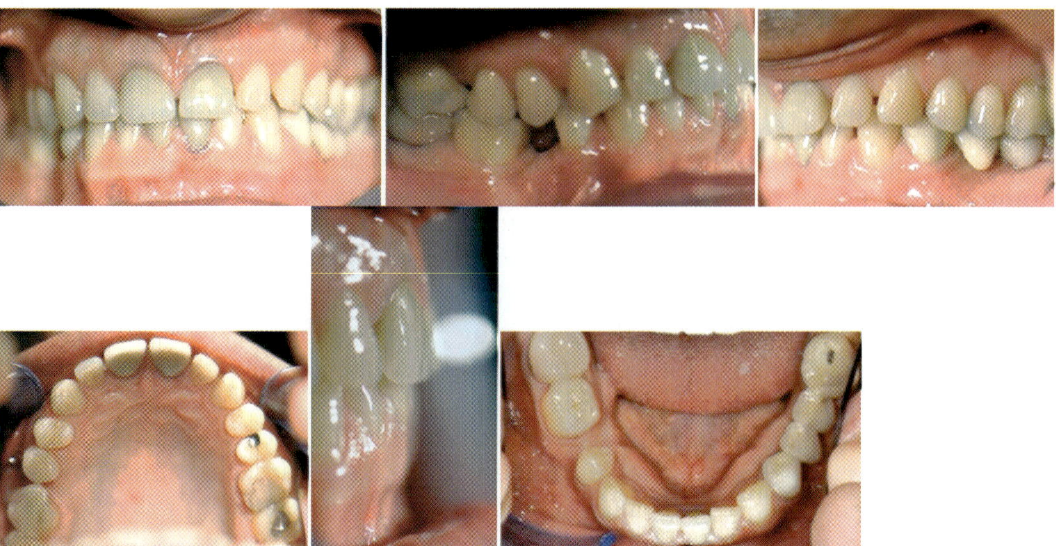
Picture 3

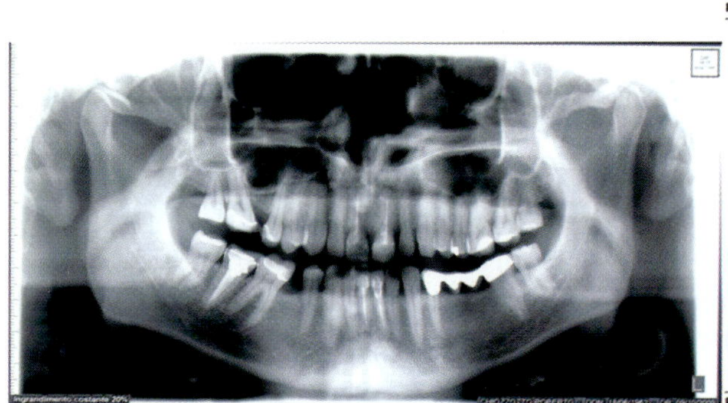
Picture 4

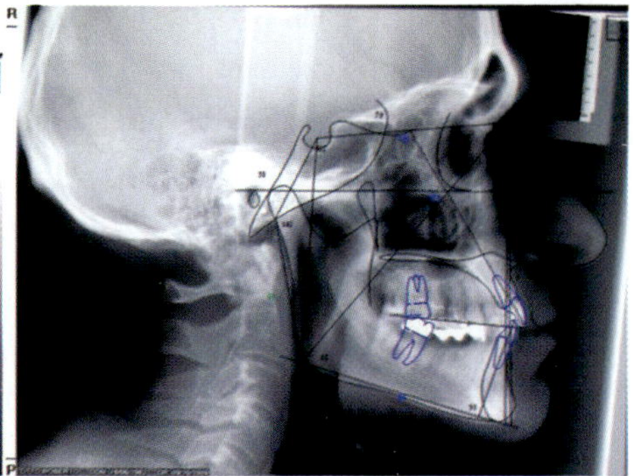
Picture 5

In order to have a comprehensive evaluation, two X-ray examinations were performed, an orthogonal panoramic radiograph (OPT) (picture 4) and a latero-lateral teleradiography (TRX L.L.) (picture 5). A cephalometric tracing was made on the X-ray obtained.

Cast models were used to evaluate of the patient and to design the bite plane. During the first visit, impressions of both arches and centric occlusion were taken. Facial arch (picture 6) models were designed at the laboratory and installed in the articulator. This method allowed us to reach a significant level of precision in reproducing the arches of the patient and their relationship. This is a fundament prerequisite in order to implement the occlusal devices correctly.

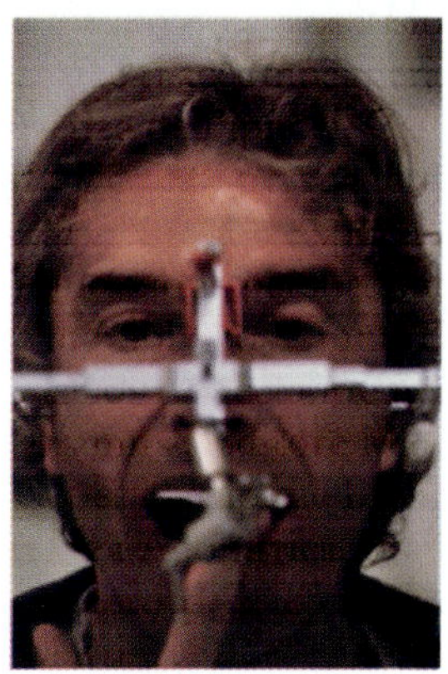
Picture 6

An electromyographic analysis was carried out using surface electrodes to test masseter and temporal muscles during three conditions – one in a resting position, one with the arches closed and one while Roberto held his breath during the last five seconds.

After these evaluations, a bite plane was designed, and Roberto tried it on so we could check if the occlusion was homogenous and balanced and delete possible interferences both in static and dynamic phases. The athlete was advised that the uncomfortable feeling of having a foreign object in his mouth tends to decrease over time, as does minor drooling and initial phonatory difficulty.

Roberto wore the bite plane during training and during competition, and he used it when he had to perform major efforts. The result of using the oral device in terms of electromyographic, subjective and qualitative athletic performance was amazing.

Therefore, we believe that an extremely specialized and targeted approach is fundamental to ensure the athlete the best possible performance.

Bibliography

Okeson J.P., Il trattamento delle disfunzioni dell'occlusione e dei disordini temporomandibolari, Edizione Martina.

Lai V., Deriu F., Chiessa G., Influenza dell'occlusione sulle prestazioni sportive, Minerva Stomatologica, 2003; 53(1):41-7.

Zucchi E., Pelosi A., Caronti A., Placche e postura. Attualità Dentale, 1996; 3/4:5-20.

Moyers R.E., Temporomandibular muscle contraction patterns in Angle class II, Division 1 malocclusions: an electromyographic anlysis, American Journal of Orthodontics, 1949; 35:837.

Angelone L., Clayton J., Brandhorst W., An Approach to Quantitative Electromyography of Masseter Muscle, Journal of Dental Reserch, 1960; 39:17-24.

Spinas E., Nanussi A., Montecorboli U., Baldini A., Lumbau A., Tripodi D., Esperienze odontoiatriche nello sport agonistico in Odontoiatria e sport, Edi.Ermes 2009, capitolo 9.

Marić M., Grampi B., Marić A., Bressani D., Odontostomatologia sportiva: proposta di un nuovo modello di aeratore, Rivista Italiana di Stomatologia, aprile-luglio 2004; N. 2, Anno LXXII, 34-38.

Marić M., Pieraccini G., Gandini P., Mergati L., Fraticelli D., Bressani D., Electromyographic evaluation of free divers wearing relaxing bite. Abstract book Blue 2005, Special Conference on Breath-hold Diving, Pisa, Italy, December 1-4 2005, 117-118. Atti IX Convegno di Odontoiatria, Nembro, 27-28 gennaio 2006 in Doctor Os, 17(1), suppl. 1, 82-85.

BIBLIOGRAPHY

Pelizzari U., Tovaglieri S., Corso di apnea, Ugo Mursia Editore.
Pelizzari U., Landoni L., Seddone A., Il respiro nell'apnea, Ugo Mursia Editore.
Platonov V.N., Fondamenti dell'allenamento e dell'attività di gara, Calzetti & Mariucci Editori.
Platonov V.N., L'organizzazione dell'allenamento e dell'attività di gara, Calzetti & Mariucci Editori.
Counsilman J, Counsilman B.E., La nuova scienza del nuoto, Zanichelli.
Sweetenham B., Atkinson J., Nuoto da campioni, Collana Tecnica e Didattica Sport Edizioni.
Monaco D., Il nuoto, Libertas Bologna.
Roberts O., Training con i pesi, Red Edizioni.
Umili A., Gli attrezzi per il corpo. Analisi muscolare degli esercizi con i pesi, Calzetti & Mariucci Editori.
Visintin G., Nuoto pinnato e orientamento subacqueo, Edizioni Fin.
Valentin P., Apnéologie – Tome 1.
Lemaître F., L'apnée – De la théorie à la pratique, Publications des Universités de Rouen et du Havre.
Mana F., Tecniche di respirazione per apnea, Magenes.
Nicoletti R., Borghi A.M., Il controllo motorio, Il Mulino.
Granchi G., Pirovano F., PNL – Comunicare per vendere, De Vecchi.
Robbins A., Come ottenere il meglio da sé e dagli altri, Bompiani.
Van Lysebeth A., Imparo lo yoga, Ugo Mursia Editore.
Il nuovo libro dello yoga, Centro Yoga Sivananda, Red Edizioni.
Platonov V.N., Allenamento Sportivo. Teoria e metodologia, Calzetti & Mariucci Editori.
Zatsiorsky V.M., Kraemer W.J., Scienza e pratica dell'allenamento della forza, Calzetti & Mariucci Editori.
Arcelli E., Il nuovo «Correre è bello», Sperling & Kupfer.
Pizzolato O., Correre… secondo Orlando Pizzolato, Edizioni Correre.
Fischi P., Ciclismo, Ediciclo Editore.
Bartoli L., Fagioli F., L'allenamento invernale del ciclista, Editrice Erika.
Stecchi A., Biomeccanica degli esercizi fisici, Editrice Erika.
Dimantini S., Allenarsi a correre, Editrice Erika.

Albert I., Williams M.H. (1975): Effects of post-hypnotic suggestions on muscular endurance. Perceptual and Motor Skills, 40(1):131-9.
Arcelli E., Acido lattico e prestazione: quello che l'allenatore deve sapere, Cooperativa Dante Editrice.
Bandler R., Il potere dell'inconscio e della PNL – Come farci aiutare dalla parte più profonda di noi stessi per vivere meglio, Alessio Roberti Editore.
Bandler R., Usare il cervello per cambiare – L'uso delle submodalità nella programmazione neurolinguistica, Casa Editrice Astrolabio.

Bandler R., Grinder J., I modelli della tecnica ipnotica di Milton H. Erickson, Casa Editrice Astrolabio.

Bandler R., Grinder J., La metamorfosi terapeutica – Principi di programmazione neurolinguistica, Casa Editrice Astrolabio.

Bandler R., Grinder J., La struttura della magia, Casa Editrice Astrolabio.

Bosco C., La forza muscolare – Aspetti fisiologici ed applicazioni pratiche, Società Stampa Sportiva.

Carnegie D., Come parlare in pubblico e convincere gli altri, Bompiani.

Casiglia E., Rossi M.A., Teoria e pratica dell'ipnosi, Libraria Padovana Editrice.

Cialdini R.B., Le armi della persuasione – Come e perché si finisce col dire di sì, Giunti.

Garratt T., PNL per lo sport, Alessio Roberti Editore.

Granone F., Trattato di ipnosi, voll. I – II, UTET.

Gribaudo C.G., Ganzit G.P., Medicina dello Sport, UTET.

Guyton A.C., Hall J.E., Fisiologia Medica, EdiSES.

Fanelli V., I poteri segreti della comunicazione empatica, Essere Felici Edizioni.

Höfler H., Terapia e ginnastica respiratoria, Edizioni Mediterranee.

Lipton B.H., La Biologia delle Credenze, Macro Edizioni.

Manno R., Fondamenti dell'allenamento sportivo, Zanichelli.

McArdle W.D., Katch F.L., Katch V.L., Fisiologia Applicata allo Sport, Casa Editrice Ambrosiana.

Milton H.E., La mia voce ti accompagnerà, Casa Editrice Astrolabio.

Milton H.E., L'esperienza dell'ipnosi, Casa Editrice Astrolabio.

Piattelli Palmarini M., L'arte di persuadere, Milano, Mondatori.

Penna R., Vercelli G., Performance sportiva – Performance di vendita, Alfa Academy.

Pirovano F., La comunicazione persuasiva, De Vecchi.

Sansavini C., Parlare in pubblico, Giunti Demetra.

Siani A., Manuale di Ipnosi, Selecta Medica.

Souchard P.E., Il Diaframma, Editore Marrapese.

Glantz S.A., Statistica per Discipline Biomediche, McGraw-Hill.

Vercelli G., L'Intelligenza Agonistica, Ponte alle Grazie.

Okeson J.P., Il trattamento delle disfunzioni dell'occlusione e dei disordini temporomandibolari, Edizione Martina.

Lai V., Deriu F., Chiessa G., Influenza dell'occlusione sulle prestazioni sportive, Minerva Stomatologica, 2003; 53(1):41-7.

Zucchi E., Pelosi A., Caronti A., Placche e postura. Attualità Dentale, 1996; 3/4:5-20.

Moyers R.E., Temporomandibular muscle contraction patterns in Angle class II, Division 1 malocclusions: an electromyographic anlysis, American Journal of Orthodontics, 1949; 35:837.

Angelone L., Clayton J., Brandhorst W., An Approach to Quantitative Electromyography of Masseter Muscle, Journal of Dental Reserch, 1960; 39:17-24.

Spinas E., Nanussi A., Montecorboli U., Baldini A., Lumbau A., Tripodi D., Esperienze odontoiatriche nello sport agonistico in Odontoiatria e sport, Edi.Ermes 2009, capitolo 9.

Marić M., Grampi B., Marić A., Bressani D., Odontostomatologia sportiva: proposta di un nuovo modello di aeratore, Rivista Italiana di Stomatologia, aprile-luglio 2004; N. 2, Anno LXXII, 34-38.

Marić M., Pieraccini G., Gandini P., Mergati L., Fraticelli D., Bressani D., Electromyographic evaluation of free divers wearing relaxing bite. Abstract book Blue 2005, Special Conference on Breath-hold Diving, Pisa, Italy, December 1-4 2005, 117-118. Atti IX Convegno di Odontoiatria, Nembro, 27-28 gennaio 2006 in Doctor Os, 17(1), suppl. 1, 82-85.

THE AUTHORS

Umberto Pelizzari

Umberto Pelizzari was born in Busto Arsizio, Province of Varese, on August 28, 1965. In 1990 he set his first freediving world record. He ended his competitive career in 2001 after setting his 16th world record in deep freediving disciplines. He was the first one to exceed 80 meters in constant weight, 130 meters in variable weight and 150 meters in no-limits variable weight. A computer science graduate, he works as journalist and TV reporter on science programs dealing with the marine environment. He founded the Apnea Academy school to disseminate spearfishing teaching and research across the world. He has been an appointed university lecturer by the Ministry of Internal Affairs to teach scuba divers and firefighters. Since 2006, he has been working as a lecturer for the second level Master's Degree in Diving and Hyperbaric Medicine at Scuola Normale Superiore Sant'Andrea University in Pisa.

www.umbertopelizzari.com

Federico Mana

Federico Mana was born in Carmagnola on January 15, 1975. He received his high school certificate in information technology, optics and optometry. He has been working as a teacher in paramedical and Continuing Medical Education (CME) sectors and has been working with multinational companies in the ophthalmic field. In 2002 he became a freediving instructor. In 2003 he decided to continue cultivating his passion by using his personal skills to train freedivers. Between 2007 and 2013 he established 8 Italian records in freediving, and in August 2009 he was the first Italian athlete to reach 100 meters in constant weight, becoming one of the deepest freedivers in the world. In 2008 he published the book "Breathing Techniques for Freediving," followed by "Equalization for Freediving" in 2010. He works with freediving magazines, and his skills on equalization techniques and stress management led him to participate as a partner of the Extreme Centre and Scuola Superiore Sant'Anna University, becoming in 2010 one of the teachers at the Master of Hyperbaric Medicine program. In 2008 he founded the Moving Limits Association, which operates in the world of wellness by offering freediving and yoga and designing training programs for the staffs of several large companies.

www.federicomana.com

Roberto Chiozzotto

Roberto Chiozzotto was born in Venice on June 18, 1962. He has a technical high school certificate and is a freediving trainer and instructor. He originally competed in cycling, starting in the beginners category and rising through the ranks with great results. After that, he turned to basketball, and won a school competition national championship in 1987. He then dedicated his time and heart to spearfishing and freediving. He started next to Umberto Pelizzari as a safety diver on the Sector No Limits Team, then became main athlete/head coach of the FIPSAS (Italian Game Fishing and Water Activities Federation) national team. He took the lead during 1999-2001 and won the AIDA World Championship in Ibiza. After a brief return to amateur cycling, he fully devoted his time and passion to the marathon, running it in 2h and 47', making ultra-rail races and running on mountains. Meanwhile, he took the course to become a FIDAL (Italian Track-and-Field Federation) instructor.

ACKNOWLEDGEMENTS

Our heartfelt thanks go to our families, who have always supported and helped us by providing us with material, pictures and advice on writing this book:

Marco Alessandria
Andrea Badiello
Igor Casabianca (personal trainer, coach, Apnea Academy instructor)
Alice Cattaneo (photographer)
Giovanni Contessa (photographer)
Cristina Giussani
Igor Liberti (photographer)
Mike Marić
Gino Passigatti
Alessandro Pilati (Genoa Football Team's sports trainer)
Andrea Primitivi (A.C. Milan FOOTBALL CLUB sports trainer)
Vincenzo Savelli (ITALIAN national TEAM swimming coach)
Daniele Tognaccini (A.C. Milan FOOTBALL CLUB trainers' director)
Stefano Tovaglieri (photographer)
Riccardo Trianni (photographer)
Paolo Zanoni (photographer)
Michele D'Incà (photographer)
Ugo Zamborlini (photographer)

Friends from athletic field in San Giuliano
Friends from multisport structure Giallo Azzurra
Friends from Apnea Academy
Friends from Apnea Planet
Friends from Moving Limits
Friends from Zero03 Fitness Club - Lodi

Published by Idelson Gnocchi Publisher Ltd.

Navy Diver, Submariner Father of American Freediving
by BOB CROFT
ISBN 1-92864945-9
Hardcover: 158 pages
$ 30.00

Bob Croft, a man who embraced adventure head-on, and accepted risk as a way of life. From helping save a submarine from sinking in Russian waters at the height of the Cold War, to volunteering as a research subject for U.S. Navy scientists, Bob is a source of vicarious pleasure for arm chair adventurers around the world. Not satisfied with "just being a lab rat," Bob took the findings of one experiment a step further. In an exploit that would rewrite the rules of human performance, he plunged below the theoretical limits of human survival, and launched the international sport of competitive apnea diving.

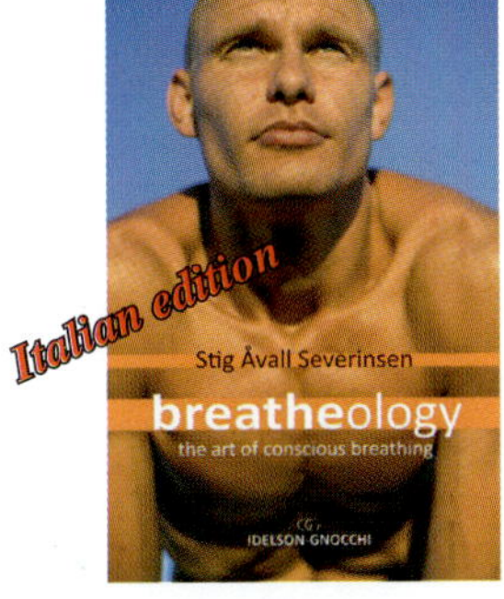

Breatheology
the art of conscious breathing
by STIG ÅVALL SEVERINSEN
ISBN 1-92864934-3
Hardcover: 300 pages
$ 39.50 - € 35,00

Most of us breathe inefficiently. Life is often lived in the fast lane, and especially when we are stressed, we tend to use only the upper part of our lungs. We forget to breathe deep down into the stomach and thereby lose out on a lot of energy. Only when you become aware of your breathing and how to train it, you will be able to learn to breathe properly. Your body will immediately absorb more oxygen and after a short time you will have more energy and gain greater mental calmness.

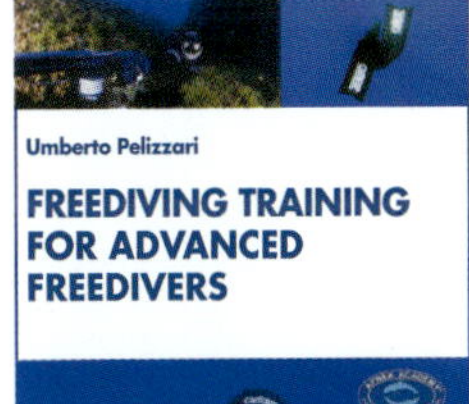

Freediving Training for Advanced Freedivers
by UMBERTO PELIZZARI
ISBN 1-928649-47-5
Softcover: 328 pages
$ 49.50 - € 50,00

This book is intended to provide information regarding the various apnea workouts. For advanced freedivers and spear fishermen. Static and Dynamic Apnea. Table of training by stages with workout examples. Training before and during competitions. All aspect of Breathing Reflex. Equalizing Maneuvers techniques.

The Ten Kings of the Sea
Salvage of Santa Isabella's Treasure
by JACQUES and PIERRE MAYOL
ISBN 1-92864924-6
Softcover: 256 pages
$ 25.00 - € 19,50

A novel based on real discoveries and experiences made by Jacques Mayol around the world during his life who was dedicated to discovering the underwater secrets of the Sea.

Manual of Freediving
Underwater on a single breath
by UMBERTO PELIZZARI and STEFANO TOVAGLIERI
ISBN 1-92864927-0

From theory to practice: the first entirely illustrated and complete guide to freediving.
The definitive guide, illustrated and up to date, for the aspiring apneist. From theory to practice this manual will accompany the reader in the discovery of a fascinating sport. A manual that should not be missing from the itinerary of any diver (apneist or otherwise) who wishes to improve their techniques of respiration, swimming and diving whilst broadening knowledge and theory.

Homo Delphinus
The Dolphin Within Man
by JACQUES MAYOL
ISBN 1-92864903-3
Hardcover: 398 pages
$ 95.00 - € 75,00

The only book written about Man's spiritual connection to the sea. The term Homo Delphinus refers to individuals who are aquatic as dolphin, share a love of the ocean. Mayol believed that some people will be, within a couple of generations, capable of swimming at depths of 200 meters and holding their breath for up to ten minutes. This book is also a limited edition coffee-table size book includes more than 300 pictures.

Deeply
by UMBERTO PELIZZARI
ISBN 1-928649-31-9
Hardcover: 224 pages
$ 50.00 - € 50,00

This book is not only an autobiography of Pelizzari, but also an incredible reflection on man's constant and irrepressible urge to exceed the limits imposed on him by nature, to experience new sensations and to go deep within himself in search of a freedom that knows no boundaries.

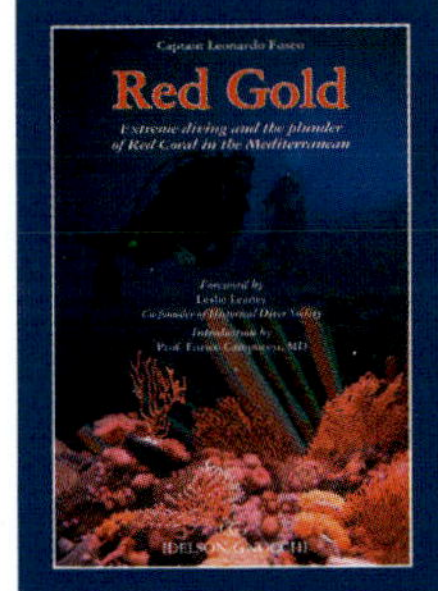

www.redcoralsociety.org

Red Gold
Extreme diving and the plunder of red coral in the Mediterranean
by Captain LEONARDO FUSCO
ISBN 1-92864929-7
Hardcover: 272 pages
$ 25.00 - € 30,00

"In 1953, at Cape Spartivento, Leonardo Fusco made his first Aqua Lung dive, and everything changed. As spearfishing led Hans Hass to an underwater career of science, film and photography, so spearfishing led Leonardo to an underwater career of coral harvesting, marine biology, mixed gas technology and hyperbaric research. Diving to recover his lost speargun, Leonardo discovered a carpet of red coral, and his life took a whole new direction."

Leslie Leaney
co-founder of Historical Diving Society

www.manualoffreediving.com www.idelsongnocchi.it